Fontenoy, Britain & The War of Austrian Succession 1740-1748

Maurice, Comte de Saxe,
Duc de Courlande et Semi-Gallie

Fontenoy, Britain & The War of Austrian Succession 1740-1748
ILLUSTRATED EDITION

Francis H. Skrine

With a Short Account of the Battle of Fontenoy by James Grant

Fontenoy, Britain & The War of Austrian Succession 1740-1748
by Francis H. Skrine
With a Short Account of the Battle of Fontenoy
by James Grant

FIRST EDITION

ILLUSTRATED

First published under the title
Fontenoy and Great Britain's Share in the War of the Austrian Succession 1741-48

Leonaur is an imprint of Oakpast Ltd
Copyright in this form © 2017 Oakpast Ltd

ISBN: 978-1-78282-644-6 (hardcover)
ISBN: 978-1-78282-645-3 (softcover)

http://www.leonaur.com

Publisher's Notes

The views expressed in this book are not necessarily those of the publisher.

Contents

Preface	7
Introduction	13
Great Britain and France in 1740	15
The Armies and Their Leaders	31
Dettingen and Marshal Wade's Campaign	62
The Advance on Tournai	95
Fontenoy	124
The Allies' Retreat	166
The Scottish Rising	196
End of "The '45	228
Siege of Pondicherry	260
Appendix 1: Existing Regiments Which Fought in Flanders, 1743–47	281
Appendix 2: British Officers Killed and Wounded at Fontenoy	282
Appendix 3: References to the Plan of Battle of Fontenoy	285
Appendix 4: Services of the Irish Brigade During the War of the Austrian Succession	287
The Battle of Fontenoy, 1745	291

Preface

Though a vast amount of research has been given to the eighteenth century, the general reader knows comparatively little of Sir Robert Walpole's long administration and the War of the Austrian Succession. The second quarter of that great century was full of peculiar colouring, and deserves closer attention than it has hitherto received. European society had not thrown off the medieval crust; formalism prevailed in religion, manners, language, and dress. But the leaven was working actively which long afterwards produced the French Revolution.

Fontenoy is one of the chief landmarks of this half-forgotten era. Carlyle pronounced it "a mystery and a riddle" (*Frederick the Great*, Book xv.), and his *dictum* holds good at the present day. The fact that the battle of May 11, 1745, was a British defeat accounts for the oblivion which enshrouds its stirring incidents.

But—

Fame is not grounded on success,
Though victories were Caesar's glory;
Lost battles made not Pompey less,
But left him styled great in story.
Malicious fate doth oft devise
To beat the brave, and fool the wise.

If wisdom was not conspicuous on our side at Fontenoy, the examples it set of calm courage, staunchness, and discipline have especial value at the present day.

For many years, I lay under the spell of the Fontenoy enigma, with little hope of solving it. A key was at length found in eight volumes of MS. despatches from our generals in Flanders 1744-45, which may be consulted at the National Record Office. The greater number

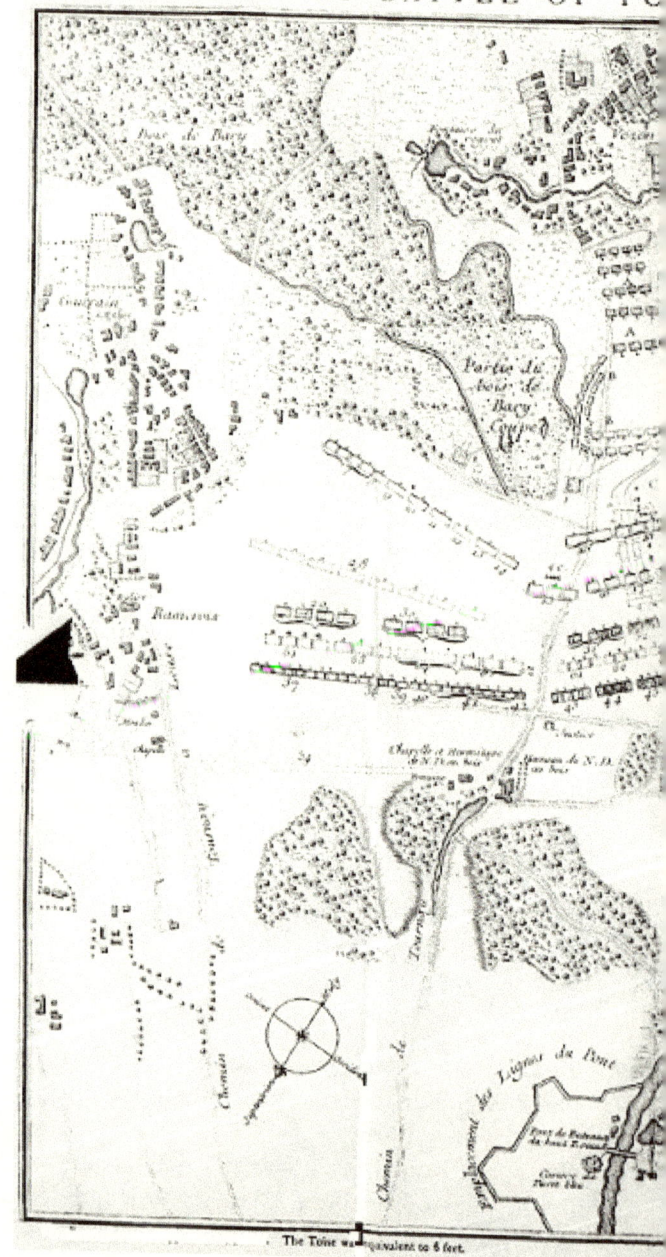

NTENOY, AFTER A SURVEY CARRIED OUT IN 1745.

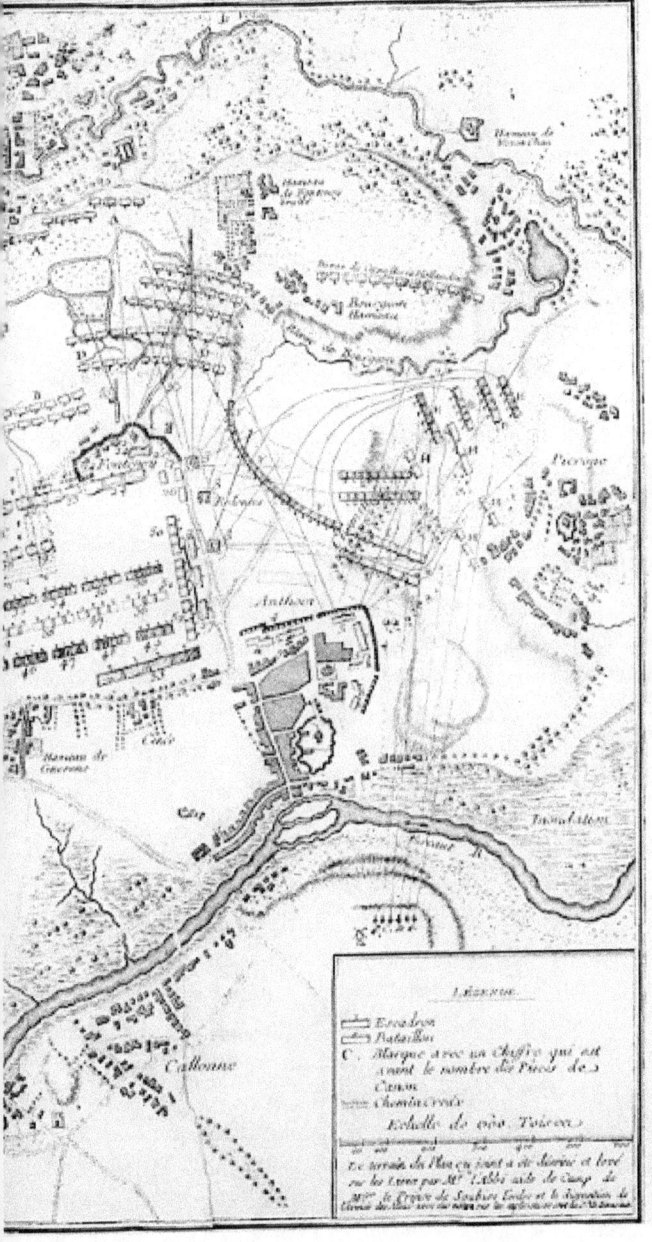

were dictated by William Augustus, Duke of Cumberland. It is a proof of George II.'s punctilious regard for the Constitution that his son should have been forbidden to address him save through the medium of a responsible minister. These quaint and stilted documents, penned while the events they dealt with were fresh in the writers' memory, enabled me to describe every incident of the drama in the chief actors' own words. The result was a picture of eighteenth century warfare in the interval between Marlborough's campaigns and the revolution wrought by Frederick II. of Prussia.

"The beginning of strife is as when one letteth out water," and he who attempts to elucidate a battle cannot foresee the point to which its ramifications may lead him. I found it necessary to compare the resources of the chief antagonists; to sketch the course of European politics which ended in the War of the Austrian Succession. Fontenoy was but a link in a chain of mighty events. Its first-fruits were the Scottish rising of 1745-46. This is indeed a thrice-told tale. Walter Scott has made it a household word, and few of its incidents have escaped the research of Robert Chambers and Andrew Lang.

The Fontenoy despatches, however, cast new light on its causation and progress, while the Hanoverian side was sustained by officers and men who had fought and suffered in Flanders. Fontenoy, too, was the parent of Rocoux and Laffeldt. In each battle did our infantry display unsurpassed valour, and the last was signalised by a cavalry charge as desperate as the ride of the Six Hundred at Balaclava without its element of heroic folly. These battles should be borne on the colours of every regiment which shared their heat and burden.

The flames kindled by Frederick of Prussia's ambition spread to North America, to India. Louisbourg taught New Englanders that union is strength, and probably suggested the combined action which won independence a generation later. The Battle of St Thomé, near Madras, revolutionised the status of European merchants in India, and launched them on a career of assimilation and conquest. During this war the foundations were laid of the United States and of our Indian Empire. A history of Great Britain's part therein must follow its fortunes far beyond the narrow limits of Flanders.

Nor could the chequered course of maritime warfare be omitted. England's sea-power was at its nadir between 1739 and 1746. Smollett has left us a lurid picture of naval incompetence—and worse—in chapters xxiv.-xxxvii. of *Roderick Random*. In February 1744, a British fleet showed its heels to Frenchmen and Spaniards off Toulon. The tide turned in 1746; and it is something more than a coincidence that low-water mark was reached with the execution of Lieutenant Baker Phillips for surrendering H.M.S. *Anglesea* to a French privateer.

During the last years of this war our seamen regained a large measure of their ancient skill and daring. The victories of Anson, Warren, and Hawke called a halt in Saxe's triumphal career. In 1757 the example made of Phillips was repeated by Admiral Byng's execution for failing to relieve Mahon. There was more truth than Voltaire intended in his famous sarcasm—that Byng was shot *pour encourager les autres*. Though naval regeneration was chiefly due to the spirit breathed into his comrades by Nelson, the stern but salutary lessons taught half a century earlier were not without result. Thenceforward every officer knew that he must "take, burn, sink, or destroy" the enemy's ships, or answer for any neglect of duty with his life.

Arma virumque cano. The hero of Fontenoy was Maurice de Saxe, whose romantic career is sketched with all its lights and shades. Beside this towering figure all others sink into insignificance; but historical details are brightened by an infusion of the personal element.

As a layman, I have felt much diffidence in commenting on the leading of our forces by land and sea. Onlookers, however, occasionally see more of the game than players. Was not the manoeuvre of "breaking the line" invented by an Edinburgh merchant? Military and nautical critics will, perhaps, judge me leniently when they learn that I have grasped the awful truth enunciated in Wordsworth's *1815*—

> *That God's most dreaded instrument,*
> *In working out a pure intent,*
> *Is Man—arrayed for mutual slaughter;*
> *Yea, Carnage is His daughter,*

. . . .that I honour their calling, and believe its development on scientific lines to be essential to human progress.

Dates have been given throughout according to the Gregorian Calendar. It was adopted by France in 1584, but England did not follow suit until 1751-52. Perfect accuracy is impossible, for "New Style" was occasionally used in this country for many years before the Act of 1751. Another difficulty was the nomenclature of regiments, which in those days were called after their colonels. In every instance save one, those which fought in Flanders have been identified with existing corps.

My chief authorities, besides the State Papers referred to, are the

Regimental Records; Chichester and Burgess's *Records and Badges of the British Army*; Campbell Maclachlan's *William Augustus, Duke of Cumberland*, with its valuable extracts from his Order Books; Beatson's *Naval and Military Memoirs*; and the *Dictionary of National Biography*. On the French side, I am chiefly indebted to Général Comte Pajol's monumental *Guerres sous Louis XV* and St René Taillandier's *Maurice de Saxe*.

It is a pleasing duty to acknowledge the ready help and encouragement given me by the great Soldier who has honoured me by permitting his name to be associated with my humble efforts; by Major-Generals D. Hutchinson and J. M. Grierson, and Colonel W. B. Robertson, of the War Office staff; by Colonels A. C. E. Welby, late of the Royal Scots Greys, and A. E. Codrington, commanding the Coldstream Guards; Lieutenant-Colonel Sir John Boss of Bladensburg; Captain Thomas B. Moody, B.N.; and Mr S. M. Milne of Calverley House, near Leeds.

Francis Henry Skrine.

Introduction

In presenting this work to the public, I need not lay stress on the tactical or strategic problems which it unfolds. They will be best appreciated by military students, whose criticism may, perhaps, be disarmed by the frank admissions in the Preface. The political issues raised are of wider importance. They are not stated explicitly in the text,—for history is one thing and speculation quite another,—but he who runs may read the morals drawn in these pages.

To exhume a dead and buried past is sheer waste of time if it be not forced to yield lessons of value to the present generation.

In 1740 the peace of Europe hung by a thread: it depended on a single aged life. When Charles VI., Emperor of Germany and last male of the House of Habsburg, was gathered to his fathers, a powerful monarch who was also a great soldier invaded Silesia, lighting up a war which drew Europe, North America, and India into its vortex. Is the equilibrium of Europe more assured at the present time? There are now potent forces in existence, dynastic, national, and military, which may seek to re-cast the old world, and in so doing may revive the struggles of a century and a half ago.

In times, so critical England is still wrapped in lethargy. It seems as though she were undergoing the evolution which brought Holland to so low an ebb in the eighteenth century. A community which has waxed rich and powerful from successful warfare and strenuous enterprise in the past, but which shirks the plain duty of personal service in defence of its possessions and rights,—which forgets that battles are won not by gold but by steel, by the sacrifices that military training and organisation entail on its population in time of peace rather than by lavish expenditure and hurried makeshifts when war is imminent,—will assuredly fail to hold its own against some more virile and patriotic neighbour.

Our regular troops are of unsurpassed quality, but, as Marshal Bugeaud remarked, "Happily for England's foes, there are but few of them." The Jacobite invasion of 1745 should serve as a warning to the school which would whittle our army down to the strength required for defending naval bases.

The natural inference is that England's military system must be placed on broader foundations. In the words of Marshal Saxe:

> Let every man be compelled to dedicate to his country the years which are often squandered in debauchery.

This work is a trumpet-call to Englishmen who do not seem to understand that alliances and ententes, though excellent in their way, are of little practical value unless we have an army powerful enough to protect ourselves and be of use to those with whom we are allied.

Roberts.

Chapter 1

Great Britain and France in 1740

Fifty years ago, (as at 1906), it was the fashion to depreciate the eighteenth century. Writers of the early Victorian era poured contempt and pity on ancestors who were guileless of steam, electricity, and the penny post. Intoxicated by a sudden revolution in the adjuncts of material existence, they fell into the common error of mistaking the means for the end. Lord Beaconsfield said with a spice of truth, "The English have stopped short at comfort, and call it civilisation." The nineteenth century has now passed into the realm of history. In weighing both periods in the balances of fuller knowledge, we are fain to admit that the earlier has received a scanty measure of justice.

In 1740 Europe was still organised on a feudal basis. International relations were swayed by dynastic ambition, by the caprice of monarchs and their favourites, by mutual ignorance and inherited prejudice. The aristocracies, with much external brilliancy and a thorough appreciation of the art of intercourse, were formal, hard-hearted, and dissolute. The middle classes were attaining wealth more rapidly than culture; the proletariat was uninstructed and often brutal. It was a time of social anarchy, when the sanction of religion and order had lost much of their force.

In such a medium charlatans of all degrees flourished apace. But greater scope was given to individualism than is possible in the vast human hives of the present day; and the social horizon was illumined by many a sweet and heroic nature, whose mould seems to have been altogether lost. The leaven of 1789 was at work fifty years before the cataclysm which modified the whole current of thought and action, producing the germs of every discovery which the men of Victoria's reign claimed as their own. The eighteenth century was indeed a time of great conceptions; and posterity may perhaps rate the age of Voltaire as highly as the age of Lord Macaulay.

France was then a factor of overwhelming importance in politics. She had a homogeneous population of twenty-one millions, gifted with marvellous ingenuity and an equal capacity for patient toil. These qualities found scope in a kindly soil and climate; and the peaceful administration of Cardinal Fleury (1726-43) had healed the scars of Louis XIV.'s disastrous wars. These mighty forces were not the sport of party government, but were, in theory at least, wielded by a single individual. Society still maintained its medieval framework, but the days were far distant when the King of France was merely first among equals. The influence of the great feudatories had been steadily sapped by a policy of centralisation, commenced in the fifteenth century by Louis XL, and brought to perfection by Louis XIV. (1638-1715). In 1740 France was ruled by a bureaucratic machine operated from Versailles, and the great nobles who served as provincial governors were little else than figureheads.

Every nation has, at some stage of its history, possessed a sovereign who united in his own person the race's salient characteristics. Louis XV., King of France and Navarre (1710-74), succeeded in early childhood to his great-grandfather's immense prestige. Naturally cold-hearted, selfish, and indolent, he received an education which fostered his worst vices. He was taught to regard France as his personal property, a toy to serve all the impulses of lust, ambition, and caprice. Unfortunately, his powers for good and evil were as absolute as those wielded by the *Sultan* of Turkey, and his subjects gave him a heart-whole devotion which he did little to justify.

Mankind, said a Greek poet, is divided into three categories—those who think for themselves, those who think as others think, and those who never think at all. The many-headed multitude was captivated by His Very Christian Majesty's imposing presence and exquisite manners, which are thus described by one of the keenest observers of the century:—

> Louis XV. had the finest head imaginable, and his mien had an equal share of majesty and grace. The best painters have failed to render the expression of that magnificent head when the monarch turned to glance at any one with benevolence. His grace and beauty constrained one to love him at first sight.... The French court was always foolishly meticulous in the matter of titles. It was averse to the appellation *monsieur*, which indeed

has become dirt cheap. Everyone who did not possess a title was addressed as *sieur*. I remarked that the king never called bishops by any other name than their own, though these gentlemen are very proud of their titles. He affected to ignore the existence of every noble who did not figure among his personal attendants. But his pride was not natural: it had been inculcated as part and parcel of his education.

When an ambassador presented one of his countrymen, the person so honoured left the royal presence with the assurance that the king had seen him, and that was all. It must be admitted that he was most polite, especially to ladies, and even to his mistresses in public. He would disgrace anyone who showed them the slightest want of consideration. No man possessed a larger measure of that peculiarly royal virtue which we style dissimulation.—Jacques Casanova de Seingalt, *Mémoires*, vol. ii.

In 1740 he was not the crapulous debauchee whose cynical disregard for the decencies of life destroyed his subjects' stubborn loyalty. But moral decadence had already set in: Louis XV. was a slave of unworthy favourites, content to be a cypher in council, and to acquiesce in measures of which his innate good sense disapproved. We shall detect in him gleams of a higher self, for "every soul bears within it the germs of a better soul." His staunchness at Fontenoy, in Napoleon's words, "gave forty years of life to the old monarchy." But a bad man must not be judged by his occasional lapses into virtue. We may safely predict that no attempt will be made to rehabilitate the character of a sovereign who ignored every duty imposed by a great position.

The French aristocracy retained most of the privileges which were essential to their status under the feudal regime, while the corresponding obligations had disappeared. Ousted by bureaucrats from the government of their country, they found scope for redundant energies in the army and fleet, and in slavish attendance on the royal person. The pleasures of rural life, which might have been a bond of union between overlord and vassal, were curtailed by the necessity of spending most of the year at Versailles.

That marvellous creation of Louis XIV. was a centre of external brilliancy such as the world had never seen, and is not likely to behold again. Its dominant note, however, was splendour rather than comfort. The eighteenth century was an age of physical darkness. Amusements were few; locomotion slow and costly. Versailles was governed by a rigorous etiquette, imposed by its founder as a means of enhancing his personal prestige, and unfriendly Paris was the centre of the kingdom's intellectual life. The sated monarch's *ennui* was shared by his courtiers, who pined to exchange their artificial environment for the free life of camp, the pomp and circumstance of glorious war.

Far worse was the plight of the lesser nobility. Confined to provincial coteries by narrow means and the great expense of travel, they still felt the drain entailed by Louis XIV.'s ambition and extravagance. Caste feeling forbade alliances with the mercantile class, whose growing wealth contrasted with their own stagnation. War was a pastime for the gilded lackeys of Versailles: for the provincial nobility, it was a necessity of existence. A soldier's career was their only resource, and lucky was he who, after spending half a lifetime with the colours, was able to retire with a pittance to his crumbling *château*.

Nobles of every degree enjoyed practical immunity from taxation, which extended to the Church's overgrown possessions. ("The clergy own at present more than a third of the estates in this kingdom."—*Journal historique du Regne de Louis XV, par* E. J. F. Barbier, vol. ii.) The whole burden fell on the unprivileged masses, and it was increased by a vicious fiscal system under which the chief sources of revenue were farmed out to a group of financiers. When Louis XV. remarked that the corporation of farmers-general was a support of the State, the Duc de Noailles, of whom we shall hear more *anon*, replied, "Yes, sire; they sustain it as the rope sustains a corpse dangling from the gallows!"

The contempt of titled drones and the bureaucrats' grinding tyranny were endured by the French people with that gay philosophy which was once a national characteristic, but has been impaired by materialism and the decay of religious belief. Beneath the mask of good humoured tolerance there smouldered a fierce hatred of Versailles and all that it represented, which burst into flames half a century later. In 1740, however, the nation accepted an absolute monarchy and all that it entailed as inevitable. Popular discontent found a safety-valve in pungent satire and rhymed lampoons, which spared no one. A display of fireworks or illuminations, a distribution of wine and food for some royal marriage, sufficed to distract the volatile Parisians' attention from their country's woes.

In 1740 France was the centre of a world-wide empire. The colonising instinct, which is stimulated by successful war, was especially active during the heyday of Louis XIV.'s career. Canada was first settled in 1608 by Samuel de Champlain, who founded Quebec; and a stream of emigrants rapidly peopled the valley of the St Lawrence. A feudal constitution was given to Canada by Jean Baptiste Colbert (1619-83), a statesman to whom France owed her financial and colonial system, as well as her marine. Newfoundland and Nova Scotia were ceded to Great Britain in 1713; but the French retained Cape Breton, an island commanding the mouth of the St Lawrence.

At its eastern extremity stood a citadel named Louisbourg, which had cost £1,000,000, and served as a centre for flourishing cod-fisheries and as a port of call for homeward-bound Indiamen. Southwards France possessed a still vaster tract, known as Louisiana. Settled in 1682 by La Salle, it stretched from the Gulf of Mexico to Lake Superior. The British colonies were a mere fringe on the Atlantic seaboard, for France claimed the entire hinterland between the valleys of the Mississippi and St Lawrence. The incubus of French annexation kept New Englanders, and the denizens of our plantations in the south, steadfastly loyal to Great Britain.

India was an arena of still keener rivalries. In Bengal, the French flag flew over Chandernagore, which rivalled Calcutta in wealth and enterprise; and French factories competed with our own throughout the Gangetic Delta. Pondicherry in the south overshadowed Madras. Dupleix (16971763), who became Governor General of French India in 1742, was the real founder of the British Empire in those parts.

The great Englishmen who translated dreams into realities built on his foundations, and imitated his policy in every detail. La Bourdonnais (1699-1753), who then governed the Isle of France and Bourbon, was greater and more resourceful than any British admiral in Eastern waters. In 1740 a French Empire over India was in the making, and, like our own, it was founded on sea-borne trade. In 1740 the French East India Company owned forty large vessels, twelve of which were despatched annually to Indian ports. (Malleson, *History of the French in India,* note). Here, however, the parallel ends. Clive, Coote, Hastings, and the galaxy of born soldiers and administrators to whose labours that pivot of our empire is due, had behind them the whole force of England.

> But the France of Louis XV. more resembled the Medea of the ancient story than the tender and watchful mother. Often did she "with her own hands immolate her offspring," and, failing this, she treated the best and bravest of her sons rather as enemies to be thwarted, baffled, persecuted, and driven to despair,

than as men who were devoting all their energies, the every thought of their lives, to increase her dominions. Yes, it was France who was their enemy; . . . that France of the eighteenth century which lay, bound and gagged and speechless, . . . at the feet of a man who, shameless himself, cared little what might become of his subjects, provided only he was permitted to wallow. perpetually in all the excesses of the vilest . . . debauchery.—Malleson, *History of the French in India.*

Her extensive seaboard and direct access to the Mediterranean gave France an immense advantage in the struggle for sea-power with Great Britain. But the navy was grossly neglected throughout Louis XV's reign. His Ministers of Marine were, almost without exception, ignorant of a profession which beyond all others calls for the specialist. Malversation of every kind was rife in the dockyards. Superior officers were too old for useful service; the seamen were herded in filthy, unventilated quarters, and decimated by scurvy.

In April 1741, a squadron of twenty-two vessels returned from American waters in a state of open mutiny, provoked by the admiral's tyranny and peculation. On February 22, 1744, our Mediterranean Fleet, under Admirals Mathews and Lestock, encountered the French and Spaniards off Toulon. The French commander, de Court by name, was eighty years of age, and had spent twenty in retirement; his ships were unseaworthy, their crews in very indifferent discipline. The incompetence—and worse—of our own admirals alone saved de Court from disaster.

Mathews and Lestock were not on speaking terms: the latter deliberately disobeyed signals, and both lost their heads. Then the action was indecisive, and much brave blood was spilt in vain. (Barbier, *Journal*, vol. ii. Diderot's *Encyclopédie,* art. "Marine," vol. x. Brun, *Guerres Maritimes de la France*, vol. i. Troude, *Batailles Navales de la France,* vol. i. Rivière, *La Marine française sous Louis XV.* Beatson, *Naval and Military Memoirs of Great Britain,* vol. i.)

Throughout the eighteenth century Great Britain, in Edmund Burke's words, was "but a moon shone upon by France." Of her sparse population in 1740 of 9,500,000, 2,200,000 inhabited Ireland, which cruel persecution had made a recruiting-ground for the French Army.

******

Of Ireland wrote Professor Stuart Blackie: "Half conquered by Henry II., and till very recently governed in the spirit of hatred, not of conciliation, it has remained for centuries in a fretful and feverish state, unparticipant alike of the blessings of a friendly union and the glory of a valiant defiance. Though possessed of the most strongly marked features of race and religion, the Irish people have been cursed with a superinduced English civilisation, which was not known to fuse itself with the native stock, as the Norman in England amalgamated with the Saxon. In consequence of this mismanagement, there has been a constant fret and discontent in that unhappy country, breaking out again and again in wild bursts of conspiracy and rebellion, a state of loveless servitude on the one side and insolent lordship on the other, similar to the relation of the Greeks with the Turks, and the Poles with the Russians."—*Essays on Subjects of Moral and Social Interest* (1890).

******

Scotland, with 1,200,000 denizens, was miserably poor; for the immediate consequence of the Union of 1707 was to check her development on national lines. Excise revenue is a fair measure of a people's prosperity. In 1708 Scotland paid £38,898 into the Exchequer under this head; in 1745 no more than £45,285. The Highlands were practically as remote and primitive as the habitat of Red Indians in our day. Their clans were despotically governed by chieftains, three-fourths of whom were hostile to the reigning dynasty.

In politics as well as physics the greater attracts the less. Court and aristocratic society in Great Britain was modelled on that of Versailles, and it was still permeated with feudal conceptions. But survivals of the past were less marked in these islands than on the Continent. The great Barons' power was shattered by the Wars of the Roses. Henry VIII.'s ability and unscrupulousness, with the added virtue of monastic spoils, made him a sixteenth-century Louis XIV. His lust of power, however, brought forces into play which his successors were unable to curb. The Reformation, which he fostered for his own selfish ends, was inimical to absolutism in Church and State alike. While in France reactionary ideals gained the mastery, with ourselves the Puritan spirit developed in an ever-increasing ratio.

It is a curious fact that conservatism is a plant of modern growth. Our eighteenth-century forbears were regarded by the rest of Europe as turbulent and mercurial folk. Elizabeth, Duchess of Orleans, voiced the opinion of her contemporaries when she wrote in 1714:—

> The more one reads the history of English revolutions, the more one is compelled to remark the eternal hatred which the people of that nation has had toward their kings, as well as their fickleness.—*Secret Memoirs of the Court of Louis XIV.* London: 18247

A habit of mind which, with all its drawbacks, is the chief source of Britain's strength, was the result of the reaction caused by the Reign of Terror in France. The last of these organic changes had placed a German dynasty on the throne; but it was endured rather than loved, because it represented principles of religion and government which were dear to the national heart. The people had wrought out in part their political salvation; they had secured a measure of parliamentary representation, freedom of the press, and control of the public purse-strings; but the process was still incomplete.

The early Hanoverian kings enjoyed a degree of personal authority which would now be regarded as unconstitutional. Secretaries of State considered themselves bound to defer to the royal will, and make it palatable to the faithful Commons by every means within their reach. The sovereign controlled foreign policy; he was his own commander-in-chief, and enjoyed a vast amount of patronage. His personal character was therefore a factor of supreme importance.

George II. (1685-1760) was honest, truthful, and conscientious within his narrow lights, and he possessed a vast capacity for business. His physical courage was as remarkable as his vanity and boyish love of fighting for its own sake. His chief disqualification for the throne of England arose from his education as a German prince. He never forgot for an instant that he was Elector of Hanover, and preferred smug Herrnhausen to Windsor's stately keep. Throughout his reign Great Britain was steered by a German rudder, and her imperial interests were subordinated to those of a paltry Continental territory.

> When any guarantee or advantage is the question, all the allies of the British crown are deemed to be allies of the Electorate; but when any danger or onus is the question, Hanover is a distinct and independent State, and no wise involved in the measures, or even fate of England.—Hon. Robert Hampden Trevor, Minister at The Hague, to Henry Pelham, May 26, 1744.

George II. detested France as the old oppressor of his fatherland, with an added zest bred by his training under Marlborough and Prince Eugene. He was, moreover, destitute of any tinge of letters; and the dull profligacy of his court was abhorrent to the thinking portion of his subjects.

Though nine-tenths of them held steadfastly by the Protestant succession, Jacobites were found in every class—even in the royal circle itself. Their eyes were turned to the representative of the Stuart cause, known to his followers as James III., or the Chevalier de St George, and to Whigs as the "Old Pretender." This amiable bigot lived at Rome on the Sovereign Pontiff's bounty. His eldest son, Prince Charles Edward (1720-88), was cast in another mould—adventurous, inured to hardships, and full of ambition. Next to his love of Hanover was George II.'s attachment to the historic throne of England. He secretly feared his young rival, and all who supported the Stuart cause incurred his deadly hatred.

The *caste* instinct, which Europe has inherited from its Indo-German ancestors, was all-powerful in Great Britain. Birth was rated far above wealth or talent, and nobles had the lion's share of high offices in the army and civil life. Their ranks were, however, constantly recruited from the commonalty, which absorbed their younger sons. Dress played an important part in men's lives. Noblemen habitually wore a star and ribbon, and incurred no rivalry from wealthy commoners. Every section of the community had its recognised social status which was marked by attire. While class distinctions were sharply accentuated, there was no gulf between the privileged and unprivileged.

Thanks to their insular position and racial energies, the middle classes were rapidly waxing rich. The twenty-five years of profound peace which followed Marlborough's campaigns were the most prosperous England had ever known. But formalism held sway in religion and manners, and an eclipse fell on British art and literature when the spacious days of Queen Anne had passed away.

While the masses were brutal, ignorant, and given to intoxication, their physical condition was superior to that of our own generation, when the brains and sinews of the countryside have migrated to enrich America and the Colonies, or to deteriorate in urban slums. Our sturdy yeomen's acres were not yet absorbed by a new landed aristocracy, founded on successful trade. The heart of the nation was sound, and it responded to generous impulses. Its most marked characteristics were insularity, bull-dog courage, and a hearty contempt for foreigners.

This sketch of the two chief antagonists in the coming struggle may serve to explain Great Britain's failure to grasp the mission imposed on her by geographical position and the genius of her people. The day was undreamt of when this little group of islands set in a northern sea became the centre of a ring of self-governing colonies and of dependencies which look thither for all the essentials of civilised life. Sea-power was neglected by George II. and his ministers. His fleets were unable to protect our commerce, and their admirals showed little of the spirit which Nelson breathed into his generation.

The country's resources were squandered on wars which had no bearing whatever on its interests. Moreover, these islands were too sparsely peopled to cope with the military monarchies of the continent, and our armies were compelled to play the thankless and undignified part of auxiliaries. Great Britain has never reaped lasting advantage from alliances. There is no surer indication of deteriorating national fibre than a tendency to rely on others rather than on our own strong arm.

In 1740 one of these dynastic controversies began which periodically drenched all Europe with bloodshed. The succession to the German Empire was at stake, which implied the hegemony of scores of autonomous states, ranging in size from a kingdom to a few barren acres. This office was theoretically elective, the great feudatories of the Empire possessing votes in a *Diet* which met at Frankfort to select a head. Chief amongst them were the Electors of Hanover, Brandenburg, and Saxony, who also sat on the thrones of England, Prussia, and Poland.

For three centuries, however, the Diets had been almost as formal as our cathedral chapters which meet to register the crown's nomination of a bishop. The vacant purple had been invariably bestowed on the head of the House of Habsburg, which by a series of fortunate marriages had acquired Austria proper, Hungary, Bohemia, Northern Italy, and Flanders. Charles VI., the last male of this illustrious family, foresaw complications after his death from his neighbours' greed and jealousy. (Born 1685, elected Emperor of Germany 1711, King of Hungary 1712, and of Bohemia 1723). He took steps to assure the succession to his realm of his daughter, Maria Theresa (1717-80), by the Pragmatic Sanction, a term employed during the Byzantine Empire to connote a solemn and public Act of State.

This settlement, dating back to 1723, was guaranteed by the Powers of Europe, Great Britain, France, and Prussia included. One essential was wanting to make the Pragmatic Sanction a reality, and that was physical force. At Charles VI.'s death (October 20, 1740), his empire had just emerged from a long and costly struggle with the Turks. The treasury was empty, and Prince Eugene's mantle had fallen on none of the Austrian leaders. Hardly had the last of the Habsburgs been laid in the vaults of the Capuchin Church at Vienna than the princes of Europe begun quarrelling for his spoils.

Charles Albert of Bavaria claimed the succession as heir in the female line to the Emperor Ferdinand I. Philip of Spain based his pretensions on the will of Charles V., which gave Austria to Spain in default of male heirs. Saxony, Poland, and Sardinia joined in the general scramble for the scattered possessions of the House of Austria. Louis XV. had not the shadow of a right to intermeddle in German affairs, nor were his country's interests in any way concerned in the dispute. But for three centuries it had been the Bourbons' settled policy to weaken Austria and thwart the Habsburg's prescriptive claim to empire.

Moreover, France was an old ally of Bavaria, which had served Louis XV. as a cat's-paw in his schemes for self-aggrandisement in Germany. Thus, his personal sympathy was enlisted on the Elector Charles Albert's side. It would probably have remained at the platonic stage but for the restless ambition of the Comte de Belle-Isle, who used his great influence with Cardinal Fleury to induce him to join a league forming against Austria.

✶✶✶✶✶✶

Louis Charles Auguste Fouquet, Comte de Belle-Isle, and his brother, the chevalier of that ilk, were grandsons of the great Finance Minister so shamefully treated by Louis XV. Parisians nicknamed them "Sensibility" and "Common-sense." Gifted with rare energy, and a rarer faculty for co-operation, they played a great part in the earlier stages of this war. The Count had distinguished himself as a soldier and diplomat, and became a great favourite with old Fleury. In 1741 he was created Marshal, and placed Charles VII. on his throne at Frankfort. In the winter of 1742 he conducted a retreat from Prague as masterly as that of Sir John Moore on Corunna.

✶✶✶✶✶✶

Foiled in this quarter by his patron's irresolution, he appealed to the bellicose spirit which was always rampant at the French court, and soon formed a war-party whose pressure Louis XV. was unable to resist. He threw solemn engagements to the wind, and gave heart-whole support to the Bavarian cause.

Maria Theresa, whose heritage stood in such jeopardy, was in her twenty fourth year, and happily married to Prince Francis Stephen of Lorraine, Grand Duke of Tuscany. Her youth, beauty, and dauntless spirit won all her subjects' hearts, and appealed with tenfold force to the chivalrous Hungarians. She prepared to defend her rights against the foes who gathered, like vultures, to despoil her.

One there was who pushed obsolescent claims with vigour, while the rest contented themselves with exchanging protocols. Frederick II. succeeded to the throne of Prussia in his twenty-ninth year, five months before the Emperor Charles VI.'s decease. He had suffered cruelly from paternal caprice, and had employed his enforced leisure in cultivating literature, music, and social intercourse.

On attaining the command of 80,000 well-drilled troops, and a treasury containing £3,200,000, he threw aside the mask which veiled his real nature, and stood before the world an almost unique example of a genius for affairs born in the purple. Measureless ambition, unwavering persistence in pursuing great ends, magical penetration, and energy which never spared itself nor tolerated sloth and incompetence in others—such qualities would have gained power and wealth in any rank of life. Their triumph was assured when their possessor had absolute power and commanding military talents.

In youth Frederick had some capacity for warm and disinterested friendships. He was soon disgusted with the ingratitude and complicated baseness which a king alone can fathom. Chamfort says, with excusable pessimism, "As one lives and sees mankind, one's heart must either break or harden." Frederick's was too strong to sink under this ordeal. He steeled it against tenderer emotions, and brought to bear on a kingdom's affairs the methods now employed by a great American trust.

The death of the last Habsburg prompted him to revive hereditary claim to certain feudal lordships in the Austrian provinces of Silesia and Glatz. Preceding Electors of Brandenburg had protested against their absorption, which dated back to the sixteenth century, but they were not strong enough to enforce legal rights. Now the tables were turned. Frederick's eagle eye ranged over the European chessboard, and his prescience told him that the mutual jealousies of the Powers might be made subservient to his ambition. Russia and Sweden were at war, and therefore negligible quantities; Denmark and Poland were too weak to cause him a moment's anxiety.

The Electors of Bavaria and Saxony would infallibly advance pretensions to the imperial crown, and France would be compelled by policy and alliances to embrace the former's cause. Great Britain was powerful only at sea, and was vulnerable in Hanover, which Frederick held in the hollow of his hand. Holland had become a republic after the death of her last *stadtholder*, William III. of England, but the spirit which wrested independence from the might of Spain was dead. Louis XIV's wars had inspired the phlegmatic Dutchmen with a fear of their mighty neighbour. Though linked with Great Britain by treaty, they would prove but lukewarm allies.

Frederick had gauged Maria Theresa's weakness, and sought to play upon it by demanding Silesia in return for help against her enemies, an alliance with the "Maritime Powers," as Great Britain and Holland were then styled, and his influence to secure her husband's election as Emperor of Germany. When these overtures were rejected with contumely, he translated words into action and invaded Silesia with 60,000 men. His first battle was a strange opening for a career of such brilliance. Mollwitz, fought on April 10, 1741, was won by the steadfast Prussian infantry. The cavalry were routed, and carried the young king far from the field of battle. He owed his life to the calculating forbearance of an Austrian trooper, who was richly rewarded by him.

Austria's foes were emboldened by their defeat, but England's generous heart went out to the injured Queen of Hungary and Bohemia. Sir Robert Walpole had vainly striven to stem the current of sympathy. His advice to abstain from meddling in Continental politics ran counter to public feeling and to the king's intense jealousy of Prussia. Resolutions were carried in Parliament for the maintenance of the Pragmatic Sanction, and a subsidy of £300,000 enabled Maria Theresa to continue the struggle. Sir Robert Walpole's influence received a death-blow at the General Election of 1741. He resigned the office of First Lord of the Treasury and Chancellor of the Exchequer, which he had held for nearly twenty-one years (February 11, 1742), and sank into obscurity as the Earl of Orford. England now rang with warlike preparations.

Danish and Hessian mercenaries were enrolled, and the Guards' brigade was ordered to embark for Flanders. King George's martial ardour was quenched for a time by one of Frederick's master-strokes. He posted an army of observation near the Hanoverian frontier, while a French force advanced on the Electorate by its western marches. George II. was unable to resist pressure at so crucial a point. He agreed to maintain neutrality for a year, and to withhold his suffrage from

Maria Theresa's husband. Frederick was now able to pursue his aggressions unchecked by British interference. It is needless to dwell on vicissitudes of the struggle for German hegemony, which deluged Central Europe with blood and stirred the *Sultan* of Turkey to offer his mediation.

******

This curious episode was a forgotten precedent for the *Tsar* of Russia's attempt to supersede war by an international tribunal. In the winter of 1743 Mohammad V. handed a document to every foreign minister at Constantinople, which began: "God, after creating the world, made man, and in order to put a finishing touch to so glorious a work He gave him dominion over land and sea. Great moderation is necessary for the good government of the human race. The refractory must be brought back to reason; but as soon as affairs proceed prosperously, we must think of peace, which is the source of all happiness. Though mankind has an instinctive horror of warfare, princes are often compelled to have recourse thereto.
But however just their cause may be, they must finish war speedily, for it has appalling consequences. . . . The Ottoman Porte hoped that the Christian princes would at length be tired of fighting, but it learns that numerous armies will take the field next spring. Now warfare pours out torrents of blood, dishonours families, and suspends the commerce and subsistence of multitudes. In a hope that the Christian princes will be touched by this representation, the *Sultan* offers his mediation." He proposed Venice as a convenient centre for a European Congress to decide all international disputes.—*The Life of Frederick II of Prussia* (anonymous translation from the French). London: 1789. Vol. i.

******

The Elector of Bavaria was duly installed as Emperor at Frankfort (February 12, 1742); but he was never aught but a pawn in the game of European politics, and died in poverty and abandonment in January 1745. Frederick II. alone profited by the sacrifice of the rest of Europe. He learnt the art of war by bitter experience, and developed the genius which welded his scattered and sparsely-peopled territories into a great Power. His arms were seconded by an astute and unscrupulous diplomacy. Watching every phase of the struggle, he threw his whole weight into the scale which seemed the heavier. After overrunning

Silesia, he made peace with Maria Theresa at Breslau (June 11, 1742), securing the coveted provinces, only to draw the sword again when a fitting opportunity offered itself.

On November 18, 1742, he concluded a treaty of defensive alliance with Great Britain. When George II. claimed the promised contingent of 10,000 Prussians, he was met by tergiversation and subterfuge. Again, on April 5, 1744, Frederick allied himself with France, and five weeks later he joined a coalition against Maria Theresa, formed at Frankfort by the titular Emperor of Germany, France, the Palatinate, and Electoral Hesse. At length, having conquered Saxony as well as Silesia and Glatz, and thus gratified his utmost ambition, he prepared to desert allies who were of no further use to Prussia.

Three weeks after Fontenoy he defeated the Austrians at Hohenfriedberg (June 3, 1745), and in notifying his victory to Louis XV. he wrote:

> My brother, I have honoured at Hohenfriedberg the bill of exchange which you drew on me at Fontenoy.

Maria Theresa held out for four months longer, but further reverses induced her to adopt George II's advice to make peace with her redoubtable foe. By the Treaty of Dresden (December 25, 1745), confirmed by the General Peace of Aix-la-Chapelle, the King of Prussia secured Silesia and Glatz, with an indemnity of a million crowns. His policy between 1743 and 1745 had an immense, if indirect, influence on the fortunes of the Flanders campaigns, and it deserves the closest study on the part of all who wish to forecast the European situation in the twentieth century.

Great Britain meanwhile was being dragged into the vortex of Continental war. Disgust at George II's pusillanimity in securing Hanover at the cost of his kingdom's honour served only to strengthen the nation's resolve to stand by the Queen of Hungary and Bohemia. In Lord Carteret, who succeeded to all Walpole's influence, the king found an agent of supreme ability, accompanied by a want of principle which led him to abet all his master's designs. Carteret won over his colleagues in the Ministry to active intervention.

★★★★★★

John Lord Carteret (1690-1763) had won his spurs in diplomacy, and in 1721 he was appointed to one of the two foreign secretaryships—that of the Southern Department. After Walpole's overthrow in 1742 he became Secretary of the Northern

Department, in whose hands was vested the management of the war. He was a brilliant scholar and wit, but was overgiven to conviviality. His influence over George II. arose from the fact that he could converse fluently in German, a rare accomplishment in those days.

★★★★★★

16,000 troops were despatched to Flanders under the veteran Earl of Stair, and Carteret betook himself to The Hague in view of securing Dutch co-operation. He found the sluggish Hollanders unmoved by his eloquence. During the winter of 1742-43 our soldiers were quartered in the cities of Flanders, "idle, unemployed, and quarrelling with the inhabitants." (Tindall's *History*, vol. viii.) But more stirring times were at hand for the British army. The thirty years' peace secured by Marlborough's glorious campaigns was at an end, and the two great Western Powers were about to renew their secular contest for supremacy. Let us pause on the threshold of war to survey the resources at the disposal of each.

Chapter 2

The Armies and Their Leaders

French preponderance in Europe rested on an army unsurpassed in spirit, numbers, and efficiency. Its origin must be sought in the guards maintained by the Capetian dynasty, and five centuries of aggressive warfare were reflected in its annals. To Louis XIV. and his great War Minister, Louvois, (see note next page), belongs the credit of making the military forces at their disposal a model for Europe.

In intervals of peace many regiments were disbanded, and others were reduced to skeleton cadres. When France returned to her almost normal state of warfare, the army was trebled by wholesale recruitments and draughts from the Militia. In 1740, for instance, the French infantry hardly reached 100,000. After three campaigns their number stood as follows:—

I. Regular Troops.

	Regiments.	Battalions.	Men.
Gardes Françaises	...	6	4,380
Gardes Suisses	...	4	2,400
Line regiments	99	160	109,940
Marines	1	1	685
Artillery	1	5	4,450
Swiss regiments	9	27	18,900
German regiments	6	18	11,880
Italian and Corsican regiments	2	2	1,200
Irish regiments	5	5	3,425
Scottish regiments	1	1	660
Total regular troops	124	229	157,920

II. Irregulars.

Free companies and arquebusiers raised in 1744	2,285
Invalides, 10 companies	10,666
Provincial Militia	93,884
Total irregulars	106,835
Grand total, infantry	264,755

The war strength of a battalion thus averaged 690 men.

✶✶✶✶✶✶

Note:—François Michel le Tellier, Marquis de Louvois (1641-91), became Minister of War in 1668. He was the real creator of the French army, to which he gave a corps of officers compulsorily recruited from the nobility—commissariat and hospital services, and all the essentials of organisation. His drill-master was the well-known Martinet, whose name has enriched our own language. Louvois was autocratic, brutal, and unscrupulous, but he sought the aggrandisement of France as ardently as he laboured to preserve his own position.

✶✶✶✶✶✶

The backbone of the old French Army was the infantry, and its flower the Household Troops, which comprised French and Swiss Guards. The first were created in 1563 by Charles IX. Foreigners were not admitted into their ranks, nor were natives of recent conquests, such as Alsace. The French Guards enjoyed extraordinary privileges. In battle array they occupied the centre of the first line; during sieges they opened the trenches, headed storming-parties, and were the first to enter a strong place on its capitulation.

Their officers were drawn from the first families in France, and had army rank much superior to their regimental status. A lieutenant-colonel was classed with lieutenant-generals, a captain with colonels, and a subaltern with captains in the line. The Swiss Guards were raised in 1616, and were brigaded with their French comrades. There was much jealousy between the native and foreign Guards. A French officer once taunted a Swiss with mercenary motives, quoting the old proverb, "No money, no Swiss." "And, pray, what do you fight for?" was the retort. "For honour, of course." "Yes, we severally fight for what we don't possess." Their staunchness won undying glory at the outset of the Revolution, and is commemorated by Thorwaldsen's famous lion at Lucerne.

A rigorous etiquette governed the precedence of the line regiments, and disputes on that score led to frequent duels. Army rank depended on the standing of regiments. Thus, a captain of the Picardy regiment took the *pas* of all company officers in other regiments, but cavalry captains ranked above their comrades in the line. Brigades were named after their senior regiment. The oldest corps that fought at Fontenoy was Normandy, raised in 1574; next came Eu, which dated from 1604. The rest had been added by Louis XIII. and his successor. Until Louvois carried out his policy of centralising all authority in his master's hands, many regiments were the property of the princes of the blood and great nobles by whom they had been raised. Hence the distinction between king's, princes', and provincial regiments, which was obsolete in 1740, but survived in the varied facings.

Grenadiers originated in 1667, when four men were assigned to each regiment who were armed with a hatchet and sabre, and carried a leather bag containing twelve or fifteen grenades. These were small cast-iron shells, weighing two pounds, which were lit at close quarters by a slow match and hurled into the enemy's ranks. They were, however, chiefly employed in the third parallels during sieges.

The introduction of grenades in line regiments dated from 1670; and before the end of the century every battalion had its grenadier company, comprised of picked men. They were first armed with muskets in 1678; and when volley-firing came into vogue, about the date of the Battle of Steenkirk (1690), the little shell to which they owed their name became obsolete. Thenceforward grenadiers were regarded as a *corps d'élite*. They guarded the regimental flag, headed storming parties, and stood on the right of the line. In 1741 grenadiers were formed into a separate force of 10,000 or 12,000 men, which was organised on a regimental basis in 1745.

France has always had a peculiar fascination for foreigners. As early as the fifteenth century the warlike and chivalrous character of her people attracted hosts of Scotch, Irish, Swiss, and German soldiers of fortune to her standard. These mercenaries were organised in regiments under their own officers. Though discipline and internal arrangements were identical with those of native troops, the words of command were given in the language of origin, and pay was on a slightly higher scale. Foreign regiments were kept at their full strength in peace-time, owing to the difficulty of recruiting them after the declaration of war. Their efficiency was very high indeed. *Esprit de corps* was strong, old soldiers numerous; and as the officers' whole life from cradle to grave was spent in the regiment, they regarded it as a home.

The Swiss element dated back to the Perpetual Peace signed by Francis I. and the cantons after the Battle of Marignan in 1516. Denizens of the little republic were regarded rather as allies or permanent auxiliaries than as mercenary troops. Their nationality was retained; they enjoyed liberty of conscience and their own military courts, from whose doom there was no appeal. First and foremost was the regiment of Bettens, raised at Berne in 1672 by a colonel of that name, whose descendant commanded it at Fontenoy. The Diesbach regiment dated from 1690, as did that of Courten, which was ruled by members of the same family until its disbandment a century later.

The revolution of 1688 established Protestant ascendancy in Ireland by methods calculated to make the island uninhabitable by all who held to the rival cult. To the monstrous system of persecution inaugurated by William III., and perfected under Queen Anne, is due the formation of the famous Irish Brigade. The oldest of its six regiments bore the name of Colonel de Ruth, subsequently taken prisoner at Culloden. It was originally James II.'s bodyguard, and followed him into exile. Lally's was commanded by Comte Arthur de Lally-Tollendal, whose strenuous work for France in Southern India was requited by an ignominious death. These fiery, chivalrous Celts took kindly to French service, and identity of religious belief was an additional bond of sympathy.

★★★★★★

Thomas Arthur, Count de Lally and Baron Tollendal (1702-66), descended from a baronial family long settled at Tullenadally, near Tuam. He covered himself with glory at Fontenoy, and was taken prisoner at Culloden. Appointed commander-in-chief of the French settlements in the East Indies in 1756, he fiercely attacked the British, overran the Madras Presidency, and laid siege to its capital. Then the tide turned: he was defeated and driven back on Pondicherry, which was captured in 1761 by an overwhelming British force. Lally was taken to England as a prisoner of war, but learning that he was accused of cowardice, he returned to Paris to vindicate his character.

After two years' confinement in the Bastille he was condemned to death by the infamous Parliament, and beheaded with every circumstance of ignominy, May 9, 1766. By such injustice did Louis XV. strangle the growth of French empire in India. Lally's great-grandson died of starvation in a Soho cellar, October 1877. (See Philip Thicknesse's *Letters from France*. London: 1768)

★★★★★★

During the wars, which darkened Louis XIV.'s declining years, the services of the Irish Brigade were out of all proportion to their numbers, and their great reputation was enhanced by Fontenoy and Laffeldt. There was one Scottish regiment, the Royal Écossais, raised in 1744, and commanded by Lord John Drummond, son of the titular Duke of Perth. It was recruited, at imminent peril to their necks, by officers sent on roving commissions to Scotland, who enlisted likely youths, ostensibly for the Dutch sea-service.

Irregular troops played a great part in the Fontenoy campaign. They offered a career highly attractive to restless spirits who were averse to discipline and the monotony of garrison life. The Arquebusiers de Grassin, raised in 1744 by a lieutenant-colonel of that name in the Picardy regiment, gave more trouble to our generals than any other corps. They were the army's eyes and ears, admirable purveyors of intelligence, and Dugald Dalgetys as foragers. ("This regiment, formed from boot-blacks and vagabonds in Paris, is becoming formidable."— Barbier, *Journal du Regne de Louis XV.* July 1745. What magnificent raw material is now rotting in our London streets!)

Invaluable as a source of supply to the regular army was the Provincial Militia, established by Louis XIV. in 1688, when he was confronted by the Augsburg League, and found no adequate reserves among the privileged classes. This citizen army was at first flouted by aristocratic officers, but its value was shown during Marlborough's and Eugene's campaigns, and it was placed on a permanent basis in 1726. Eighteen years later Marshal Saxe induced his master to use the militia as a source of supply for the standing army. It was divided into garrison and field forces, the latter including younger and more vigorous men. In the winter before Fontenoy (1744-45) the standard of height and age for recruits in the regular army was perilously low. A call for militia volunteers was responded to with such enthusiasm that no place could be found for many promising candidates.

In 1740 the French cavalry stood without rival in Europe. As was the case with the sister arm, their germ is found in the royal guards. The cavalry, however, resisted Louis XIV.'s reforms with greater vigour than their comrades. They clung stubbornly to their feudal basis, and many regiments were still the personal property of noble families. The effective in that year stood as follows:—

	Squadrons.	Men.
The King's Household Troops, *Maison du Roi* . .	12	2,544
Gendarmerie de France and Chevau-Légers, ranking with the Household	8	1,280
French and foreign cavalry, 60 regiments . . .	164	26,240
Dragoons, 15 regiments	60	9,920
New levies and irregulars	12	1,920
Total	256	41,904

A squadron was the unit. It stood in peace-time at 130 files, but on a war footing was raised to 160. An average regiment included 4 squadrons, which were divided into as many companies of 40 files.

The Household Cavalry was placed on a permanent footing by Louis XIV. in 1675, and it was officered by members of the high nobility.

Traces of the ancient alliance between France and Scotland survived in the first company of Body-Guards. It was styled *Écossaise* because for upwards of a century it was recruited exclusively from the little northern kingdom. The last Scots captain was the Comte de Montgommery, who slew King Henry II. by mischance in a tournament (1559). The oldest companies, however, were the *Gardes de la Porte et de la Prévôté de l'Hôtel*, whose annals ran back to the age of St Louis (1261-70). The *Mousquetaires* were a creation of Louis XIV. There were two companies, styled Grey and Black from the colour of their chargers, entirely composed of young nobles who sought opportunities of access to the royal person, and disdained to draw their daily pittance. The *Gendarmerie de France* was founded in the fifteenth century, and ranked immediately after the Body-Guards. The first of its 16 companies, making 8 squadrons, was styled *Gendarmes Écossais*, and had an unbroken existence of 366 years, extending from the days of Joan of Arc to the Revolution.

Among cavalry regiments of the line the senior was *Colonel Général*, raised in 1635. Officers and men rode grey chargers: they were saluted by all other cavalry corps, but rendered similar honours only to princes of the blood, marshals, and full generals. But the most distinguished was the Royal Carabiniers, so styled because troopers carried a rifled musketoon. Its strength was equal to that of five ordinary regiments. The *Carabiniers* were indeed a crack corps, and their splendid services during Eugene's and Marlborough's wars justified the proud device emblazoned on their standards, "Always on the path of honour." Immense pains were taken to preserve the highest standard of efficiency. The officers underwent a special scientific training, and in the *Carabiniers'* cavalry school originated the famous institution at Saumur. So high stood their reputation for discipline that all other regiments were compelled to send representatives every year to undergo a course of training with them.

Dragoons were first employed in the sixteenth century by the Duc de Brissac, who, while operating in broken country, conceived the idea of mounting his foot-soldiers on wiry hill-ponies. At their reorganisation by Louis XIV., between 1656 and 1674, they retained most of the characteristics of mounted infantry; and their superior mobility was employed with terrible effect during the cruel dragonnades directed by that crowned bigot against Protestant congregations. We shall see that this quality was conspicuous at Fontenoy.

Hussars were a lighter description of mounted troops. They were first enrolled by Louis XIV. from Polish and Hungarian deserters, and retained the picturesque *pelisse*, shako, and curved sabre of Eastern Europe. Bestriding undersized horses with short stirrups, they circled round the enemy's heavy cavalry with blood-curdling yells. In order of battle they took positions which enabled them to pursue retreating troops and foil attempts at re-forming. Their chief utility, however, was in harassing hostile camps, cutting off stragglers, and intercepting supplies.

The French artillery was placed on a modern basis in 1732 by Valliere, who standardised the calibres while he reduced the weight of cannon. The latter were 4-, 8-, 12-, 16-, and 24-pounders, but the two first alone had any pretensions to mobility. Both carriages and tumbrils were still extremely cumbrous. Charles XII. of Sweden took the first step towards creating a field artillery about 1703. It was left to Frederick the Great, nearly forty years later, to give this indispensable arm the organisation which it still retains. In 1743 Marshal Saxe copied that great innovator by furnishing each battalion with a couple of 3-pounders, drawn by a pair of horses. In practice these little guns proved terribly embarrassing to infantry officers. Speaking generally, the science of artillery was imperfectly understood in 1745, but French guns almost invariably outclassed our own.

Like our regulars in the present year of grace, the old French Army was a mercenary force. The recruiting sergeant installed himself at a wine-shop while some rural festival was in full swing. His dazzling uniform, martial air, and upturned moustache proved irresistible to bumpkins, whom he lured with tales of love, plunder, and adventure. One of the advertisements issued by these notorious deceivers is still preserved:—

> Regiment of Rouergue, in garrison at Thionville; Colonel, Vicomte de Custine. Brilliant youths, who aspire to serve your king, satisfy your laudable ambition by addressing M. Vinot, sergeant of that regiment, who lodges with M. Hardi, Rue Thibaudin, third floor. He will accept recruits 5 feet 6 inches in height. *N.B.*—Anyone who brings him a likely fellow will be well rewarded.

The sergeant's purse was at his dupe's disposal; and after a prolonged carouse the poor victim awoke with aching head to find himself irremediably committed to a life as toilsome and arduous as a galley-slave's.

The minimum height for admission to the Household troops was 5 ft. 7¼ in.; in line regiments the standard was an inch less. Recruits were received between the ages of sixteen and twenty-five. When war broke out, these rules were set at nought. Six years was nominally the period of service, but as only a limited number of discharges were granted annually, recruits might calculate on spending ten or twelve years with the colours. When the hour of freedom struck, every inducement was offered to secure re enrolment, and the bounty of 30 *francs* was seldom resisted. Thus, the ranks included a large proportion of old soldiers with twenty and even thirty years' service to their credit, and this stiffening was the chief source of the army's strength.

In those days' soldiers were not clad in the neutral tints imposed by long-range weapons and smokeless powder. An army arrayed in order of battle was as variegated as a well-ordered flower-garden, and presented a scene of dazzling beauty of which we can form no conception in this prosaic age. The general effect was heightened by a host of waving banners, termed "flag" in infantry and "standard" in cavalry regiments. They were delivered to colonels with pomp and religious ceremony, and were revered as the Ark of the Covenant. Colours were much ampler and more numerous than at present. Those of the Guards were gorgeous with gold and silver embroidery, and bore grandiloquent mottoes. Every regiment had a white "colonel's flag," which was of larger dimensions than the rest. All flags had a white cross in the centre, while standards displayed the rising sun, an emblem adopted by Louis XIV.

Uniforms were introduced into the infantry by Louvois in 1668-70, but twenty years elapsed ere the semi feudal cavalry adopted the king's livery. The most conspicuous item was a short overcoat with voluminous skirts turned back, termed justacorps. In French infantry regiments the prevailing hue was white or grey, in Irish and Swiss regiments red; in irregular regiments blue was conspicuous. Greater diversity was seen in the Household troops' attire. They wore the Bourbon colours—red, white, or blue. A vest, small clothes, and white linen gaiters fastened above the knee with black buttons completed the infantry uniform. Troopers wore heavy jack-boots, which impeded their movements when dismounted. A few cavalry regiments retained the *cuirass*, almost the last relic of medieval armour.

The picturesque three cornered hat, which is a distinctive mark of eighteenth century attire, was almost universal. Its material was thick felt, and it was worn well over the eyes, with a point turned slightly to the left. Officers' hats were trimmed with gold or silver lace; those of inferior grades displayed an edging of the regimental colours, which were repeated in the collar, cuffs, and lapels. The trooper charged home with an iron skullcap under his three-cornered hat, which at other times dangled from the saddle bow. Dragoons wore a brass helmet; hussars their national shako. A tall bearskin cap was given to the grenadier companies of the French and Swiss Guards in 1730. The soldier's hair was dressed in a compact mass with a nauseous mixture of grease and flour, and clubbed in a long pig-tail. Hussars, however, wore their long locks arranged in pleats.

Uniforms were showy rather than serviceable. The hat was reduced to a shapeless mass by rain, and then impeded its wearer's vision. The linen gaiters were equally unsuited to rough work. Moreover, the soldier's misfortunes were aggravated by a vicious system of army clothing, under which the captain contracted for supplying his company. By economising at the cost of his men's health, he largely supplemented his pay, which ranged from £80 to £120. He was apt to regard his squadron or company as a farm from which the maximum amount of profit was to be screwed. Thus, uniforms which were supposed to last for three years were made to do duty for five, and even seven. They were donned only at reviews and in battle order, and were then replaced by linen rags, which were a fertile source of chills, filling the military hospitals.

Arms and accoutrements were clumsy to a degree which would not be tolerated in our day. The infantry musket was 3 ft. 8 in. in barrel, .670 in. in gauge, and threw an ounce ball to a maximum range of 80 or perhaps 100 yards. Cartouche-box with twenty rounds of ball, and haversack containing necessaries, were suspended from buff-leather cross-belts, from which hung the bayonet and a short sword, derided by the cavalry as a *briquet* or steel for striking fire. In full marching order the load carried was more than 64 lb., *viz.*:—

	lb.
Haversack, with kit	15.4
Firelock, with strap and bayonet	15.4
Sabre	2.6
Share of portable tent, blanket, and cooking-pot ..	4.9
Cartouche-box with 20 rounds	5.0

3RD REGIMENT OF DRAGOONS

Four days' rations	21.0
Total	64.3

Infantry captains and majors carried a spontoon six feet long, armed with a steel lance head; subalterns, a light fusil. Sergeants were armed with sword and halberd.

The private's pay was on a meagre scale, and it was generally several months in arrears. Linesmen drew 6 *sols* 9 *deniers per diem*, equivalent to 33.75 *centimes* of modern currency. In the Guards, foreign regiments, and cavalry the rate was fifty *per cent* higher, and a *Carabinier* was passing rich on 10 *sols* a-day. These pittances were subject to deduction of 2 *sols* for the bread and 1 *sol* for the meat ration, leaving a soldier of the line a penny *per diem* as pocket-money. The infantry bread ration was 26 ounces; troopers enjoyed 28. The meat allowance was nominally 17 ounces, and a quart of sour wine was served out daily.

Much suffering was caused by the peculation of army contractors, belonging to the gang of harpies termed Farmers General, who battened on the French people. Bread, in the shape of biscuit, was generally forthcoming; but the meat was irregularly given out, and of wretched quality. When commissariat arrangements broke down, the men received the money equivalent to their rations, to their intense satisfaction.

The private soldier's spartan fare contrasted strangely with the unbridled luxury affected by his superiors. The aristocracy, as one of them remarked, had no other career open to them but "to go and get themselves knocked on the head, like fools, in the king's service." They sought relief from the boredom of garrison life and the fever of campaign in riotous living. Magnificent were the equipages of wealthy officers, and others were half ruined by an attempt to vie with their luckier comrades. Thus, transport and mobility were impeded; and the sight of their chief's profusion was a direct incentive to pillage and excesses of every kind for the rank and file.

An effort was made to cope with this growing evil by royal ordinances. In 1734 officers were strictly enjoined to reduce the dimensions of their outfits, and to keep more frugal tables. In 1735 grades below that of general officer were forbidden to use silver plate except in the form of spoons, forks, and goblets. Daily fare was to consist of plain joints; fruit was not to be served on porcelain or crystal dishes. Two ordinances appeared in 1741 regulating private transport. A commander-in-chief might do as he pleased, but lieutenant-generals were restricted to 30 pack horses or mules, colonels to 16, and inferior officers to a number proportionate with the fodder rations drawn by them.

Small effect was produced by these fulminations, because the king and his favourites drove a coach-and-four through them. Louis XV. started at the campaign of 1744 with his entire household; and two sisters (the Duchesses of Lauraguais and Châteauroux), who were his acknowledged mistresses, joined the royal headquarters at Lille. His tent in the Fontenoy campaign was a gorgeous structure of silk and brocade, presented by the Sultan of Turkey. Marshal Saxe was accompanied in camp by a complete operatic troop. The Prince de Conti left Paris in February 1744 to take command in Italy with a train of 84 mules, 36 led horses, more than 20 mounted attendants, 2 campaign coaches for his superior officers, and 5 or 6 waggons. (Barbier, *Journal historique et anecdotique du Regne de Louis XV,* vol. ii.)

The soldier's dreams of a peaceful old age were encouraged by the sight of the Invalides, which Paris owes to Louvois. But only the lucky few who had interest at court or in the War Ministry could hope to enter its stupendous portal. Inns and post-houses throughout France were beset with old soldiers, who appealed for alms by displaying maimed limbs or honourable scars. In the case of officers, pensions depended on royal favour; and all who had access to the royal person were besieged by suppliants, who too often found "what hell it is in suing long to bide."

Heart-rending cases of distress were common. E. J. Barbier, who was an eighteenth-century Samuel Pepys, records in December 1749 the arrest of a man for begging in the streets who proved that he had maintained a Knight of St Louis for fifteen years by these ignoble means. His master admitted that he would have died of hunger but for the few *sous* brought in daily by this faithful servant. Barbier adds an *on dit*, which one devoutly hopes was true, that the king granted a pension to his pauper knight, with remainder to his valet. (*Journal historique*, vol. iii.)

The Order of St Louis, to which this officer belonged, was founded in 1693 by Louis XIV. as a recompense for long and faithful service. There were three grades—the Grand Cross, Red Ribbon, and Knighthood. The cross, of gold and white enamel, displayed on one side the patron saint, with a sword and olive-branch on the reverse. *Bellicae virtutis Premium* was the device; and the ribbon was flame-coloured. Every officer could claim this decoration after a given number of years' service, those spent in campaigning and with the colours counting as two. The cross was also conferred, irrespective of service, for actions of special gallantry. The *Roi Soleil* was far in advance of his age in adopting this cheap and effective method of encouraging emulation among his troops.

During the discussions in council which preceded the institution of the Legion of Honour, Napoleon said: "Never would Louis XIV. have withstood a European coalition had he not been able to pay his soldiers with crosses of St Louis." In 1740 privates had no incentive to good conduct save a distribution of two months' pay, which generally followed a successful campaign. Medals and stripes were introduced only in 1771. Our own army chiefs were slow to follow suit. The first medal issued in modern times was that for Waterloo, which was distributed in 1816. Peninsular heroes had to wait for a similar recognition until 1847, when most of the officers and men who had shared in the undying glory of those campaigns had passed beyond the reach of human reward. In our days, the pendulum has, perhaps, swung too far in the opposite direction.

Ill-fed and worse clad as he was in 1740, the French soldier found solace in his loyalty, his passion for glory, and the national disposition to make the best of things. Songs were a great resource. A library might be made of the ditties which enlivened eighteenth-century barracks and bivouacs. Tobacco was eschewed by aristocratic officers, save in the form of snuff. The rank and file were great smokers, and they prized the privilege of buying the much-loved weed at six to nine and a half *sous* per pound. Discipline was by no means oppressive. Privates saw but little of their superior officers. They were at liberty to follow any trade, and to engage in harvest or other field work, provided that they returned to barracks at 8 p.m.

The fearful floggings so common in the British Army were unknown across the Channel, but death penalties were much more frequent than with us. The gallows or firing-party awaited all who were convicted of desertion, marauding, disobedience to orders, and the thousand and one offences defined by comprehensive military code. These punishments were seldom necessary in the field; for the ardent French nature rebelled against the boredom and routine of garrison life, while it bore hardships involved by war with equanimity.

In 1748 Lord Albemarle was watching a thousand prisoners, who had been taken with a convoy for Bergen-op-Zoom, file past his lodgings. One of these "ragged scarecrows," seeing the earl's ribbon and star, remarked gaily, "Today it is your turn, sir; tomorrow it will be the king's."

"If they all have this spirit," adds the chronicler, "no wonder they beat us."

Before the revolution in the art of war wrought by Frederick II. of Prussia, a European army's manoeuvres retained many survivals of the middle ages. In the days of Conde and Turenne the fate of battles was decided by the shock of dense masses of men. During Louis XIV's wars, battles were battles of position. Those fought by Marshal Saxe and his school were outpost affairs, and governed by no prearranged design. Frederick the Great astonished the world by dealing unexpected blows on an enemy's weakest point, and introduced battle manoeuvres.

In 1740 deep formations were still in vogue. The infantry were massed in ranks four to eight in depth. Cavalry was employed to cover the slow and punctilious evolutions preliminary to formation in order of battle, and then took position in the infantry's rear. An extensive plain was necessary for these parade ground movements; while modern armies seek the cover afforded by woods, villages, and inequalities of the ground.

In 1740 the French Army was the first military school in Europe. Among the host of able men who led their soldiers to victory, or preserved them from utter disaster, Maurice de Saxe stands preeminent. He was born on October 28, 1696, the illegitimate son of Augustus II., Elector of Saxony, and afterwards King of Poland, whose vices were thrown into the shade by a rare degree of courage and political foresight. Maurice de Saxe's mother was the lovely, wayward Aurora von Königsmarck, descended from a long line of distinguished warriors, whose influence with Augustus II. gained the unique privilege of recognition for her child.

Thus, the stars of heredity fought for the young Comte de Saxe, and they overcame the disadvantages of equivocal birth. It has often been remarked that the bar sinister is attended by a bold and enterprising spirit, as though its wearer were conscious that social position must be won sword in hand. This militant instinct appears in tenfold force in illegitimate scions of a royal race. To come into the world on the steps of a throne and yet be separated from it by an impassable gulf—such was the fate of Maurice de Saxe. It serves to explain his nobility of soul, his breadth of view, his boundless ambition. He was throughout life a sovereign in quest of some shadowy realm, and once at least he nearly grasped the reality. His childhood was spent under the eye of one who worshipped his beautiful mother with chivalrous devotion.

This was Marshal Count von der Schulenberg, a soldier of fortune cast in the same mould as Gustavus Adolphus of Sweden. Vigilant, intrepid, resourceful, and God-fearing, he was one of the few heroic figures which shine in the darkness of a corrupt and self-seeking age. Far different would have been his pupil's fate, and perhaps that of Europe, had he followed this mentor's advice:

Be irreproachable in morals, and you will rule mankind; be industrious; strive for great things; love worthy friends.

Such were Schulenberg's maxims, and they served to counteract in some measure the indulgence of a doting mother. Maurice entered the imperial army at twelve, under the marshal's wing, and his daring elicited a word of warning from Prince Eugene:

Young man, you must not mistake rashness for valour.

In 1714 his mother's baleful influence led him into the first false step of a stormy career. She wedded him to a child of fifteen, who was a great heiress, but possessed no personal quality fitting her to fix the affections of one who was already convinced that "a wife is no part of a soldier's baggage." After many infidelities on both sides, the young couple drifted apart. In 1721, after obtaining a divorce, Maurice de Saxe sought a new career in France. He arrived at Paris during the mad carnival of the Regency, and plunged into the vortex of dissipation with all the zest of a novice gifted with a stock of energy which must find an outlet. His escapades bordered on madness. He was idolised by the women of the Regent's court, and the chosen companion of his orgies.

But the good seed cast by Schulenberg preserved the youth from moral shipwreck. In the intervals between his long debauches he found time to study mathematics and every branch of military science. He purchased the colonelcy of a foreign regiment in the French service, and took delight in devising new methods of drill and firing exercises. "One of the first geniuses for war I have ever known,"—such was the verdict of Charles Folard, the capable translator of Polybius, who knew the young colonel well.

In 1726 came an opportunity of gratifying his passion for rule. The duchies of Kurland and Semigallia had for centuries been governed by a family descended from those Teutonic knights who imposed Christianity and feudalism on the heathen of the Baltic coast. On the death of the last grand duke, Maurice tore himself from the arms of his mistress, Adrienne Lecouvreur, to stand as candidate for the vacant throne.

******

Adrienne Lecouvreur (1692-1730) was a great actress and a fascinating woman. She was the only mistress who ever fixed Maurice's inconstant heart. Adrienne died of poison, believed to have been administered by the Duchesse de Bouillon. This tragedy is the motive of Scribe and Legouvé's well-known play, in which Rachel and Sarah Bernhardt gained fresh laurels.

******

The sinews of war were provided by Aurora von Königsmarck, who had become Abbess of Quedlinburg, and by the sale of Adrienne's jewellery. It would be difficult to unearth a more startling instance of the social anarchy of that age.

The campaign opened well. Maurice won the active support of two Russian princesses, both of whom loved him devotedly, and both succeeded to the purple. Had he but played his cards with discretion, Maurice de Saxe would have found scope for even his energies in governing All the Russias. Thanks to this powerful influence, he was elected as duke by the national *Diet* of Kurland. His dreams of sovereignty were of short duration, for the duchy was coveted by Russia and Poland alike. Saxe found himself between the upper and the nether millstone, and was compelled to relinquish the sceptre. The dethroned Duke of Kurland and Semigallia found oblivion for his disappointment in the whirlpool of Paris.

In 1732 came another crisis in his life, which was pregnant with lucky consequences for the world. He was brought to death's door by a violent fever, the result of mad excesses of all kinds, and employed the long evenings of convalescence in giving shape to the grandiose dreams which filled his brain. The outcome was his famous *Rêveries*, which were published posthumously in 1757. (*Les Rêveries de Maurice, Comte de Saxe, Duc de Courlande et Semigallie*. Edited by M. de Bonneville, Captain-Engineer to the King of Prussia. 2 vols. large 4to. Paris: 1757. Reprinted at The Hague in 1 vol. small folio in the following year.)

An autograph inscription in one of two manuscripts preserved at Dresden runs thus:—

I have completed this work in thirteen nights. It may well show traces of the fever which was consuming me. This consideration will, perhaps, excuse defects in arrangement and style. I have written it as a soldier, to dispel my *ennui*. Done in the month of December 1732.

The *Rêveries* are in two parts—the first dealing with details, the second with the "sublime" side of the military calling. In treating this problem from a technical aspect Saxe anticipates Napoleon's dictum, "*The whole art of war lies in the soldier's legs.*" He advocates universal military service in supersession of a system by which mercenary armies were recruited from the dregs of the population:

> Let every man be compelled to dedicate to his country the years which are often squandered in debauchery.

In criticising the uniform in vogue, he condemns the white linen gaiter as being expensive, fitted only for the barrack-yard, and injurious to health. The three-cornered hat he considered equally unpractical, for it was reduced to a shapeless mass by heavy rain. He advocated the cadenced step. Arguing on the analogy of dancing, he believed that soldiers would forget their fatigue if they marched in unison. This immense revolution is due to his teachings. Saxe preferred the bayonet, after a volley at close quarters, to the rolling fire then employed. He recommended a breech-loading carbine for cavalry.

Chapter 9 treats of "Redoubts, and their Excellence in Order of Battle." He wrote:

> I never hear of entrenchments, without thinking of the Great Wall of China.

The best entrenchments are those which nature made. They are wise dispositions and the maintenance of a high standard of discipline.

> Put the best troops in the world behind entrenchments, and you ensure their discomfiture; or at any rate you lead them to think of defeat rather than victory.

On the other hand, nothing is more calculated to harass an enemy than redoubts. They must attack at great disadvantage, and hesitate to leave them in their flanks or rear. The army that adopts them has a rallying-point, and protection in case of retreat; for it is aware that the enemy will not venture to press far beyond these improvised citadels in pursuit. A strong point in favour of redoubts is, that they can be created at almost a moment's notice. Five hours and 1488 men suffice for constructing a redoubt which would stop an army.

In discussing discipline the young soldier anticipated Ruskin's golden words, which should be taken to heart by all who are entrusted with authority over their fellows:—

> Man is an engine whose motive power is the Soul; and the largest quantity of work will not be done by this curious engine for pay, or under pressure, or by the help of any kind of fuel which may be supplied by the chaldron. It will be done only when the will or spirit of the creature is brought to its greatest strength by its own proper fuel, namely, by the affections.

In Saxe's opinion pipe-clay is a good thing in its way, but a knowledge of the human heart is better. Death was far too common a punishment for military crimes.

> It is absolutely necessary to make the soldier work. Read in history the multifarious functions undertaken by Roman *legionaries*, and you will see that the Republic regarded idleness and leisure as its most redoubtable, foes. The consuls fashioned their troops for victory by making them almost impervious to fatigue. Rather than permit a soldier to remain idle, they employed him on useless work.

Passing from the technical to the sublime side of the *Rêveries*, we see that this young dreamer is no longer an idle man of pleasure. He has developed into a chief who is planning an expedition to conquer some shadowy realm. The habit of manoeuvring a battalion has inspired him with a craving to remodel human society. Having recast in theory every method of destroying human life, he sketches one for repeopling the devastated world. Jean-Jacques Rousseau must surely have studied this noble passage:—

> What a spectacle is offered by nations in our time! We see a few rich, indolent, and voluptuous beings finding happiness at the expense of the multitude, which natters their passions and subsists by finding new pleasures for its masters. This assemblage of oppressors and oppressed we term Society, and we gather all its vilest and most despicable elements to turn them into soldiers.

In these *Rêveries* we see the germ of Saxe's triumphs at Fontenoy, Rocoux, and Laffeldt. They inspired many of Frederick the Great's reforms, and were taken to heart by Napoleon. But so ingrained is the conservatism of the military mind that many of the most obvious reforms suggested by Saxe are still to seek. The *Rêveries* are as worthy of the closest study by soldiers as they were one hundred and sixty years ago.

On the death of Maurice de Saxe's father in 1733, his half-brother became Elector of Saxony, and the nobles of Poland called him to her uneasy throne. This election was made to the prejudice of Stanislas Leczinski, father-in-law of Louis XV. Despite Cardinal Fleury's pacific counsels, France leagued herself with Spain and Sardinia, and plunged into war with the Emperor Charles VI., who was the new King of Poland's mainstay. Saxe was placed in a sore dilemma, from which he escaped by consulting his conscience. He wrote:

I have thought less of the ties of blood, than of my honour, which binds me to the king's service.

In the ensuing war, he won his spurs as a leader under the Ducs de Berwick and Noailles. In command of a division of the army of the Rhine, he distinguished himself at the siege of Phillipsburg (1734), and won the Battle of Ettingen by a desperate charge. Then he outmanoeuvred his old master, Prince Eugene, who threatened the French army on both flanks, dislodged him from an advantageous position, and frustrated the junction of two hostile forces. These signal services were requited by promotion to the grade of lieutenant-general (1736).

On the outbreak of the War of the Austrian Succession Saxe seized every opportunity of enhancing his reputation. He captured Prague by escalade on the night of November 25, 1741, and displayed a humanity rare indeed in that age, by putting a stop to pillage. In the following April, he drove the Austrians from a strong position at Egra. His victorious career was stayed by the ineptitude of colleagues. Belle Isle's retreat from Prague was one of the greatest feats of the campaign; but he brought only 12,000 men back to French territory of 50,000 who had crossed the Rhine. This check called a halt in operations on German soil.

Saxe's acknowledged master in the art of war was the old marshal, Duc de Noailles. Illustrious birth smoothed his upward path; and not less, perhaps, did his marriage with a niece of Madame de Maintenon, who was the uncrowned Queen of France.

******

Adrien Maurice, Duc de Noailles (1678-1766), was chief of

one of the greatest feudal houses. It was illustrious in Limousin as far back as the eleventh century, and could show an unbroken descent since 1230.

★★★★★★

He gained the confidence of Louis XIV., who employed him in 1700 as an agent to place the crown of Spain on the head of his grandson, Philip V. Noailles had entered the French army at fourteen, and saw much service during the disastrous war of the Spanish Succession, provoked by his master's ambition. He was a *preux chevalier*, well versed in affairs and knowledge of the human heart, and given to speak his mind with uncourtier-like frankness. Marshal Noailles was a profound tactician. He would have ranked among the greatest leaders of his century had he not been liable to lose his head in the stress of battle.

Louis Armand Duplessis, Duc de Richelieu (1696-1788), was the antithesis of high-souled Noailles. Like Saxe, he was one of the Regent's *roués*, but owed his elevation to the highest military rank by pandering to Louis XV.'s worst vices. He married thrice in as many reigns, and traversed the century triumphing like a god. Great ladies fought for his notice, and Voltaire distorted history to flatter him. In him splendid courage and mother-wit were united to pride, which was not justified by his birth, and a cynical contempt of religion, morals, and public opinion. Richelieu was, in fact, an epitome of the best and worst characteristics of his caste.

All born leaders of men succeed, perhaps unconsciously, in gathering round them a school of devoted followers, who imbibe a measure of their genius. Maurice de Saxe owed much of his success in war to a knot of able men whom he attracted by personal fascination and moulded by his example. Chief amongst them was Ulric Frederic Waldemar, Count de Löwendahl. Royal blood ran in his veins, for his grandfather was a natural son of King Frederick III. of Denmark. Entering his kinsman's army at thirteen, he practised the soldier's art in every country of Europe. Löwendahl was one of the galaxy of military adventurers who took service under the Tsaritsa Anne of Russia.

On the accession of Elizabeth these were scattered to the winds. While Keith, Earl Marischal of Scotland, and a mirror of chivalry, became Frederick the Great's most trusted adviser, Löwendahl sought glory and plunder under the French king's banner. Sieges were his forte. He curtailed the slow and methodical approach by means of zigzags and parallels by mounting batteries of the heaviest ordnance, whose concentrated fire no garrison could resist. Löwendahl was much more than a soldier. His accomplishments and linguistic skill were as phenomenal as his wit.

The brilliant soul was enshrined in a frame cast in a herculean mould, and Löwendahl's strength was as prodigious as Maurice de Saxe's. Unlike his chief, he had much of the hardness of heart which was common in men of the eighteenth century. In 1736, on the eve of quitting Poland for Russia, he eloped with the young Countess Braniçka, leaving at Warsaw his wife and children, with whom he held no further communication.

While the French Army was an adjunct of the sovereign's state, the docile instrument of his designs, with centuries of tradition behind it, the military strength of Great Britain was of recent origin, and its growth was jealously controlled by Parliament. Cromwell's army of 80,000 yeomen was the most efficient ever possessed by this country. At the Restoration, the great bulk was disbanded, about 5000 men only being re-embodied on the same day. The new Parliament grudgingly assented to the formation of a Brigade of Guards composed of three regiments.

In 1740 the Grenadier Guards ranked as "First," although priority belonged to the Coldstream Regiment, then styled "Second Foot Guards." The latter was raised at the Border village of that name in 1660. In 1661 its colonel was General Monk, who rather by good fortune than merit was enabled to play the part of king-maker. In deference to him, the regiment was not included in the disbandment, but was honoured by its inclusion in the Brigade of Guards. Grenadiers were introduced from the French model in 1677, and James II. gave most battalions a grenadier company.

They were all picked men. In column, they occupied the front ranks; in line, they stood on the right. It was their privilege to lead in all services of special danger, and they suffered in proportion. In 1740 grenadiers still carried pouches containing the hand shell to which their name is due. The words of command are given by Walter Scott in *Rob Roy*, "*Open your pouches—blow your matches—fall on!*" One of the Duke of Cumberland's general orders, issued ten days before Fontenoy, directs "the train to deliver immediately 12 inches of match to each grenadier."

The Line dated from 1661, when the "Royals," afterwards the 1st Foot, were re-embodied. They were the bodyguard of Scottish kings in the ninth century. Passing into the service of the kings of France, they won glory in the Thirty Years' War as the Regiment of Douglas, and at its close they returned to the British service. But for the break of continuity caused by their disbandment under the Commonwealth, the Royals, or Royal Scots, would be the oldest regiment in the world. Most of the other regiments of the line in 1740 were called after their colonels for the time being—a most inconvenient practice, which greatly increases the difficulty of identifying units.

Then the 3rd Buffs, so styled because their facings and small clothes were buff coloured, were raised in 1661, and eighty years later they were styled "Lt.-General Howards." The 21st, or Royal Scots Fusiliers, were named "Campbells," or the "Royal North British Fusiliers," in 1740. The *rationale* of fusiliers was to guard artillery, and for this purpose they carried a *chevaux de frise* in sections, with which they surrounded the guns. While officers in other regiments carried spontoons six feet long, those of the fusiliers were armed with light muskets, termed "fusils."

Charles II.'s reign witnessed the revival of our much-neglected citizen army, whose history stretches back to the days of Alfred. On the abolition of feudal tenures, £70,000 *per mensem*, raised by poundage on real and personal estates, were assigned to meet the cost of training 30,000 militiamen. No attempt was made to link the resuscitated force with the regular army. During the quarter of a century of peace which was secured by Marlborough's wars the militia had become obsolete, and the London Train-Bands, which were its only survival, were the object of much cheap ridicule.

In this respect, we are not one whit more patriotic than our ancestors of 1740. The evolution of defeat always proceeds on similar lines. A community waxes rich on the fruits of successful war and conquest, and is then inclined to shirk the responsibility of national defence. Now the race is, and will always be, for the strong. A time comes when men who have lost the instinct of self-preservation are attacked by warlike neighbours, and are compelled to disgorge possessions which they cannot guard.

In 1740 the Household Cavalry consisted of the Royal Horse Guards Blue, the Horse Guards, and Horse Grenadier Guards. The first were raised in 1661, and commanded by Aubrey De Vere, Earl of Oxford, whose memory lingers in the popular appellation given to this splendid regiment. The other corps traced their origin to three troops of mounted attendants on the royal person, whose gorgeous attire was conspicuous in Restoration pageantry. Until the Revolution of 1688 they served ceremonial purposes. William III., however, was often in the thick of battle, and his bodyguard developed into an efficient part of the fighting machine.

At this period, too, the Royal Horse Guards were styled "Blue," to distinguish them from William III.'s Dutch attendants, who wore red. There were two troops of Horse Guards and as many of Horse Grenadier Guards in 1740, a Scots troop having been added to each corps after the Union of 1707. They were reorganised in 1788 as the First and Second Life Guards.

At the epoch of which I am writing our cavalry of the line was of two descriptions. There were four regiments of Horse, or "Heavies," raised by James II. between 1685 and 1688. The oldest was the King's Regiment of Horse (1st Dragoon Guards). Another, styled in 1740 Ligonier's, or the Black Horse, owed its wonderful efficiency to the care for discipline and internal economy exercised by the brothers John and Francis Ligonier, who successively commanded it.

During five years' active service in Germany and Flanders (1742-47) Ligonier's never lost a trooper by desertion, or had one tried by general court-martial. The deaths from sickness were only six, while thirty-seven non-commissioned officers and men won commissions for special gallantry. With such a record, the *esprit de corps* was especially strong. Every man took pride in being "a Ligoneer," as the name was pronounced. Their glorious traditions have been inherited by the 7th Dragoon Guards. Dragoons were introduced from France by James II., and they were still considered mounted infantry, carrying a long musket, with the butt in a leather bucket, and the barrel passing up under the sword arm. In point of fact they were a hybrid force, which often proved a broken reed in the day of battle. A brilliant exception was the Royal North British Dragoons (Royal Scots Greys), raised in 1681. The troopers wore tall grenadier caps, rode white or grey chargers, and were armed with bayonets besides broadswords.

The fluctuations in our standing army during its earlier days reflected every phase of that struggle between conceptions of royal prerogative and popular rights which culminated in the Revolution of 1688. Under Charles II. it grew apace, and at his death the original force of 5000 men had swollen to 16,500. His absolutist successor, James II., made Monmouth's rebellion and Irish troubles an excuse for raising the standing army to 28,000. The Declaration of Rights of 1689 forbade the "raising or keeping of a standing army in times of peace except with the consent of Parliament." Hitherto military government had rested on Articles of War which emanated from the royal will.

The Mutiny Act of 1689 transferred its regulation to the omnipotent Legislature. In 1691, however, the Commons voted 67,000 men in furtherance of William III.'s Continental designs. Under Queen Anne the stress of Marlborough's campaigns raised the standing army to 200,000, of whom the bulk were foreigners in British pay; but on the return of peace this huge force was reduced to 19,000.

The outbreak of the War of the Austrian Succession found our cavalry about 9000 strong, consisting of the Blue Guards, four troops of Horse and as many of Horse Grenadier Guards, four regiments of Horse, and ten of Dragoons. The war strength of the squadron was 150 files. The infantry numbered 21,600, including the Guards' Brigade and thirty line regiments, with an average of 650 per battalion.

In 1745 foreign mercenaries—Hanoverians, Hessians, and Danes—brought up the total force at Great Britain's disposal to 74,600 men. The most notable addition under George II. was the famous Black Watch.

In 1729 General George Wade, who commanded in Scotland, formed three companies of clansmen, whose chiefs adhered to the Hanoverian cause. This small force proved useful in counteracting Jacobite intrigues and repressing the Highlander's love of cattle-rieving. They were afterwards increased to six companies, and in 1739 these were embodied into a regiment under John, Earl of Crawford. Hitherto officers and men had worn their clan tartan. They were now given a most picturesque uniform of dark green, blue and black checks, and were styled the "Black Watch," to distinguish them from King George's scarlet-clad soldiers. Retaining ancient tribal customs, with broadsword and target in addition to the regulation firelock, these Highlanders were an object of curiosity and terror on the Continent.

The Royal Artillery were organised as a regiment in 1716, though officers were not regularly commissioned until 1741. Guns were still very unwieldy, and calibres were so small that they were valued rather for moral effect than practical utility. They were horsed by contractors, whose servants could not be relied on in action.

Our army 160 years ago, (as at 1906), was recruited from the dregs of a proletariat which was brutal, lawless, and given to strong drink. Indeed, a considerable proportion of those who fought in Flanders belonged to the criminal classes, for it was quite common to pardon convicted felons who were willing to serve in His Majesty's army or fleet. Such material needed a tight hand, and the general orders of 1745 record a grievous amount of scourging, shooting, and hanging.

But the British soldier, led by generals whom he trusted, and fed with regularity, displayed a bull dog staunchness which nothing could resist.

His uniform and equipments were cumbrous and ill adapted to speedy movement, but were not so absurd as the skin-tight garb borrowed from Germany after the Seven Years' War. They consisted of a red coat, with voluminous skirts which were buttoned back, forming lapels; small clothes and gaiters, which were a sorry protection against wet or mud; and a three-cornered felt hat, which collapsed when rain-sodden. Stiff leather belts supported a wallet for kit, cartouche-box, and bayonet. The atrocious stock had not yet been imported from Germany, but the soldiers were compelled to shave clean, below an imaginary line from nose to ear, with cold water, poor razors, and worse soap. Their hair and pigtail were besmeared with a nauseous mixture of flour and tallow. It was common to see a row of men in barracks bestriding the same bench, and each rendering the service of hairdresser to a comrade in front.

Some curious light is cast on army clothing at this era by the report of a Parliamentary Commission appointed in 1746. Privates of the Guards and line received an outfit annually, consisting of coat, waistcoat fashioned of the previous year's coat, shirt, small clothes, shoes, stockings, and laced hat. Troopers in the Horse and Horse Grenadier Guards drew a new kit every two years; in heavy cavalry and dragoon regiments this distribution was triennial. The cost was met by deductions from pay, termed "off-reckonings."

Clothing was provided by regimental colonels, who made an average profit of £578 *per annum* in infantry and £641 in cavalry regiments. Distinctive facings were still in embryo, deep yellow being common to thirteen line regiments. Colours were not so liberally allotted as they were in the French Army. Most foot battalions possessed two flags, and every squadron had a standard.

On the other hand, pay was on a far more liberal scale. Troopers in a heavy cavalry regiment drew 2s. 6d.; dragoons, 1s. 9d.; privates of the Foot Guards, 10d.; and of line regiments, 8d. *per diem*. This was subject to many oppressive deductions. Besides "off-reckonings" for clothing, there was a "stoppage," amounting to a penny *per diem*, to meet the salaries of paymaster and surgeon, and "poundage" to provide for pensions and the upkeep of Chelsea Hospital. Queen Anne's first Mutiny Act fixed three years as the term of service, but great inducements were offered for re-engagement on its expiration.

The army owed its staunchness to the large proportion of seasoned men in its ranks. The splendid establishment at Chelsea, whose creation is one of the few worthy actions standing to the credit of Charles II., accommodated 400 inmates, who were boarded and lodged, with an allowance of 8d. per week as pocket-money. Out-pensioners drew £7, 12s. 6d., which probably went as far as £20 in these days. (At Fontenoy a grenadier whose leg was carried off by a cannonball exclaimed, "*Dead as Chelsea, by God!*" using a proverbial expression well known in the army—Dictionary *of the Vulgar Tongue,* 1758).

Drill was almost incessant, and intolerably irksome. In war-time manoeuvres were carried out under a heavy fire with as much precision as though the troops were on parade. The "Hyde Park" movements of martinets of the old school were derided by more enlightened officers. Shoulder-to-shoulder formations three deep were usual. During the heat of action the front rank must have been placed between two fires, and rapid movement was out of the question.

On the other hand, these dense masses were often irresistible by sheer impetus. The proper role of cavalry was not grasped until Frederick the Great brought this arm to miraculous perfection, and demonstrated the value of shock tactics. In order of battle the cavalry were posted on the infantry's flanks or rear. Their function was to cover extension from column into line and protect retreat.

Optimists who hold that the opportunity produces the man, find no confirmation of this comforting theory in our military annals during the eighteenth century. There was, indeed, a curious dearth of supreme talent in the British Army throughout that era. Between the close of Marlborough's active career in 1713 and the dawn of Wellington's, which dates from the Battle of Assaye in 1803, Great Britain passed through thirty-seven years of war. *A priori* one might suppose that generals would have learnt their craft by long experience of its practical side. This assumption is belied by facts. Good soldiers, in the ordinary sense of the term, we had in abundance—men devoted to their profession and versed in its minutiae. With two, or at the utmost three, exceptions no British leaders displayed a spark of that genius which should be the sole passport to supreme command.

Among generals who led our armies to disaster, chequered by gleams of victory, John Dalrymple, second Earl of Stair (1673-1747), was the most conspicuous. Like most of the seniors in 1740, he had been educated in Marlborough's school and fought in all the great battles of the war of the Spanish Succession. His laurels, however, were won in diplomacy, and Lord Stair was unquestionably the greatest ambassador who ever represented his country at a foreign court. In that capacity, he resided in Paris during the momentous years between 1715 and 1720, and displayed a genius for intrigue which made him a leading factor in the European situation. As a general, Stair stood on a much lower plane. He was no strategist, and lacked the essential virtues of tact and patience. George II. was the last king of England to lead his troops in the field, but undaunted courage and a high sense of duty were his only military virtues.

His son, William Augustus, Duke of Cumberland, was better qualified for command. He was born in 1721 at Leicester House, a gloomy pile on the northern side of the fields of that name, which was the Prince of Wales' official residence. His love of soldiering was shown in infancy, for in 1726 he appeared at a St James's birthday parade at the head of a battalion of tiny Guardsmen, to the intense delight of his grandfather, George I. The young prince was fortunate in a tutor named Stephen Poyntz, who imbued him with a love of literature, very rare indeed in the House of Hanover. His mother, the cultured and charming Queen Caroline, took pleasure in bringing her children in touch with men of science.

Among the intimates of his childhood was Sir Isaac Newton, whose funeral, in 1727, the child attended at his own request. From this "pride of the human race" he imbibed a love of mathematics. He also became a fair classical scholar, and was an adept in all manly sports. At fifteen the king placed him in the navy, in view of reviving the long disused office of Lord High Admiral. When war broke out with Spain in 1739, he served as a volunteer in a fleet destined to intercept the enemy's squadron off Ferrol. His admiral was Sir John Norris, whose proverbial ill-luck won for him the sobriquet "Foul-weather Jack." It did not desert him on this occasion. The *armada* was dispersed by a terrific gale, and Cumberland was heartily disgusted with this experience of nautical life. He was gazetted to the First Guards, and threw himself, heart and soul, into his new profession.

William Augustus, Duke of Cumberland, was a dutiful son, steadfast in his loves and hates, and honest in all his dealings. As a soldier, he was brave to a fault, and spared neither himself nor others. A strict disciplinarian, and prodigal of his soldiers' blood, he won their attachment by unswerving justice and regard for their comfort. There was a strain of true nobility in this much-maligned man's character, alloyed with a large share of the brutality and hardness of heart which characterised his age. Horace Walpole, who was intimate with many of the duke's favourites, wrote:—

> His understanding was strong, judicious, and penetrating, thoroughly incapable of resisting partialities and *piqûres*. He was proud and unforgiving, and fond of war for its own sake. He despised money, fame, and politics; loved women, gaming, and his own favourites—and yet had not the social virtue.—Horace Walpole, *Memoirs of the Reign of George II*, vol. i.; and *George III*.

A more kindly light is shed on this complex character by James Wolfe, who served under him for several years, and was incapable of truckling to any man. Writing to his father, in 1750, he says:—

> The letter you sent me came, as you guessed, from Goldsmith. I wrote to him, by the duke's direction, to inquire after an officer's widow in Ireland, who, he was told, had a son fit to serve; and H.R.H., who is ever doing noble and generous actions, wanted to provide for that child. The father was killed at Fontenoy.—Wright, *Life of James Wolfe*, chap. xiv.

Field-Marshal George Wade (1673-1748) joined the army at seventeen, and commanded the Third Brigade of British Infantry, which bore the brunt of fighting on the fatal day of Almanza (1707). At the incoming of the Hanoverian dynasty he was sent to the west of England, where he rendered conspicuous service by unearthing Jacobite plots and depots of concealed arms. The two first Georges never pardoned disaffection to their cause, or overlooked zeal displayed in promoting it.

In 1724 Wade was despatched on a roving commission to report on the state of the Highlands, which was seething with suppressed excitement. He curbed the clansmen's love of cattle-rieving and organised the loyal portion in companies, who kept the Jacobite element under control. Wade's greatest service, however, was his network of military roads, which linked the innermost recesses of the Highlands with centres of civilised life, and will remain a lasting monument of his energy and science.

※※※※※※

The famous distich which was once inscribed on an obelisk between Inverness and Inverary, "If you had seen these roads before they were made," &c, is often quoted as a bull by people who are not aware that to "make" a road was to convert a cattle-track into a paved and bridged thoroughfare.

*****

George Wade left behind him in Scotland the reputation of a firm but kindly administrator. He was unfitted to direct operations on a large scale in the field by a lack of will-power and initiative.

Society in the eighteenth century was hasting to decay, and racial ties were of small account. Louis XV.'s best generals were Germans. Lieutenant General John Ligonier (1680-1770) was born a subject of Louis XIV. He came of a noble Huguenot family in the south of France, and, with several brothers, was driven from his country by Louis's insane persecution. He obtained a commission in the British army in 1703, and fought in all Marlborough's battles.

That Ligonier was a splendid cavalry officer was evidenced by the unequalled efficiency attained by his regiment (7th Dragoon Guards). We shall see him resourceful in action and undismayed by defeat. His letters, which are a delightful medley of English and French, display the courtier's instinct and all the vivacity of his race. It is not surprising that he rose to high favour with the royal family, and was loved by comrades of all degrees.

Another knight without fear and without reproach was John Lindsay, 20th Earl of Crawford (1702-49). He obtained a captaincy in the 3rd Guards in 1734; but a thirst for glory led him to join an imperial army fighting the French under Prince Eugene in the following year. Passing into the Russian service in 1738, he greatly distinguished himself in two campaigns. Then he returned to the Emperors banner, and was severely wounded at the Battle of Krotzka (1739). Lord Crawford never wholly recovered from this mishap; but suffering could not quench this heroic spirit. He shared Ligonier's reputation as a cavalry leader, while his judgment was superior to the ardent Frenchman's.

Lieutenant-General Sir James Campbell of Lawers was in no wise inferior to this gallant pair. Born about 1670, the second son of the Earl of Loudoun, he became colonel of the Scots Greys in 1708, and won his spurs under Marlborough. He was chosen M.P. for Ayrshire, and afterwards Governor of Edinburgh Castle.

Of a very different stamp was Lieutenant-General John Hawley. Popular rumour explained the persistent favour shown by the royal family to this ruffian by a theory that he was King George's illegitimate son. This, however, was physically impossible, and is disproved by his cynical and blasphemous will, which expressly states that he "began the world with nothing." Moreover, the State Papers contain a curious letter, addressed to Field-Marshal Wade, under whom Hawley served in 1744, which shows that the flintiest heart had a soft spot, and dispels the myth of his royal descent. He wrote:

> When my father was killed, King William gave my two brothers and myself commissions. They two were both killed since in the service. He also gave a pension of £300 a-year to my mother and sister to maintain them, which a few years ago, His Majesty ordered to be struck off, as I was then one of his *aides-de-camp*. I gave my sister the pay of that post (being called £200 a-year). When His Majesty was pleased to employ me abroad he also took that away. I then was forced to make my sister the same allowance out of my pay; and what with making my little equipage and the great expense here, the little I have saved, which is about £500, is all gone.
>
> As I am far from being thought extravagant, so I am unable to run into debt, since if anything happens to me, an only sister will come to want. And as there are fourteen officers of an inferior rank, and all those in the same rank, now employed, who have either governments or good employment, and some have both besides their pay. As I flatter myself that I have served at least as well as those under me, I hope His Majesty will be pleased either to honour me with a government also or that he would be graciously pleased to have some compassion and give me leave to dispose of my own troop to a worthy man, to save a sister from starving; which will encourage me to serve with more pleasure and gain a good officer to the regiment.— Lieutenant-General Sir John Hawley to Field-Marshal Wade, undated, but docketed July 27, 1744.

Hawley's first commission was dated 1694. He served with the cavalry throughout Marlborough's campaigns, and commanded a dragoon regiment at Sheriffmuir (1715). He was a rapacious marauder; but while he allowed himself unbridled licences, he visited any infringement of discipline with the severest penalties. James Wolfe, who was his *aide-de-camp* and knew him too well, wrote on November 3, 1755, from Canterbury:—

> General Hawley is expected in a few days, to keep us all in order. The troops dread his severity, hate the man, and hold his military knowledge in contempt.—Wright, *Life of James Wolfe*, chap. xiv.

His nickname in the army was "The Hangman"!

The influence of this scoundrel with the royal family was probably due to secret services rendered to the dynasty during Queen Anne's reign. Whatever the cause, it was wholly bad, and the evil reputation which clings to Cumberland is in large measure the result of Hawley's misdeeds.

Such were the chiefs to whom was intrusted the task of upholding British honour during this disastrous war. Though none of them attained the first rank as generals, almost all of them did their duty according to their lights. The absence of systematic training is responsible for every miscarriage between 1744 and 1748.

CHAPTER 3

Dettingen and Marshal Wade's Campaign

Great Britain was now deeply involved in the Continental imbroglio. The flower of her standing army, which had wintered in Flanders, was reinforced by 6000 Hessians taken into our pay. But when Carteret proposed to entertain 16,000 Hanoverians, he was met by a chorus of indignation. William Pitt, who led the Opposition, exclaimed in Parliament:

> It is now but too evident that this great, this powerful, this formidable Kingdom is considered only as a province of a despicable electorate!

Yet, on a division, the Ministerial scheme was carried by a large majority; and popular susceptibility was soothed by the addition of 6000 Hanoverian troops, paid for by that State. With these reinforcements, George II. felt himself strong enough to take the field. In April 1743, the British contingent in Flanders quitted their winter quarters, under the Earl of Stair, and joined an Austrian Army commanded by the Duc d'Aremberg. (Leopold, Duc d'Aremberg, b. 1690, wounded at Malplaquet. In 1716 became commander-in-chief in the Austrian Netherlands, and held that post till his death in 1764).

In mid May, the allied forces, 40,000 strong, mustered at Höchst, between Mayence and Frankfort, and then advanced to Aschaffenburg in order to separate the French from their Bavarian allies.

George II. was eager to emulate the policy of William III. in assuming the command of a confederate army for the protection of his Continental dominions. He resolved to take the field in person, and hastened to Hanover, immediately after the prorogation, with the young Duke of Cumberland. Thence he proceeded to the Allies' headquarters on the Main.

Meanwhile France was straining every nerve to meet her new antagonist. The one moderating influence disappeared with Cardinal Fleury, who succumbed, after a stubborn fight with death, on January 29, 1743, leaving his master a puppet at the mercy of mistresses and court cabals. His successor was Cardinal de Tencin (1680-1758), whose career is an instance of the success so often attained by mediocre talents when they are associated with a supple backbone.

★★★★★★

André Hercule de Fleury had been Louis XV.'s tutor, and attained almost complete mastery over his sluggish mind. Becoming Prime Minister at seventy-three, he clung to power for seventeen eventful years. He loved peace, but was dragged into two unjust wars. He carried economy to a point which seriously impaired the nation's resources, while he allowed them to be depleted by a swarm of greedy favourites and farmers-general. Like many statesmen, Fleury lived too long for his country and his reputation.

★★★★★★

This crafty churchman stood pledged to pursue the German war with vigour. In May 1743, Marshal Noailles was despatched with 60,000 men to cross the Rhine and join forces with Bavaria. He dogged the Allies' footsteps, and established himself on the left bank of the Main only four miles from their camp. In the movements, which followed, Noailles completely out-manoeuvred Stair and his royal master. He occupied the Main on either side of Aschaffenburg, cutting off supplies. King George found his army reduced to a desperate plight. Men and horses were starving; Stair and d'Aremberg were not on speaking terms; while a superior French force overlooked his camp from the opposite side of the Main.

No course remained but to retreat by the right bank to Hanau, where well-filled magazines and 12,000 British, Hanoverian, and Hessian reinforcements awaited him. No sooner did this retrograde movement begin than it was detected by Noailles. He crossed the Main above Aschaffenburg, and occupied that base immediately after its evacuation by the Allies. A battery of Impounders was sent forward by the left bank, which sorely harassed the retreating enemy. Noailles' nephew, the Duc de Gramont, was detached with 30,000 men to cross the river at Selingenstadt, three miles in advance of the Allies, and oc-

King George II at Dettingen

cupy the denies of Dettingen, through which they must pass.

On June 27, 1743, they reached the spot which should have been their Caudine Forks. They were completely entrapped. To retrace their footsteps was impossible, for Aschaffenburg was occupied by the enemy. On one flank was an unfordable river, with heavy guns playing on them from the opposite bank. Retreat eastwards was barred by densely wooded hills. In their front was a strong position held by 30,000 foes.

But a little patience was needed on the French side to ensure the total destruction of the retreating enemy. This quality was not conspicuous in the national character, and Gramont had less of it than the majority of his comrades. He quitted an impregnable position to offer battle on the plain to superior forces, placing his own between the Allies and the 18-pounders cannonading them from the opposite bank. Noailles' hand was forced by this insane movement. No course was open to him but to extricate Gramont, if possible, from the consequences of his rashness.

The battle commenced by a furious charge of the French Household Cavalry and *Carabiniers*, who rode down two lines of Anglo-German infantry. Troops so staunch were not to be dispersed. They speedily re-formed, and presented an unbroken front to fresh attacks. Then the *Gardes Françaises* advanced in line against the Anglo Hanoverians. Received with a terrible rolling fire, they recoiled, leaving forty-two officers killed and wounded. The same fate attended isolated attacks by units without order or cohesion, which dashed against the dense masses of our infantry, only to retreat in confusion. Disheartened by repeated failure, the French regiments ignored their officers' entreaty to rally once more. Vainly did the French Household Cavalry strive to retrieve the day by desperate charges.

They rolled back our Horse Guards Blue and the Royal Regiment of Dragoons, only to be overthrown in their turn by the Scots Greys and Ligonier's Black Horse (7th Dragoon Guards). In the words of a contemporary chronicler:—

> After the enemy began to break, they closed again and made a more obstinate stand than before; but James Campbell, (mentioned in previous chapter), at the head of the Greys, put them out of their sullen humour, and made them take to their old route again. They grew confused, and our dragoons pursued and made a dreadful slaughter.—*Record of the Scots Greys*. In this

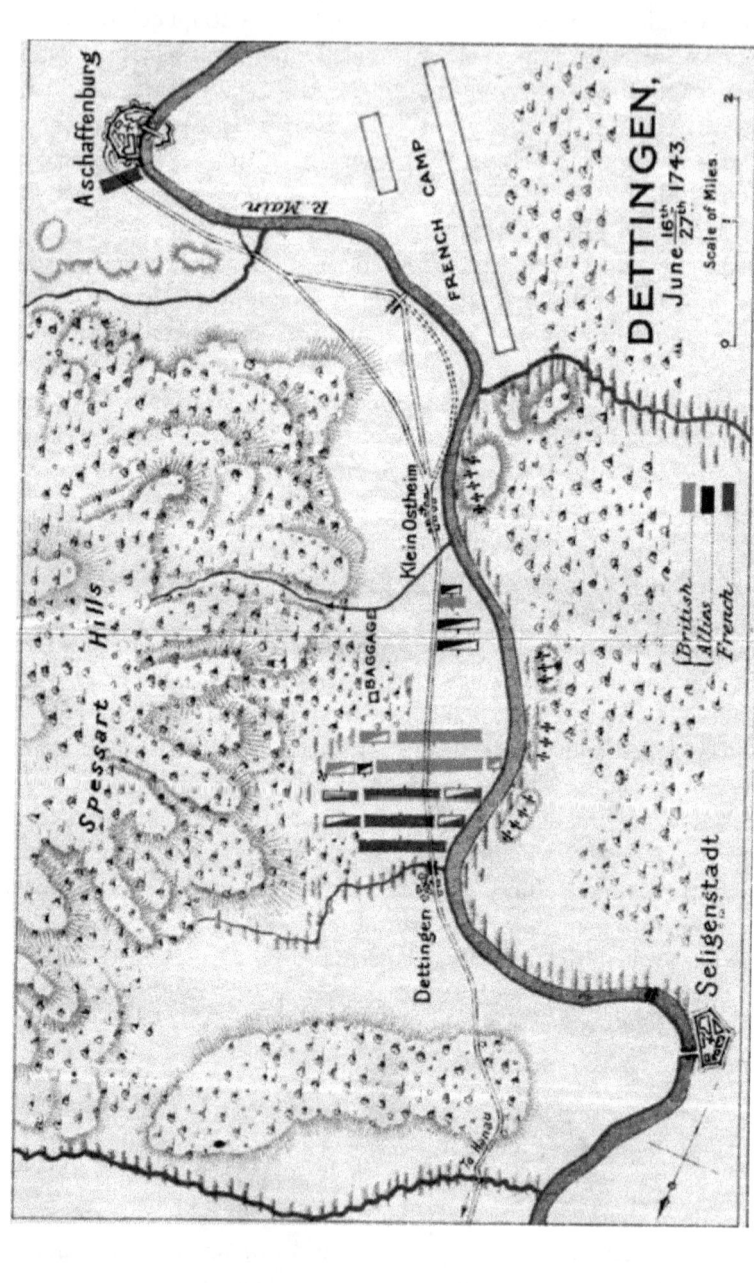

pursuit, the 1st (Royal) Dragoons captured the white standard of the *Mousquetaires Noirs*.

The Greys captured a standard of the *Chevau-Légers de la Garde*, which is officially described as:

> Of white damask, finely embroidered with gold and silver; thunderbolt in the middle, with a blue-and-white ground; motto, *Sensere Gigantes*.

On the French side Louis XV.'s Household Cavalry were more than decimated, losing ninety-three officers. On ours, the burden and heat of the day were borne by the British and Hanoverian infantry. The Guards Brigade, who marched in the rear, had a narrow escape of being cut off by the French occupation of Aschaffenburg. They were placed by George II. under a Hanoverian general named Ilten, who wheeled them to the right in order to avoid the fire of Noailles' 18 pounders across the Main. They were kept by their "Confectioner," as they nicknamed him, unwilling spectators of the conflict from a hill in the rear. One of them left a quaint picture of eighteenth-century warfare in a letter to his wife:—

> Our men and their regimental officers won the day, not in the manner of Hyde Park discipline, but our foot almost kneeled down by whole ranks, and so fired on 'em a running fire, making almost every ball take place; but for ten or twelve minutes 'twas doubtful which would succeed, as they overpowered us so much, and the bravery of their *Mason du Roy* coming upon us eight or nine ranks deep; yet our troops were not seen to retreat, but to bend back only—I mean our foot—and that only while they fresh loaded; then, of their own accord, marched boldly up to 'em, gave them such a smash with loud huzzas every time they saw them retire, that then they were at once put to flight. The English infantry behaved like heroes, and as they won the major part of the action, to them the honours of the day were due. They were under no command by way of Hide Park firing, but the whole three ranks made a running fire of their own accord, and at the same time with great judgment and skill, stooping all as low as they could, making almost every ball take place. ...The enemy, when expecting our fire, dropped down, which our men perceiving, waited till they got up before they would fire. .... The French fired in the same manner, I mean like a

running fire, without waiting for words of command, and Lord Stair did often say he had seen many a battle, and never saw the infantry engage in any other manner.—Lieut.-Colonel Charles Russell to his wife, June 29 and August 6 and 7, 1743. (Historical MS. Commission's Report on the MS. of Mrs Frankland-Russell-Astley of Chequers Court, Bucks, 1900, hereafter referred to as "Chequers Court Papers.")

After four hours' fighting Noailles recalled his wearied and disheartened troops. The Allies were permitted to continue their retreat on Hanau, not before King George II. had dined, by way of bravado, on the battlefield, and created Campbell and Ligonier Knights Banneret under the royal standard. Lord Stair was eager to launch his cavalry in pursuit of the discomfited foe, but he was overruled by d'Aremberg and the Hanoverian generals. Out of 35,000 engaged, the French lost at least 6000 in killed and wounded, including hundreds of the *Gardes Françaises*, who perished in an attempt to swim the Main. The Allies numbered about 40,000, and had 2381 *hors de combat*. Their wounded, 600 in number, were perforce left on the battlefield at Noailles' mercy, and it is pleasant to add that an appeal to his chivalrous nature ensured the utmost care for these poor creatures.

Dettingen was emphatically a soldiers' battle, and our infantry proved, as they did in the Boer War, that thirty years of peace had in nowise impaired their proverbial steadiness. Colonel Russell, whose letters to his wife have been quoted above, remarked that "the superior officers rode about bravely enough, and exposed themselves, but gave no sort of orders." King George, however, was excepted from this general censure. His defective strategy was more than compensated by a rare degree of personal courage. He fought, dismounted, between the first and second lines, and cheered on his men in guttural English. Colonel Russell wrote—

> His Majesty was in the field of battle the whole day, and behaved very gallantly; went himself and placed a battery of Hanoverian cannon, which was of the utmost service and did great execution. The Duke d'Aremberg rode up to him and begged him not to expose himself in the manner he did,—that he was liable to be surrounded by the enemy and taken prisoner. He answered, "What do you think I am here for—to be a poltroon?"—Chequers Court Papers

Equal bravery was displayed by the Duke of Cumberland, who

BATTLE OF DETTINGEN

left his regiment, the First Guards, to fight on the right of the first line. James Wolfe, then adjutant of Duroure's regiment (12th Foot), recorded that—

> The duke behaved as bravely as a man could do. I had the honour of speaking to him just as the battle began, and was often afraid of being dashed to pieces by cannon-balls.

Though wounded by a bullet through the leg, he refused to quit the field, and when he came under the surgeon's hands he insisted on a *mousquetaire* more grievously hurt being attended to before his own injury was examined. Though still in early manhood, Cumberland was corpulent and plethoric. Russell wrote:

> Our colonel, was thought yesterday (July 7) to be in some danger, and his body being gross, makes it go but ill with him. His papa, they say, was in tears for him yesterday.—Chequers Court Papers.

The victory of Dettingen was a triumph of discipline over untrained valour. Noailles' tactics were pronounced by so consummate a judge as Frederick of Prussia "worthy of the greatest captain," (Frederick II., *Histoire de mon Temps*, vol. ii.); those of the allied generals were below contempt. On the other hand, our regimental system, with all its brutality, ensured absolute steadiness amid the carnage of battle, while French morale had deteriorated in the riot and rapine of two German campaigns. The defeated general placed his finger on an ulcer which was destroying the finest army in Europe in a letter addressed to Louis XV. on the morrow of Dettinefen:—

> The manoeuvres of yesterday were due to the enemy's discipline alone, and to their officers' strict subordination and obedience to commands. I am grieved to inform your Majesty that these qualities are unknown among our own troops, and that, unless we apply ourselves with seriousness and perseverance to remedy this evil, your army will be utterly ruined.—Pajol, *Les Guerres sous Louis XV.*, vol. ii.

In his despair, the Comte d'Argenson, then War Minister, turned to Maurice de Saxe as the only man capable of bringing the army to heel. He was appointed to command the debris of the forces under Noailles, and succeeded in restoring discipline by adopting the severest measures. (Saxe to d'Argenson, July 18, 1743).

Noailles' position was extremely critical. Prince Charles of Lorraine, ablest of Austrian generals, was advancing through Suabia at the head of 60,000 men. The King of England, strongly reinforced, had arrived at Worms with a half-formed intention of joining forces with Prince Charles. Noailles was between the upper and nether millstones; and everything pointed to an invasion of Alsace in overwhelming strength. Again, did Saxe preserve his adopted country from disaster. By skilful manoeuvring, and those Fabian tactics in which he was a past master, he hindered Prince Charles from crossing the Rhine. Well might he exclaim, "I have been the shield and buckler of Upper Alsace!"

King George's army, too, was no longer formidable. His undisguised partiality for Hanoverians provoked keen displeasure among his English subjects, and destroyed all the popularity he had won by his conduct at Dettingen. Lord Stair and the Duc d'Aremberg had been on bad terms throughout the campaign. The first was hot tempered and punctilious; the second "a proud, rapacious glutton, without talent or sentiment." (Smollett, *Continuation of Hume's History of England,* vol. iii.)

Their dissensions soon reached such a pitch as to render further co-operation between them impossible. Stair sent his master a memorandum containing broad hints of the latter's Hanoverian leanings, and with the pride that apes humility he asked permission to "return to his plough." George II. accepted this resignation of command with marks of excusable displeasure. At the end of October, he quitted headquarters for London, and, in accordance with the leisurely methods of those days, his army retired to winter quarters in Flanders.

Dettingen served but to exasperate the virulence of party warfare. England was inundated with pamphlets, which attacked the king's partiality for his Hanoverian troops and retailed all the flouts sustained by Lord Stair and the British contingent at the hands of their allies. When Parliament assembled in December 1743 motions condemning the war were brought forward in both Houses. But the Ministry, strong in royal support, had still a solid majority at their command. Supplies of £10,000,000 were voted, and large subsidies allotted to the Queen of Hungary and Bohemia and a host of minor potentates.

At this period our naval efficiency was at its nadir. Numerical strength was not wanting. Marines were first raised in 1741; and throughout the war estimates provided for 11,500 of these troops and 40,000 seamen. But the fleets of France and Spain contended with our own on equal terms. Privateering was active on both sides, and the balance of gain from this thinly veiled form of piracy was little, if at all, in our favour. 1744 is a year of sinister memory in our naval annals. Rottenness was revealed in Admiralty administration; want of patriotism, and even physical courage, in superior executive officers.

At the very close of 1743 Admiral Mathews, commanding the Mediterranean Fleet, learnt that a French squadron under M. de Court had sailed from Brest to rescue twelve Spanish vessels blockaded in Toulon by Vice Admiral Lestock. He joined the latter on January 3, 1744, in the Bay of Hyeres, and mustered twenty ships to attack the enemy. In a few days, his forces swelled to thirty sail-of-the-line, and as the Franco-Spanish squadron numbered only twenty-six line-of-battle ships, he anticipated an easy victory. Unhappily a bitter feud raged between the two admirals. Mathews was pointedly discourteous to Lestock, who nursed his wrath, to vent it at the cost of his country's honour.

On February 9, 1744, the enemy's ships were seen under sail and in order of battle off Toulon. In the manoeuvres, which followed, our own were miserably handled. Lestock's division lagged far in the rear; and while the Franco-Spanish line kept perfect order, Mathews' ships covered nine miles of water. On February 11, the enemy was observed steering S.W. towards the Straits of Gibraltar under easy sail. Mathews gave chase, while Lestock lingered five miles astern. At 1 p.m. our foremost vessels came up with the enemy. A few of the captains proved worthy of their race. Cornewall, in the *Marlborough*, was beset by overwhelming force. He refused to go below when both legs were carried off by a cannon-ball, and fought the ship till his fate was sealed by the fall of her main and mizzen masts.

But none of the captains astern were moved by the *Marlborough's* plight to come to her assistance. At sunset Mathews intended the fleet to remain in line of battle throughout the night, but the signal code then in use did not admit of his communicating these simple instructions. The action, such as it was, dragged on till February 13, and during its whole course Mathews never succeeded in giving orders to form line of battle parallel with the enemy. Then he lost his head, hoisted contradictory signals, which at one time brought about manoeuvres strongly resembling a flight.

The tale of wrong doing was complete when Mathews desisted from pursuit, although a few hours more would have compelled the enemy either to abandon their damaged vessels or engage on very disadvantageous terms. Our losses were insignificant, except on board the *Marlborough*, which had 161 killed and wounded.

Matters were even worse with the combined fleet. De Court was eighty years of age; his ships were too weak to bear the concussion of repeated broadsides; and he was on bad terms with the Spanish Admiral Navarro. On his return to Brest he was superseded on a complaint preferred by Navarro of want of co-operation, and thus defended himself in a letter addressed to the Minister of Marine:—

> It was not I, my Lord, who forced M. Navarro to fight against all the rules of war and prudence; it was not I who separated his ships from him and threw him into danger. But after he had taken so much pains, in spite of all that I could do, to get himself handsomely beaten, it was I who came to his assistance and gave him an opportunity of getting away, which otherwise he never could have had.—Translation of despatch in Beatson's *Naval and Military Memoirs,* vol. i.

This disgraceful affair excited a storm of indignation at home, and became the subject of a Parliamentary inquiry. In the end courts-martial were held on Mathews, Lestock, and eleven of their post-captains. The first was cashiered; but Lestock, who was a far greater sinner, escaped on technical grounds. Five captains were cashiered, a sixth was declared unfit for further employment, and a seventh dismissed his ship. One of the culprits died before being brought to trial, another escaped punishment by flight, and only two were acquitted.

Popular clamour was stilled by news that an invasion of England was contemplated by her ancient foes. This design was prompted by old Fleury's successor, Cardinal Tencin, who owed his position as a prince of the Church to the Chevalier de St George.

******

> Barbier writes, in February 1739: "M. de Tencin has obtained a cardinal's hat by the nomination of the Chevalier de St George, who is at Rome, and is the son of King James of England, who died here. They say that it has cost him 600,000 *livres*."—*Journal,* vol. ii.

******

His influence on the pliable King of France was aided by reports from a swarm of Jacobite agents, who returned from England with stories of the growing attachment of the people to their rightful sovereign. The tactics of party government were misinterpreted by Louis' advisers, who firmly believed that if James III. or his son were to land on British soil, they would be acclaimed by the whole population. The time seemed opportune for an invasion, for the flower of our army was wintering in Flanders, and barely 7000 men were available for the kingdom's defence.

The scheme promised other advantages, which appealed to the selfish instincts of Versailles. The exiled Stuarts might well serve as a pawn in the game of European politics. If the design miscarried, it would, at any rate, engross the attention of Great Britain, which was the backbone of the anti-French coalition. A few weeks after Dettingen Tencin requested the Chevalier de St George, who was then residing at Rome, to allow his son, Charles Edward, to take part in an invasion of England. The utmost secrecy was enjoined, lest the British court should take alarm.

The *chevalier* was overjoyed at the prospect of regaining his lost inheritance; and Tencin's offer appealed with greater force to his son. Charles Edward Stuart, then in his twenty-third year, was romantic, adventurous, and consumed with ambition. He had smelt powder at the siege of Gaeta in 1734, and was inured to all war's hardships. With the utmost impatience, did he await the signal that all was ready for his advent. Meantime 15,000 chosen troops converged on the ports of Picardy, and transports assembled at Dunkirk to carry them across the Channel. A squadron was fitted out at Brest to serve as convoy, under Admiral de Roquefeuille, reputed to be a skilled and energetic seaman. Supreme command was given to Saxe, who was instructed by a secret memorandum to:

> Embark the troops and conduct them to the river of London, where a revolution would break out immediately after their landing.

On learning that his hour had struck, Charles Edward left Rome in disguise, and after running the gauntlet of our Mediterranean Fleet, he landed at Antibes and posted to Paris. Though he was not received by Louis XV., his movements were watched by King George's emissaries. Mr Thompson, who represented England at the French court, was directed to invoke existing treaties in support of a demand that "the Young Pretender should be banished from French soil" (February 3, 1744).

Eight days later George II. revealed the impending invasion in his speech to Parliament. The effect on public opinion was electrical. Each

House presented an address expressing the indignation and abhorrence excited by a design formed in favour of a "Popish Pretender." All the cities of Great Britain joined in a chorus of loyalty. Lord Stair forgot his grievances, and accepted the post of commander-in-chief. The States of Holland were reminded of their obligation, under the Treaty of April 14, 1719, to furnish 6000 men in case of invasion, and England rang with preparations to repel attack.

In the interval, Prince Charles Edward arrived at Dunkirk, where he was received with the utmost enthusiasm. On February 4 Roquefeuille quitted Brest with twenty-two warships, and sailed up the Channel for his rendezvous. This movement was detected by a British cruiser, which brought the news to Portsmouth. Admiral Sir John Norris promptly mustered the Channel Squadron at Spithead, and weighed anchor for the Downs, where he was to join another, fitting out at Chatham.

On February 28, 1744, Roquefeuille, who had been delayed by contrary winds, appeared off the Isle of Wight, in view of preventing the junction of our Portsmouth and Chatham Squadrons. He came too late. Norris had already quitted his anchorage for the Downs. Finding Spithead deserted, Roquefeuille imagined that the enemy had sought refuge in Portsmouth harbour. Blocking egress, as he supposed, with the bulk of his ships, he despatched five of them to Dunkirk with a message urging Saxe to embark his men forthwith. 7000 troops, with immense war material, were hurried pell-mell on board the transports, Saxe and Prince Charles Edward sailing in the same vessel, and the armada got under weigh.

At this crisis, a frigate despatched by Roquefeuille to gain intelligence of the British fleet returned under full sail, with signals that it was actually rounding the foreland. She was followed by the appearance of a much superior force, advancing with light winds towards the French squadron. A council of war was hurriedly convoked, and, as is generally the case, timid counsels prevailed. Roquefeuille made the best of his way back to Brest, leaving the luckless transports to their fate.

"Foul-weather Jack" did not belie his reputation. The Channel was swept by a tremendous gale, which hastened Roquefeuille's retreat, but wrought havoc with Saxe's flotilla. Seven vessels were lost with all hands; others received serious damage, the ships that bore the hopes of France and Jacobite England making Dunkirk with the utmost difficulty. Charles Edward returned to Paris, where he vegetated on an allowance of £3000 a-year from the French court.

Despair at the failure of so deeply laid a scheme for placing James III. on the throne is reflected in his letters to Saxe. The attraction which that magnetic personality carried with it incited the young prince to offer his services in the forthcoming Flanders campaign. But for the earl marischal's urgent remonstrances, Charles Edward would have witnessed his countrymen's disappointments and defeats. No student of history can doubt that a mortal blow was dealt at the Stuart cause by this dalliance with the French. It fully accounts for the cool reception vouchsafed to the prince when he penetrated to the heart of England in 1745.

Our ancestors might possibly have overlooked his dissidence from the national faith. They could not pardon a close alliance between the fallen dynasty and a nation which they had come to regard as hereditary and inexorable foes. The *Vergilian Non tali auxilio, nee defensoribus istis, Tempus eget* should have been the Stuart motto. Nor was this attempt to make capital out of George II.'s hated rival less disastrous to French interests. British opinion ran strongly on Maria Theresa's side from generous sympathy with the oppressed. The king was incapable of such sentiments. But for this abortive invasion he might have consulted his selfish instincts by withdrawing from a coalition which promised no advantage to the Electorate of Hanover.

Great Britain and Spain had been at war since 1739; but despite the intimate connection between Bourbon dynasties on either side of the Pyrenees, despite our huge subsidies to the German coalition, despite Dettingen and the attempted invasion, we were still nominally at peace with France. Our troops on the Continent were regarded as mere auxiliaries of the Queen of Hungary and Bohemia. Louis XV. now threw off a transparent mask and put an end to the highly anomalous conditions which had lasted for three years. On March 17, 1744, Mr Thompson, British Minister at Paris, wrote to Lord Carteret:—

> I received last night a billet from M. Amelot, Secretary of State, desiring me not to fail going this afternoon to Versailles. . . . There I found M. Amelot, who began to make excuses for having sent for me on such an occasion. Afterwards he went on, saying that what he had to communicate might not, perhaps, be very agreeable to me, and that it was with great regret that he found himself obliged to make so indifferent a compliment, as they had nothing to lay to my charge personally; but that,

in short, things were come to such a pass between the two nations that France could no longer avoid declaring war. Here he made a stop, and I replied that, for my own part, I was sorry to see things were carried to such extremities, but since it must be so, it was some satisfaction for me to think we were as ready as they.

The French declaration of hostilities, dated March 15, 1744, set up a distinction between the King of England, Elector of Hanover, and his people, whose susceptibilities were spared as far as possible. Of the former it alleged that—

> Not content with dissuading the Court of Vienna from reconciliation, and displaying his animosity by the most violent designs, he has sought to provoke France by molesting her maritime commerce, in entire disregard of international law and solemn treaties. Personally, a foe to France, he has endeavoured to stir up other enemies against her on all sides. The piracies of English men-of-war increased in cruelty and savageness: our ports afforded no refuge against their insults.
> At length, an English squadron had the audacity to blockade Toulon, to stop our vessels, impress their crews, and seize munitions of war on their way to his Very Christian Majesty's fortresses. So many repeated insults and outrages have at last exhausted his Majesty's patience. He can no longer submit to them without disregarding his duty to his subjects, his allies, and his own honour and glory. Such are the motives which forbid his Majesty to continue longer within the bounds of moderation which he had imposed on himself, and compel him to declare war by land and sea against the King of England and Elector of Hanover.

The British counterblast was issued on March 29, 1744. It charged the French king with violating his own guarantee of the Pragmatic Sanction; with wantonly attacking England's ally, the Queen of Hungary, in view of destroying the balance of power and extending his dangerous influence; and with assisting the Spanish fleets in their struggle with those of Great Britain. The peroration is not devoid of eloquence:—

> The notorious breach of treaties by repairing the fortifications of Dunkirk; the open hostilities lately commenced against our

fleet in the Mediterranean; the affront and indignity offered to us by the reception of the son of the Pretender to our crown in the French dominions; the embarkation actually made at Dunkirk of a considerable body of troops notoriously designed for an invasion of this kingdom, ... will be lasting monuments of the little regard had by the French court for the most solemn engagements, when the observance of them is inconsistent with interest, ambition, or resentment.

Austrian Flanders became the arena of the next campaign. It came to the House of Habsburg in 1477, by the marriage of Charles the Bold's only daughter with Maximilian, afterwards Emperor of Germany. These outlying provinces were governed by viceroys of the imperial family, termed Stadtholders. Geographical position, within easy reach of England, France, and Germany, made their rich and well-peopled plains the "Cockpit of Europe." In Lord Beaconsfield's words:

> Flanders has been trodden by the feet and watered with the blood of successive generations of British soldiers.—Mr B. Disraeli's speech at the Literary Fund Dinner, May 8, 1872, the King of the Belgians in the chair.

Early in the spring of 1744, the allied army began to assemble at Brussels and Ghent. All the contingents fell short of the strength agreed on between the confederates, for 55 Dutch battalions were locked up in the chain of fortresses termed the "Barrier." The force available for field operations was only 40,388 bayonets and 14,370 sabres. Lord Stair was offered the command of the British contingent, and on his refusal to serve with the Duc d'Aremberg, the thankless post was conferred on Wade. In the previous December, he had been made a field-marshal, in order to give him prestige in his colleagues' eyes. He was then seventy-three, and advancing years had impaired his vigour. An excellent soldier of the old school, he did not possess the precious gift of patience which enabled Marlborough to overcome the obstructions of jealous associates.

Arriving at Brussels in mid April, the new field-marshal held frequent councils of war, attended by d'Aremberg, Prince Maurice of Nassau, and Prince Charles of Lorraine. It is probable that the general last named undertook to invade Alsace, as a diversion from the main operations in Flanders. On his departure for Vienna, the inherent evils of divided command began to show themselves. The allied generals wasted precious time in wrangling, and June was well advanced ere they could agree on a plan of operations. On the 10th of that month they had advanced southwards by the right bank of the Scheldt, and halted between Audenarde and Bottelaere. Here a general review was held; and Wade told Carteret that the Allies' effective strength was under 40,000, while the enemy's were at least double.

In response to his entreaty, reinforcements were hurried over from England, and the Dutch frontier garrisons were weakened in order to swell the army in the field. Its strength on paper soon rose to 64,000; but Wade's command of 22,000 British and 16,000 Hanoverians was all that could be relied on. These troops were in a high state of discipline, and on excellent terms with each other. The Dutch contingent, 20,000 strong, were of inferior material. Holland had lost the flower of her infantry at Malplaquet (1709).

During a generation of profound peace her citizens had grown rich, and they chose to pay in purse rather than person for national defence. The Dutch Army contained a large German element. Now, Marlborough's and Wellington's campaigns prove that mercenaries make excellent fighting material if only they are well fed, treated with justice, and subjected to strict discipline. These essentials had been notoriously neglected since the Peace of Utrecht (1713). The successors of men who had defied the might of Spain in the sixteenth century had degenerated into a spiritless rabble.

While the Allies were hampered by hesitation and discord, their foes acted with the vigour of unfettered genius. During the winter 120,000 men had been massed on the Austrian frontier, where they awaited orders to take the field. Supreme command was given to Noailles, much against his will, for he would have preferred to keep his place in the Council of State. The other Ministers, however, dreaded his great influence with the king, and combined to secure Noailles' appointment as commander-in-chief in the hope that his credit might be impaired by another Dettingen. Such miserable intrigues were at the root of many a French disaster. On this occasion Noailles checkmated his ill-wishers by persuading Louis XV. to take the field in person. His advice, too, procured for Saxe the coveted grade of marshal, which he would have attained much earlier had he not clung to the Lutheran faith.

The king left Versailles for the front, May 3, and on his arrival at Lille he reviewed the field army, 62,000 strong, on the plain of Cysoing. Then a plan of campaign was elaborated. In those days, frontiers were defended by a chain of strong places, and an invader's efforts were concentrated on the task of reducing them successively. The vices of this system have long been admitted. Permanent defensive works have been superseded by strategic camps, which are too extensive to be invested; and the smaller fortresses have been dismantled.

The French Army was now divided: 47 battalions and 70 squadrons were assigned to Noailles, with instructions to besiege the frontier citadels of western Flanders. Saxe was given 33 battalions and 43 squadrons, with which he was to hold the enemy in check during his colleagues' siege operations. This duty was highly congenial to the author of the *Rêveries*, who wrote—

> I am by no means for pitched battles, particularly at the commencement of a campaign. Indeed, I feel sure that a really skilful general might wage war throughout his life without being compelled to offer battle. . . . I do not mean to say that one should not attack the enemy when an opportunity offers of crushing him, or that one should not profit by his false moves. But I wish to emphasise the fact that one may fight without leaving anything to chance, and that is the highest pitch of perfection and ability in a chief.

He began by framing rules for the discipline and internal economy of his army, which are a masterpiece of lucidity, combined with attention to the minutest details. After one hundred and sixty years, this code is still the basis of French organisation in the field. On May 17, the two forces separated. Noailles, accompanied by Louis XV., laid siege to Menin. After its capitulation (June 4) he invested Ypres. This was so strong a place that siege operations had to be shielded from interference on the enemy's part. Saxe, therefore, occupied Courtrai, which had been evacuated by its Dutch garrison, with 35 battalions and 52 squadrons, while Noailles detached 55 squadrons to hold the left bank of the Lys below that fortress. Other forces were despatched to secure Maubeuge, which was the key of Hainault, and the line of the Sambre. Some regiments of light cavalry, and the much-dreaded Grassins, were ordered to contain the garrison of Tournai and check foraging by the Allies on the left bank of the Scheldt.

These dispositions produced the effect anticipated; but the fate of the campaign was decided by Saxe's resolve to cling to Courtrai. If the Allies approached him by the right bank of the Lys, he could draw reinforcements from Noailles' army before Ypres. Should he be compelled to repel an attack, he could cross the Lys under the guns of

Courtrai. On June 25, Ypres surrendered to Noailles. Three days later Fort Knocke hung out the white flag; and on July 1, Furnes followed its example, the garrison defiling before Louis XV. as prisoners of war. We learn how impatient the allied army was of their long inaction in a letter addressed to his wife by Colonel Russell of the First Guards:—

> We have our club every Thursday night, and one might think it was at Pontac's: a long table, well set out and illuminated, never less than four-or five-and-twenty officers, and the music of our regiment playing all the time. General Ligonier and Lord Albemarle have gladly accepted our invitation to join us. All this seems pleasant, and for the time it is so, provided one could divert one's self of thought, and not consider what can be the consequences of such a campaign as we are likely to have,—to see the French taking all the towns with so much ease, scarce meeting with the least resistance, and we not in a capacity to act, or likely to be in one.—Chequers Court Papers.

The Allies' vacillation was due to d'Aremberg's persistent obstruction and the Dutch generals' timidity. France was still at peace with the Republic, whose troops were deemed to be auxiliaries of Maria Theresa. The states-general knew that a too active participation in the campaign would provoke a declaration of war, and probably a French invasion. They were quite willing to give moral support to the coalition, but they declined to take part in aggressive operations. On July 6, the harassed marshal informed Carteret:—

> I was of opinion that we should have passed the Scheldt when the French first invested Ypres, placed ourselves on strong ground, and covered Ghent, whence we received our bread and forage. But as that did not meet with the approbation of the Austrian general (d'Aremberg) at that time, when it might have given the enemy some interruption in the carrying on of the siege, it would be rash to think of it, now Count Saxe has been so considerably reinforced.

Wade occupied his enforced leisure in corresponding with Noailles on the exchange of prisoners. Among many medieval usages which clung to warfare in the eighteenth century was the "Cartel" system, which established a tariff of ransoms to be paid for prisoners of war. The Cartel of Frankfort, signed by the belligerent Powers in July 1743, laid down the following scale:—

		£	s.	d.
For a Field-Marshal		2000	0	0
" Lieutenant-General		200	0	0
" Maréchal de Camp		60	0	0
" Brigadier		36	0	0
" Colonel		24	0	0
" Cavalry captain		4	0	0
" Infantry captain		2	18	0
" Sergeant		0	8	4
" Trooper		0	2	4
" Foot soldier		0	1	8

******

The Marechal de Camp held rank between lieutenant-generals and brigadiers. His duties were those which were assigned to generals of brigade in subsequent years. In 1740 he was the marshal's or lieutenant-general's *factotum*, and rode on his right in battle order.

******

The ransoms of non-commissioned officers and privates were paid by their company officers.

Noailles' letters breathe a spirit of chivalry which characterised the best elements in his order:

> I am too jealous of the sentiments with which you honour me not to appreciate your remarks on that score.
> Whatever may befall us, I will strive to do nothing calculated to lessen the share you have given me of your esteem; and I am confident of gratifying the king, my master, by behaving with truth, simplicity, and straightforwardness. The zeal and fidelity I owe to all that concerns his honour and glory have nothing incompatible with what an honest man owes to others and to himself. Warfare need not lessen our mutual esteem.
> Let us hope that happier times may bring with them the added sweetness of confidence and friendship. I cannot end this letter without assuring you, sir, how deeply I feel the sentiments with which you honour me. You will always experience in my case those of an old soldier, who will lose no opportunity of displaying them. The long years during which you and I have served afford a reciprocal guarantee that we are animated by the perfect frankness which ought to be maintained by warriors.—
> Marshal Duc de Noailles to Field-Marshal Wade, July 6, 1744.

Such men had no difficulty in coming to terms on this point.

They even agreed that fishing-boats in the English Channel should be protected from seizure during the rest of the war. This concession, however, was vetoed by George II. after consulting the mayors of his Cinq Ports. Some curious light is thrown by this correspondence on Channel fisheries in past ages. The Mayor of Hastings wrote—

> Formerly the French were not permitted to fish on this coast, or presume to come for that purpose beyond mid-Channel. In the reigns of Queen Elizabeth and King James they were not permitted to fish within our headlands, except eight or nine vessels allowed to fish on our coast for the French King's table. Now they are large and numerous, and sweep all the bays, even to low-water mark.—T. Collier, Mayor of Hastings, to the Earl of Winchelsea, Lord of the Admiralty, June 5, 1744.

During the War of the Spanish Succession, French boats, full of men, used to cross the Channel. They made a pretence of fishing while English warships were in sight, and when the coast was clear they became privateers. Moreover, the French Channel fisheries were on a far larger scale than our own. The embargo laid upon them during the recent attempt at invasion caused infinite distress at Dunkirk, Calais, and Boulogne. "A clog on fishery is much more intolerable to the French than English." (T. Lamb, Deputy-Mayor of Eye, to the Admiralty, June 10, 1744).

Weightier matter soon engaged the generals' attention on both sides. On July 7 news came to the French camp of Prince Charles of Lorraine's irruption into Alsace. He crossed the Rhine with 70,000 Austrians on July 1, captured Lauterburg, and stormed the French lines at Weissenburg. Public rejoicing for the surrender of Ypres was damped by accounts of his ravages. Barbier writes:—

> Hussars and *Pandours* have laid part of Lower Alsace under contribution, destroyed the crops, cut down trees in the Forest of Hagenau for their entrenchments, pillaged convents, turning the nuns naked into the fields, and been guilty of a thousand cruelties.... Such are the results of an invasion which might surely have been prevented with a little foresight.—*Journal*, vol. ii.

Louis XV. decided that the conquest of Flanders was of less importance than security on his eastern frontier. He despatched the Duc d'Harcourt, to Alsace with 26 battalions and 23 squadrons drawn from the army in Flanders. (François, Duc d'Harcourt; 1679-1750. Fought at Ramillies at seventeen; created Marshal of France, March 19, 1746). On July 19, he followed slowly with his *harem* and favourites. History records how, three days after reaching Metz, he was seized with apparently mortal illness, the retribution for gross excesses; how he did public penance for his misdeeds and dismissed the Duchess of Châteauroux, only to recall her when danger was past.

******

Marie Anne de Nesle (1717-44) was the last of three sisters who were mistresses in succession of Louis XV. She was an ambitious, headstrong, and vindictive woman, who might, if she had lived, have wielded all the power afterwards attained by the Marquise de Pompadour. Created Duchesse de Châteauroux in 1743, she was publicly dismissed while her lover was, as he supposed, on his deathbed at Metz, but soon recalled to favour. Her death, in the hour of triumph, is one of history's unsolved enigmas.

******

The English Cabinet had earlier intelligence of Prince Charles's diversion in Alsace, and George II. saw clearly that the psychological moment had come for utilising the greatly superior forces idling in Flanders. On July 13, 1744, Carteret informed Wade that—

> It is his Majesty's pleasure that the army in Flanders should no longer remain inactive, but that you immediately consult with the Austrian and Dutch generals, and settle together such methods of acting offensively against France as shall best be suited to the present situation and circumstances, the choice of which must be left to those on the spot. But I repeat that it is the King's positive command that the army should forthwith enter upon action.

On July 17 the Secretary of State becomes more pressing:—

> The strongest representations have been made on the part of the Archduchess, (see note following), to His Majesty, desiring that the army might ... attack with a spirit suitable to the glory of the British nation, in order to find its subsistence in French countries. The army is 60 battalions and 106 squadrons. His Majesty does absolutely command you to commence hostilities of all kinds forthwith against the French, and take the first opportunity, in correspondence with ye Austrian and Dutch generals, of attacking them with the whole force of the Con-

federate Army.

✶✶✶✶✶✶

Note:—She was Stadtholder of Flanders. Colonel Russell was presented to her before leaving Brussels for the front, and thus describes the *vicereine*: "She seems to be an agreeable woman, and has a tolerable good person, does not look quite so well at present, as she is with child. Her dress was plain, had on some very fine diamonds; her maids of honour, of which she had three or four, were very plain, and had but disagreeable persons. Duchess d'Aremberg, who is with them, is really a very fine woman of her age; appears to be about forty, but must have been very handsome."—Chequers Court Papers,

✶✶✶✶✶✶

That King George's very natural impatience was not without its effect is proved by Wade's next despatch:—

Upon frequent advices of considerable detachments being sent from the French Army to the Rhine, it was thought proper to call a council of war, which was held yesterday at my quarters, as it was the general opinion that we should not continue any longer inactive, when assured that the whole detachment was really intended for the Rhine, and out of reach of returning to us. Two different proposals were made—the one to march towards Tournai, on this side of the Scheldt, and the other to cross the river and march towards Count Saxe's army; and the latter ... was carried by a considerable majority.—Wade to Carteret, Berlegem, July 25, 1744.

Nearly a week was spent in preparing for this advance; and on July 30 Wade told Carteret that:

The whole body of 60 battalions and 105 squadrons would pass the Scheldt on the morrow, as the first step towards putting in execution his Majesty's commands.

He added some significant information bearing on Anglo Dutch relations. According to a report from the Comte de Chanclos, an active Austrian general commanding at Ostend:

Great disputes and animosity had arisen between soldiers of the two nations, and he had the greatest difficulty to prevent their falling one upon another with the utmost rage and violence.

After traversing the Scheldt, the Allies moved slowly westwards and took up a new position in a semicircle, stretching from Anseghem to Waereghem, nine miles from Courtrai. Saxe declined to believe that they would attack or mask that fortress, because they had withdrawn the garrison from Ghent, which held all their heavy baggage, leaving that line open to a *coup de main*. He nevertheless took measures to strengthen his defences: 32 battalions, with cavalry reserves, were posted on the ramparts and glacis of Courtrai, and three redoubts were erected on the left bank of the Lys, to defend a bridge thrown across it at Harlebeck.

Should the enemy cross the Lys and advance by its left bank on Courtrai, he, too, would cross it, placing this serious obstacle between himself and them. These precautions proved unnecessary, for the Allies abandoned a movement which was evidently intended to lure him from his coign of vantage into the open field. On August 3, they broke camp, and pursued the left bank of the Scheldt in a south-westerly direction, halting between Espierre and Avelghem, where Wade fixed his headquarters. He hints at the *rationale* of this move in a despatch to Carteret of August 5:—

> The Court of Brussels complain of the inactivity in which I have encamped on the other side of the Scheldt. They may blame their own generals; for I often proposed that our army should pass that river, when our generals might choose a strong ground, our right extending towards the Lys and our left towards the Scheldt.
> In such a position, we covered Ghent, and might wait for the arrival of reinforcements, or annoy the enemy as occasion might offer; but the fear of being drawn too far from Brussels always prevented their assenting to this proposal. If I had always agreed with them, the French would have been possessed of Flanders long ago.
> If Count Saxe continues in his present camp on the Lys, I believe it will not be difficult for us, by a detachment of 5000 or 6000 men, to destroy the works they have been making for some time at Tressin and other places beside the River Marque; but if he should march his army to take post there, I hope, in this season of the year, the river will be no hindrance to our attaquing with our whole force, and bringing matters to the decision of a general action, in which I think we can't fail of

success, for a finer body of troops or a more complete one I never saw drawn together, the number of squadrons amounting to 112, and 69 battalions of foot, the regiments from Mons, Tournai, and Audenarde having joyned us after our passing the Scheldt.

On August 9, the Allies pushed farther southwestwards, to the left bank of the Marque. Their right wing, composed of British troops, occupied Tressin, the Hanoverians being posted in the centre, while the Dutch stretched leftwards as far as Peronne. In this position, they threatened Lille, Douai, and Condé. On the morrow Wade wrote to the Secretary of State:—

> We have passed the River Marque unopposed, and encamped about a league from Lille. We have a spacious plain in our front, sufficient to draw out our whole body in line of battle, and where our fine body of cavalry might have an opportunity of exerting themselves; but as by our last advices Count Saxe's main body continues still behind the Lys, between Courtrai and Menin, he does not intend to give us an opportunity to make use of them.

These manoeuvres did not escape Saxe's penetrating glance. The Allies' object was evidently to make use of Tournai as a base for subsistence, and decoy him from an impregnable position at Courtrai by threatening Lille. He reinforced the garrison of that great citadel by regulars drawn from Dunkirk and Ypres, bringing its defensive strength up to 12 battalions and 3 squadrons.

At the same time, Lieut.-General Du Chayla was sent with 48 squadrons to secure the lines of the Deule and Scarpe between Courtrai, Douai, and the allied army's new position. He knew that their numbers were fifty *per cent* greater than his own, for spies reported that they drew 85,000 bread rations daily. Allowing for the extra portions then served to superior officers, he computed the allied force at 70,000.

That this surmise was pretty accurate is proved by an elaborate "plan of battle" sent home by Marshal Wade on August 19. It showed 71 battalions and 114 squadrons ranged in two lines, nationalities being distinguished by colouring. The right wing was composed of British and Hanoverian troops, the left of Dutch and Austrians. The cavalry were disposed on either flank, the artillery in the rear. The whole army was now at its maximum strength, the relative proportion

	Cavalry.	Infantry.	Total.
British	4,281	17,492	21,773
Hanoverian	5,530	10,633	16,163
Dutch	5,620	16,848	22,468
Austrian	3,601	8,950	12,551
Total	19,032	53,923	72,955

being—

Saxe was not dismayed by the Allies' numerical superiority. He learned that Frederick II. of Prussia, had invaded Bohemia with 40,000 men, and foresaw that this diversion would deliver Alsace from the Austrian incubus. In that event, the detachment made under Harcourt would return to strengthen his forces. In a letter to the Duke of Saxe-Weissenfels, commanding the Saxon auxiliaries of France in Germany, he disclosed the situation with characteristic bluntness:—

> The Allies are two leagues from Lille. They apparently thought they had put me off the scent, but I believe that I am hampering their projects. They cannot bring up siege artillery by the Bruges canal to Ghent, nor yet by the Scheldt from that base to Tournai. They dare not advance on Douai, for they would be unable to keep communications open with Tournai, whence their bread rations come. In order to prevent them from extending posts in the plain of Leuse, I have stationed 24 squadrons below Douai and as many below Lille. These forces will cut off the retreat of any corps that may advance beyond the Scarpe and the Deule, which they have not yet attempted to do. I hope to get out of the scrape, although I am confronted by a far superior force. The Allies came in my direction with the object of attacking, but they have changed their minds—I believe, wisely—Pajol, *Les Guerres sous Louis XV,* vol. iii.

The writer divined that the Allies' advance on Lille was but a feint. In point of fact, they were not in a condition to attack a first-class fortress. A complete siege-train had, indeed, been supplied from Woolwich, but it stuck fast at Antwerp, owing to objections raised by the Dutch against furnishing any *quotum* of the cost of transport. Colonel Russell wrote on August 14 from the Guards' camp near Anstain:—

> There seems no chance of our laying siege to Lille, as the Dutch have not yet declared war, though they have joined us as allies of the Queen of Hungary, and they will not agree to the ex-

pense of carrying on a siege. When the Duke of Marlborough took it the expense was two millions of money, of which the Dutch bore the greatest share, besides the cost of twenty thousand lives.—Chequers Court Papers

At a crisis when Wade's hands were tied by his colleagues' indecision, George II. must needs hamper him by putting forward a plan of campaign which had been drawn up by that inveterate meddler, Lord Stair. Its leading idea was to strike at the heart of France. Antwerp and Ostend were to be garrisoned, in order to maintain communications with England. Saxe was to be allowed to amuse himself by reducing the minor Flemish strongholds, while 60 battalions and 100 squadrons were to advance on Paris. That capital being unfortified, its capture would be an easy matter. If, however, Paris proved untenable, the Allies might take up winter quarters at Rouen. This preposterous scheme was scouted by the allied generals. In forwarding their unanimous opinion from his headquarters at Anstain—only five miles from Lille—Wade wrote, August 14:—

> This was under the consideration of the Cabinet Councill two years ago, when France had so small a force in the Netherlands. I think it now much more impracticable, and, if attempted, must be attended by very fatall consequences, if not with the destruction of the whole army. The repeated commands your lordship has sent me from His Majesty, that we should immediately enter upon action, I have constantly communicated to the generalls who have the command of the troops of the severall nations; and I have, on my part, done all I could to excite 'em to it in one shape or other.
> And as Count Saxe seems determined to continue in the strong post he is now possessed of, I have for ten dayes past solicited the Duke (d'Aremberg) to move our army to some other camp, which might induce the enemy to change their situation, and thereby some favourable opportunity might offer of attacking them. Besides this, there are several other reasons why we should march from this place.
> The desertions of our men (especially among the English) increase dayly; and by our near neighbourhood to Lille, many of our straglers and moroders are taken and carried prisoners to the town. Notwithstanding all the precautions we can take to prevent it, forrage is grown scarce..... These are, in my humble

opinion, sufficient reasons for changing our situation; but I fear there is another, which has more weight with the Austrians. They are raising contributions, and some of them owned they can by no other means find money to pay their troops....

By your lordship's letter to Mr Trevor, (see note following), I find the Pensionary complains of the want of discipline in the allyed army; and I allow it to be so, since the junction of the Dutch troops, who fell to plundering the day after their arrival in the camp, and set the example to our soldiers, who before were very orderly. They had this excuse for their licentiousness, that they had no ammunition-bread provided for them.—
Wade to Carteret, September 5, 1744.

******

Note:—Robert Hampden Trevor (1706-85) had been our Minister-Plenipotentiary at The Hague since 1741. His correspondence with Henry Pelham, which has been preserved, shows that his attachment to the all-powerful brothers was stronger than his loyalty to King George. In a letter of May 15, 1744, he reported that "the cause of the sluggish conduct of the war by Holland was its want of a due reliance upon our royal master, through its discovery of the prevalency of his electoral bias." Trevor succeeded to his half-brother's barony, and was created Viscount Hampden in 1776.

******

These pessimistic views were echoed by Colonel Russell, who gives a gloomy picture of the sufferings entailed on the civil population by warfare in his day:—

Our bawmen, (bau-men, villagers in the Allies' pay, employed in collecting supplies.), still go on foraging daily by stealth, and every three or four days publicly by order, and therefore our horses fare well; but I cannot help thinking what a miserable thing it is to live in a country that is subject to become the seat of war. It is sad to see the fine groves and avenues daily made a sacrifice to our common use, and yet we do nothing but what necessity requires.

At our first coming the Dutch and Hanoverians marauded in a shocking manner, contrary to all orders, and set so bad an example to the English that they also made havoc enough; but severe orders to the provost to hang up all offenders, and to the pickets to prevent such outrageous doings, soon put a stop to them; and now we have what the country affords brought to us, but the best of our provisions comes from Tournai. . . . We hear that every one in England is dissatisfied with our inactivity, but there is nothing we can do without cannon, and of that all sides seem to avoid the expense; and as to marching into and ravaging great part of France, which we certainly could do with such an army as ours, the Dutch absolutely refused to join in it. In short, an allied army like ours, with as many different commanders, each pulling their several ways and influenced by their separate interest, can never undertake what an army should do that has but one head, are under one interest, and understand all the same language.—Chequers Court Papers

Lille proving obviously too hard a nut to crack, the question of besieging Maubeuge was mooted in a council of war. This idea was abandoned when the Allies learnt that the garrison had been strongly reinforced by troops returning from Alsace. That province no longer needed protection. Prince Charles of Lorraine had recrossed the Rhine on August 24, to assist in repelling Frederick II.'s invasion of Bohemia. The Allies had lost a unique opportunity of profiting by the enemy's weakness.

Saxe was now in a position to assume the offensive. In the assurance that he would soon receive reinforcements, he sent forth a swarm of light troops, which destroyed the Allies' magazines; while detachments under D'Estrées and the Prince de Pons threatened their communications and flanks. At length starvation stared them in the face. Wade set his back against the wall and insisted that the army should quit its position east of Lille. He even declared that, if pushed to extremities, he would act independently of the Dutch and Austrians. (Wade to Carteret, Camp Anstain, September 27, 1744).

The threat was effective; but, as irresolute men are wont to do, d'Aremberg and Nassau passed from timidity to rashness at a bound. They urged an advance on Courtrai, and the occupation of the Lys between that city and Ghent. This was the very scheme which Wade had advocated three weeks previously, and it had been rejected by his colleagues at a time when Saxe's forces were at their lowest ebb. (Wade to Carteret, September 27, 1744).

On September 28, the dispirited army began its retreat on Tournai, and three days later it followed the left bank of the Scheldt towards

Audenarde. During this weary march intelligence came to Wade that a French force of 14,000 men had got into their rear. He promptly informed d'Aremberg of this movement, and on getting no reply from the fatuous Austrian, he continued his march. On the morrow a council of war was held to decide whether this small body was to be attacked. It was too late.

> Twenty-four hours' delay ruined all: the enemy decamped. As your lordship knows, I am by his Majesty's command to submit my opinion to the judgment of a council of war. I can't be assured what will be our further proceedings.—Wade to Carteret, Avelghem, October 3, 1744.

October 2 found the Allies encamped on the left bank of the Scheldt: British and Hanoverians at Avelghem, Dutch and Austrians at Helchin. During their halt, Count Chanclos, who was one of the few able generals on the Austrian side, led a detachment towards the main body from the Bruges Canal, pursuing the left bank of the Scheldt. This bold movement led Saxe to suspect that the enemy at length intended to attack him. He issued orders for a concentration, recalled his cavalry from Lille to Courtrai, and waited for the Allies to make up their minds to recross the Scheldt or act offensively, with Courtrai as their objective.

As the country between the Scheldt and Lys had been swept bare of supplies, their decision could not be long delayed. On October 4, they continued their march, taking a northern route, and three days later they took up a new position, covering Ghent. The right wing encamped at Nazareth, the left extended to Huysse; and they established a strong post at Deynze, on the Lys. Wade's next despatch is in the querulous tone which was habitual to him.

> I am sorry to inform you that my predictions have been verified, for, though it was agreed that the army should continue their march for four days, till they had passed the Lys at Deynze, it is now thirteen days since we began our march for the plains of Lille, and we have not yet passed that river. I am always obstructed by the Duc d'Aremberg and the Dutch generals, (Prince of Nassau, Ginkel, and Cronstrom, the latter was 83 years of age). It is now too late. The country is impracticable; we must give up the campaign, and encamp at Ghent, to save the Queen's country from being foraged.—Wade to Carteret, October 1, 1744.

The dearth of supplies which guaranteed Saxe from attack also rendered Courtrai untenable. Despite his earnest wish to remain in that strong position until the Allies had recrossed the Scheldt, he was constrained to evacuate it on October 9 and retire on Menin. His three months' sojourn at Courtrai won for him a European reputation as a master of the art of war; but it had consequences still more momentous. A period of inaction was employed by Saxe in perfecting the moral and disciplinary training of his troops. The army which triumphed at Fontenoy, Rocoux, and Laffeldt was fashioned for its task at Courtrai.

While Saxe's Fabian tactics were crowning him with bloodless laurels, the Allies were battling with the elements in a comfortless camp. Winter's approach was heralded by a tremendous storm, which levelled the tents and filled the hospitals with sick men. (Wade to the Earl of Granville, October 21, 1744. Carteret had succeeded his mother in the higher dignity).

No choice was left them but to seek shelter in adjacent cities. On October 13, these less than lukewarm associates separated. The Dutch and Austrians betook themselves to St Denis, three miles S.E. of Ghent, while Wade concentrated on Deynze. Generals Ginkel and Cronstrom of the Dutch service, who had been obstructionists throughout this ignominious campaign, sought to make a scapegoat of the old marshal. On October 19 Lord Granville sent him extracts from Mr Trevor's despatches, which contained:

> An account of your having withdrawn the English and Hanoverian troops from the allied army, leaving the Dutch and Austrians, as they alledge, exposed to many insults on the part of the French.

These aspersions stirred the old marshal to fury, he asked:

> How could the army be exposed to insults from the French in camp almost under the walls of Ghent, and eight leagues from the ennemy, encamped on the other side of the Lys, and then actually separating their troops? For what sinister end this clamour has been raised, these false, absurd, and scandalous misrepresentations dispersed abroad, let the authors of them answer; but sure, it is the endeavouring to create misunderstandings between England and Holland, can be calculated only for the ruin of the Queen's affairs and the common cause.—Wade to Granville, November 7, 1744. 37

After disposing his troops in their winter quarters, Wade obtained the king's permission to return home—

> There being very little probability, in the present condition I am in, of my being able to serve in another campagne, which I hope may be attended with better success than this has been.— Wade to Granville, October 17, and reply, October 23, 1744.

On November 13, he resigned command in Flanders to Sir John Ligonier, and returned, crestfallen, to England.

The storm which broke up the Allies' camp hastened Saxe's resolve to seek winter quarters. After distributing his army over a chain of strong places on the French frontier between the river Meuse and Channel, he went to Paris to render an account of his stewardship. Comte d'Argenson, Minister of War, assured him of the king's entire satisfaction, and directed him to prepare a plan for the operations of 1745.

Marshal Wade became the object of endless diatribes at home, and his exploits were travestied in the Paris theatres. Public indignation on our side was intelligible enough; for an army fifty *per cent* stronger than that which won the Battle of Blenheim had spent six months in objectless manoeuvres. But Wade was far less to blame for the fiasco than was a system which linked Great Britain with allies whose interests differed widely from her own. Our generals' initiative was paralysed by the necessity imposed on them from above, of consulting jealous colleagues at every turn. The moral cowardice which is bred of divided counsels led them to avoid rather than meet a foe.

"I don't like all this moving about," exclaimed a young officer who saw the grim humour of the situation. "I should not wonder if some day we were to fall in with the enemy!" (Mackinnon, *Origin and History of the Coldstream Guards*). Under such conditions Frederick the Great or Napoleon themselves could never have dealt those sledgehammer blows which decide a nation's fate.

Undignified as was his leaders' plight, the British soldier was more to be pitied. The cause for which he was called upon to die never enlisted his love or sympathy. His endurance was strained to breaking point by fruitless marches and counter-marches, without a hope of indulging his fighting instinct. Instead of meeting a glorious death on the battlefield, or returning home to reap a rich reward for duty faithfully rendered, he too often found a grave in a foreign land.

Chapter 4

The Advance on Tournai

The ignominious campaign of 1744 proved a terrible weapon in the hands of Lord Granville's foes. Their name was legion, for his habitual truckling to King George had rendered this powerful minister highly unpopular with all classes. But, "drunk with wine, ambition, and royal favour," he scorned to conciliate public opinion, and was blind to the signs of the approaching storm. A Cabinet crisis was precipitated by the Flanders fiasco. The Duke of Newcastle and his brother, Henry Pelham, formed a Ministerial cabal against Granville during his attendance on George II. in Hanover.

✶✶✶✶✶✶

Thomas Pelham Holies, Duke of Newcastle (1693-1768), and his half-brother, Henry Pelham (1696-1754), led the faction known as "The Pelhams," which succeeded to all the influence wielded by Granville. The first was nominally Secretary of State for Foreign Affairs, the second First Commissioner of the Treasury and Chancellor of the Exchequer. The duke was a prey to morbid vanity, but not quite such an egregious fool as his enemies averred him to be.

✶✶✶✶✶✶

On November 12, 1744, Newcastle presented a memorial to their master, which told him plainly that he must choose between Granville and the rest of his colleagues. The king clung desperately to a minister who had always been a pliant agent of his will and was able to converse with him in German.

After twelve days' hesitation, he sulkily yielded, and Granville was compelled to surrender office. His successor as Secretary of State was William Stanhope, Earl of Harrington, who was versed in court usages and those of diplomacy, but had not a tithe of his ability.

✶✶✶✶✶✶

At this epoch, there were two Secretaries of State, who shared in the direction of home affairs and divided those relating to other countries. Granville had been "Secretary of State for the Northern Department," and in that capacity, had charge of the war portfolio.

✶✶✶✶✶✶

When Parliament assembled, King George found that the sacrifice of his faithful adherent would serve his ambition to pose as an arbiter of Continental affairs. The reconstituted Ministry proved as eager as Granville himself to promote measures which they had ascribed to his base subservience. They were joined by the self-styled Patriot party, prototypes of the Little Englanders of our day, and found an unexpected convert in William Pitt himself.

✶✶✶✶✶✶

William Pitt the elder, afterwards Earl of Chatham (1708-78), was the leader of the "Patriots," recruited from younger members of the Whig party. He took the side of Frederick, Prince of Wales, in the bitter family feud which ended only with the latter's life, and incurred the King's deadly hatred by so doing.

✶✶✶✶✶✶

In supporting a motion for a parliamentary grant to continue the war, he voiced the general feeling of relief caused by Granville's disappearance, he exclaimed:

> We are now free from that minister who, when not ten men in the nation were disposed to follow him, supported himself in the royal closet on that broken reed—dependence on foreign princes!

During the remainder of this war George II. and his ministers had little to fear from the once virulent and powerful opposition.

They took advantage of the lull in party strife to plunge the country more deeply in the Continental quagmire. On January 8, 1745, a Quadruple Alliance was concluded at Warsaw between Great Britain, Austria, Holland, and Saxony. Maria Theresa's subsidy was raised to £500,000, enabling her to equip and maintain at least 50,000 men; and a host of minor German potentates were allotted doles from the British Exchequer. Lord Chesterfield was despatched on a mission to The Hague, in view of reviving the tepid zeal of our Dutch allies.

✶✶✶✶✶✶

Philip Dormer Stanhope, fourth Earl of Chesterfield (1694-1773), was equally famous as an orator, a man of letters, and a wit. His spirit was essentially French. He was one of Walpole's bitterest enemies, and was cordially disliked by George II. Nevertheless, he was admitted to the Pelhams' Ministry, and became Secretary of State in 1746. Two years later he was driven by increasing deafness from political life.

✶✶✶✶✶✶

On December 16, 1744, Sir John Ligonier wrote from Brussels:—

> I am extreamly glad to find, from His Majesty's speech from the throne, that the number of troops which each of the Allies is to furnish here, and the proportion of the expenses of sieges, is to be settled. I hope the plan of operations will be so too, and that it be an offensive war. A defensive one will tire you out in England, and never bring a safe and honble. peace. I would not venture my opinion to anybody but my Lord Harrington, that being, perhaps, much above my sphere.

The general's deference was appreciated by the new Secretary of State, who sent him to The Hague (December 28) to assist Chesterfield in concerting measures with the Dutch and Austrian leaders. The earl's insinuating address succeeded where Granville's overbearing manner had failed miserably. The states-general undertook to furnish 52,000 men, against 40,000 to be supplied by Great Britain. (Hon. Philip Yorke to Horace Walpole, May 16, 1745).

Some light is thrown on the genesis of the Fontenoy campaign by despatches from our generals in Flanders. Hawley, who commanded 11 battalions and 15 squadrons at Ghent, kept Harrington informed of French movements during Ligonier's absence at The Hague. On February 6, 1745, he wrote:—

> By Sir John Ligonier's instructions left with me, I am directed to acquaint your lordship with anything that may occur in these parts during his absence. I have a pretty good emissary in all of theyr frontier garrisons, especially a good one at Lille. Hitherto they are all very quiett. Theyr usuall way of talke is the same everywhere—of the great things they are to do as early as the monthe of Marche.... They talk of attacking Tournai and St Ghislain at the same time.... The new regiment, called Royal Scotche (which lyes at St Omer, Lord John Drummond, Coll.), is pretty near compleated, and new cloathed; and about three

weeke ago one Captain Glengarry and three more Scotts officers came from Scottland with ninty odd recruits to Dunkirke, and a fortnight later came one Keizer with eleven more. He is a Jew, and a lieutenent, but they have also all nations in the regiment; but then they have 150 of our deserters, mostly Scotche.

The regiment alluded to was raised in August 1, 1744, and placed under the command of Lord John Drummond, son of the titular Duke of Perth, and a man of great personal charm. The uniform was blue; collar, cuffs, and lapels red; brandenburgs, buttons, and cockade white. Its flag bore a white cross on yellow ground bordered with red.

On February 9, 1745, Sir John Ligonier reported progress at The Hague to Harrington:—

> I saw my Lord Chesterfield and Mr Trevor together; and I own my surprise and concern was great at hearing that the king's part of the Flanders Army will be so considerably diminished as 22,000 men, and that at a time when the States are willing to give all the troops they have. If I was to give my opinion at first sight, it would be that the French will take the field with great superiority, which will oblige us to leave great garrisons on Namur, Charleroi, Mons, Ath, Tournai, and Audenarde; and if that should be the case, what army can we expect to bring into the field? They must, by their situation, be masters of besieging wherever they please.
>
> Put us in a condition of acting offensively, and the disadvantage falls on the enemy. We begin the war where the Duke of Marlborough left it, and may perhaps end it in one campaign with honour and safety to Britain and all Europe by an honble. peace; whereas a defensive, lingering war must produce the contrary effects. £100,000 bestowed on the siege of Maubeuge and Landrecies last campagn might have saved the nation £6,000,000 this year.
>
> Your lordship may say, What is this fellow prating for? Why, my lord, he has a mind to say, if he durst, that there are Danes, Munsterians, and, I believe, 10,000 or 12,000 Hessians to be had for money. I think so, but these are things above me, and which I hope your lordship will forgive me for mentioning, as knowing me guided by a faithful zeal for the king's service and glory, and *un parfait dénouement* à my Lord Harrington.

On March 23 the vivacious Frenchman wrote as follows to Harrington:—

> *En gros*, what I can find by the marshal, (Marshal Königsegg, who commanded the Austrian contingent), is that we shall assemble the army early, having our artillery and all other things necessary. If we are stronger, we shall immediately enter upon action; if weaker, we must trye to hinder the enemy from doing anything; and if they undertake a siege, fall upon them. As to what your lordship mentions of Lord (illegible in the MS. probably James, 14th Earl of Morton, imprisoned in the Bastille 1746, died 1767), if your lordship and Lord Cholmeley desire that he should be with me this campain, he is very well come, though I confess to you I shall alwais be in some pain lest some accident should happen to him, especially if he is not designed for our trade.
>
> As for his equipage, a bed, some cloathes, a couple of horses for himself, and horses for what servants he designs to have with him, is enough for the necessary. *Pour le superflu, cela dépend de la fantaisie*; a good groom is absolutely necessary. As I have two *aides-de-camp* in pay, and that His Majesty allows me no more, I can't give it to my lord. But I presume H.R.H. will permit me to have him given in orders as a supernumerary, which I believe will be better than being a volunteer at large. Your lordship may be sure, all old gentlemen being fond of giving advice, that my lord will have mine, *gratis*.

The Duke of Cumberland had sued in vain for permission to serve during the campaign of 1744, and his father was loath to entrust supreme command to so young a soldier. Lord Stair, our "only general," was again appealed to; but he had taken Wade's failure to heart, and scouted the notion of co-ordinate authority in the field. No course remained but to give Cumberland the nominal rank of commander in chief. It was hoped that his royal birth would give him prestige in the eyes of colleagues; while he was assigned a mentor in the person of the impetuous Ligonier. Lord Chesterfield's silver tongue won over the Dutch to this proposal.

The *London Gazette* of March 12, 1745, recorded the issue of a commission under the Great Seal appointing William Augustus, Duke of Cumberland, &c. &c.:

> Captain General of all and singular his Majesty's land forces employed within the Kingdom of Great Britain, and . . . in

conjunction with the troops of his Majesty's Allies.

His Austrian *adlatus* was Marshal Joseph George Lothaire, Count Königsegg, who had won great distinction in the Turkish wars, but was now in his seventy-third year, and half-crippled by gout. His rank technically implied a joint authority with Cumberland, and but for the veteran's infinite tact, his appointment might have involved us in even worse disasters than Fontenoy. The trio of generals was completed by the Prince of Waldeck, who numbered as many years as Cumberland, and was already famous for impetuous courage. He commanded the Dutch contingent, but was nominally subordinate to the young duke.

Cumberland was accompanied throughout his Flanders and Scottish campaigns by Sir Everard Fawkener (1684-1758), whose career aptly illustrates the social confusion of his age. The son of a London mercer, he followed the paternal business until late in middle life. In 1735 he was knighted and sent as ambassador to Constantinople. This sudden metamorphosis has never been explained, but the amazing sycophancy disclosed in Fawkener's letters leads to a surmise that he served the Hanoverian dynasty as a secret agent.

He was a man of some culture, became a close friend of Voltaire's during the latter's residence in England (1726-29), and shared his philosophic views. In 1743 he obtained the post of private secretary to the Duke of Cumberland, and grasped the fact that to succeed in life one must become indispensable. There is ample evidence that most of Cumberland's despatches were drafted by Fawkener's facile pen. The new commander-in-chief arrived at The Hague on April 17, 1745, and wrote in a cheerful vein on the 23rd to Lord Harrington:—

> I met with very friendly reception from the government, and was spared many points of ceremony which I should be very glad to dispense with. I am under difficulties to express the great pleasure I feel to have found Marshal Königsegg answer so fully with the character which had been given of him, and the expectations he had raised by his behaviour on my recommendation to the command of the army and since in everything relating to me. My intentions are to imitate his example, as well as to follow his advice; and I persuade myself there is a sure foundation laid for a thoroughly good understanding between us. I have good reason to be satisfied with the Prince of Waldeck and General de Wendt, (commanding the Hanoverian contingent), and I promise myself great advantage to the gen-

DUKE OF CUMBERLAND

eral cause by their good disposition.

Which of the frontier fortresses would bear the brunt of French attack? This question was eagerly debated at daily councils of war. In the end, Mons, Namur, Tournai, Ath, and Charleroi were strongly garrisoned, and provisioned for a long defence. To the consternation of their inhabitants, orders were issued banishing from the fortified *enceinte* all who had omitted to lay in six months' supplies. When concentration was complete, the field force was reviewed near the encampment at Anderlecht, a south-western suburb of Brussels. According to a "State of the Allied Troops," sent home by Cumberland, its effective strength was 12,000 sabres and 30,550 bayonets.

The British and Hanoverians, who again composed the right wing, made a brave show in their new clothing; and the Dutch occupying the left were roused from their habitual phlegm by the excitement of approaching battle. Neither contingent was up to promised strength; and owing to the ever-present Prussian incubus, Maria Theresa was able to supply only six weak squadrons for the defence of her possessions as Countess of Flanders. In view of the huge force mustering across the frontier, it was a perilous adventure to attempt the offensive with less than 43,000 men, and old Königsegg advised the adoption of harassing warfare. He was overruled by his youthful colleagues and the equally ardent Ligonier. There should be no repetition of the aimless gropings of 1744. The tactics of the opening campaign were as simple as Nelson's at Trafalgar.

"In immediate prospect of the day of action"—so ran the general orders of April 29, 1745—Cumberland organised his staff. Most of his six *aides-de-camp* bore names which became household words in our military annals. They were Lieut.-Colonels the Earl of Ancrum and Hon. Henry Seymour Conway; Captains Lord Bury, Lord Cathcart, Hon. Joseph Yorke, and Robert Napier; with a Captain Vendermeer, unknown to fame. See notes following).

******

Note:—Earl of Ancrum, eldest son of the third Marquis of Lothian; Captain and Lieutenant-Colonel in the First Guards. He was severely wounded by a musket-ball at Fontenoy. Commanded the left wing of the English cavalry at Culloden as Lieutenant-Colonel of the 11th Dragoons, and strove in vain to save the life of a heroic Highlander named Gillies Macbane, who stood up single-handed to a cavalry charge and slew thirteen dragoons ere he succumbed. In 1758 he is referred to by Horace Walpole as "my friend Lord Ancrum, who loves a dram of everything, from glory to brandy!" Died 1775, Marquis of Lothian, K.T., and senior general in the army.

Henry Seymour Conway was brother of the first Earl of Hertford. He was at Eton with Horace Walpole, whose lifelong friend he became. Joined the First Guards in 1737; promoted Captain and Lieutenant-Colonel in 1741, and served with his regiment at Dettingen. Five years later he became Colonel of the 48th Foot, and was taken prisoner at Laffeldt (1747). Conway shared in the failure of one of those foolish and disastrous raids on the French coast which diminished the lustre of our victories during the Seven Years' War, and George II. would not hear of his being again employed.

In the following reign, he obtained command of a British division in Germany, but won no new laurels. He died in 1795, a Field-Marshal and the father of the British Army, and with him snapped the last link which binds our own age with Fontenoy; for Conway lived to see Napoleon's star rise. He owed much to Walpole's extreme partiality; but the verdict of posterity is that of Macaulay, "Conway was versed in the learning of his profession, and personally courageous, but wanted vigour and capacity" (*Essay on Lord Clive*).

Lord Bury was the second son of the second Earl of Albemarle; Captain-Lieutenant in the Coldstream Guards; *Aide-de-camp* to the duke during the Culloden campaign. On the morning of the battle he was nearly slain by a Highlander, who penetrated the English lines and fired point-blank at Bury, whom he mistook for Cumberland. In 1749, while Colonel of the 20th Regiment, he incurred the censure of his major, James Wolfe of Quebec fame, who wrote:

"Lord Bury promises fairly and means nothing. In that he resembles his father and a million of other showy men who are seen in palaces and the courts of kings. He desires never to see his regiment, and wishes that no officer would ever leave it. This is selfish and unjust. They have a way of trifling with us poor soldiers that gives many honest, poor men high disgust" (Wright, *Life of Wolfe*, chap. vii.).

Lord Bury succeeded to his father's peerage and much-dilapidated property in 1754, and attended Cumberland in his last command, which ended so disastrously with the Convention of Klosterseven (1757). As Lord Albemarle, he commanded the British forces which captured the Havannah in 1762. Cumberland wrote to congratulate him in terms which prove that he was, at all events, capable of sincere friendship: "No joy can equal mine. I strut and please myself as if it was I who had taken the Havannah." Meeting his friend's mother at St James's, he exclaimed, "By God, my lady, if it wasn't in the drawing-room I would kiss you! "After a career facilitated by royal favour, Albemarle died in 1772 a Knight of the Garter and Governor of Jersey (Campbell Maclachlan, *Life of the Duke of Cumberland*).

Lord Charles Cathcart, ninth Baron Cathcart in the Scottish peerage, entered the Third Guards at an early age. He was very severely wounded at Fontenoy. In his diary for March 3, 1773, Sir Joshua Reynolds wrote of Lord Cathcart: "He is proud of his Fontenoy scar, and requests Sir Joshua to arrange that the black patch on his cheek maybe visible. It is not often that a man has had a pistol bullet through his head and lived."

Cathcart and the Earl of Sussex were selected as hostages to be given to France under the ignominious Treaty of Aix-la-Chapelle (1748), which provided that "two persons of rank and distinction" should be assigned to French custody as pledges for the surrender of Cape Breton. Cathcart afterwards exchanged soldiering for diplomacy, was ambassador at the court of Catherine of Russia, and died in 1776.

Hon. Joseph Yorke, Captain Yorke of the Coldstream Guards was third son of Lord Chancellor Hardwicke, emphatically a strong man, and the founder of a family which wielded immense influence in the eighteenth century. He, too, embraced diplomacy in later life, was created Lord Dover in 1788, and died *sine prole* 1792. His name lingers as that of the builder of Dover House, Whitehall.

Captain Robert Napier's name is that of a galaxy of heroes whose fame is still with us. He entered the army as ensign in the 2nd Foot. Napier was gazetted Lieutenant Colonel and Deputy Quartermaster-General on June 25, 1745, in reward for his services at Fontenoy. Died 1766 as Lieutenant General and Colonel of the 12th Foot.

******

The "Inspection" of the cavalry was assigned to the gallant Sir James Campbell, whose career has been sketched in chapter 2. Majors-General the Earl of Rothes and Humphrey Bland commanded the first line of cavalry, Hawley and Major General Richard Onslow the second. The Household Cavalry was placed under Lord Crawford. (See notes following).

******

Note:—John Leslie, eighth Earl of Rothes, commanded the second line of infantry at Dettingen, and a brigade of cavalry at the battle of Rocoux, where, according to the historian Smollett (vol. ii. chap, ix.), he "behaved with splendid gallantry." Commander-in-Chief in Ireland 1760; died 1767.

Humphrey Bland's service dated back to Queen Anne's wars; Colonel of the King's Own Regiment of Horse. In 1727 he published a guide to the whole duty of a soldier, entitled *A Treatise on Military Discipline*, the sixth edition of which appeared in 1746. At Dettingen he attended George II. on foot, after his own horse had been shot under him. Completed the Highland rout at Culloden, in command of the cavalry of the right wing; wounded at Laffeldt.

Bland was a martinet, and, while Governor of Gibraltar, was thus stigmatised by James Wolfe: "I am afraid General Bland is not quite so well-bred and polite as might be wished. He has a roughness about him that breaks out sometimes into ill-manners when he is in authority" (January 1, 1750). Commander-in-Chief in Scotland 1755; died 1763.

Richard Onslow was brother of Arthur, Speaker of the House of Commons, and, like many of his family, was M.P. for Guildford; Governor of Plymouth; presided at a court-martial which tried Lord George Sackville for misconduct at Minden, but died of apoplexy soon after proceedings commenced, 1760.

******

The British cavalry which fought at Fontenoy included the following corps:—

Household.

Horse Guards, 3rd and 4th (Scots) Troops; Horse Grenadier Guards, 2nd (Scots) Troop. These now form the 1st and 2nd Regiments of Life Guards.

The Royal Horse Guards, styled officially "Blue Guards."
Regiments of Horse.
The King's Regiment of Horse (1st Dragoon Guards).
Ligonier's, or the Black Horse (7th Dragoon Guards).
Dragoons.
Hawley's, or the Royal Regiment, 1st (Royal).
Campbell's, or the Royal North British (Royal Scots Greys).
Bland's, or the King's Own (3rd Hussars).
Cope's, or the Queen's (7th Hussars).
Stair's, 6th (Inniskilling).

Sir John Ligonier was entrusted with the "Inspection "of the British infantry; Lord Albemarle, Colonel of the Coldstream Regiment, with that of the Guards. Command of the first line of infantry was given to Majors-General Hon. H. Ponsonby and W. Pulteney that of the second line to Majors-General Hon. C. Howard, Hon. J. St Clair, and John Campbell. (See notes following).

******

William Anne Keppel, second Earl of Albemarle, owed his second Christian name to his godmother, the queen; Colonel of the Coldstream Guards, 1744; second in command at Culloden; succeeded Cumberland as Commander-in-Chief in Scotland, and led the British infantry at Laffeldt. Albemarle is reprobated by James Wolfe and Lord Chesterfield as owing everything to his airs and graces. Stanhope (*History of England*, vol. iii. chap. xxxii.) hints that he sold Government secrets to a French mistress while ambassador in Paris. Casanova tells us that this lady's nickname was "Lolotte." That she utterly ruined him admits of no doubt. "He chided her one night for praising the beauty of the stars which shone in the firmament, albeit she knew he could not bestow them upon her" (*Mémoires*, vol. ii.) He died almost penniless at Paris, 1754.

General Ponsonby was second son of Viscount Duncannon; Colonel of the 37th Regiment; served at Dettingen; killed at Fontenoy at the head of the First Guards.

W. Pulteney, son of the first Earl of Bath; served in the First Guards under Marlborough, and Brigadier at Dettingen. He quitted the army on succeeding to his brother's vast possessions.

Hon. C. Howard, son of the third Earl of Carlisle; Captain-Lieutenant, Coldstream Guards, in 1719; M.P. for Carlisle; Brigadier at Dettingen. Wounded in four places at Fontenoy; died 1765, General and Colonel 3rd Dragoon Guards.

Hon. J. St Clair, son of eighth Baron Sinclair; served in the 3rd Guards under Marlborough; was ordered, on returning to England after Fontenoy, to select a site for a fixed camp to protect London against Prince Charles Edward, and reported in favour of Finchley Common. Thither marched the Grenadier companies of the Guards, furnishing a subject for one of Hogarth's caricatures. Commanded a futile attack on the port of Lorient, August 1746; succeeded his brother in 1750 *de jure*, but did not assume the title; died a full general in 1762.

John Campbell of Mamore was first cousin of the Duke of Argyle, whom he succeeded in 1761; Colonel 21st Regiment, and Brigadier at Dettingen. Rendered yeoman service to the Hanoverian cause during the '45 by bringing "loyal" Highlanders to the king's standard and hunting Prince Charles Edward. He figures in *Redgauntlet* as "a tall, thin, gentlemanly man, with a look and bearing decidedly military." Died 1770.

******

The Guards constituted a brigade, the seventeen line regiments being divided into four others, named after the senior regiment of each, *viz*.:—

Royals, Brigadier George Churchill
Howard's, H. Skelton.
Onslow's, J. Ingoldsby.
Sowle's, Thomas Bligh.

******

Note:—George Churchill was commonly supposed to be a natural son of the great Duke of Marlborough, but in a letter to the Earl of Harrington, dated June 13, 1745, he states that his father was "the late Admiral George Churchill." His first commission is dated 1707, and in 1743 he was Lieutenant-Colonel of the Coldstream Guards. Wounded at Fontenoy; Commander of the Forces in Scotland, where he died after a very long illness in 1753.

Brigadier Skelton had served for many years in the Third Guards; Colonel, 32nd Foot, 1742. Died 1757, leaving his ancestral home, Branthwaite Hall, Cumberland, to a former A.D.C., Captain James Jones of the Third Guards, who had saved his life in Flanders.

James Ingoldsby was junior major of the First Guards, ranking as lieutenant-colonel. He is often referred to in the Chequers Court Papers, and appears to have been an amiable man of convivial habits. His want of nerve was the principal cause of our defeat at Fontenoy.

Thomas Bligh became Colonel of the 20th Foot in 1740. We shall see him behaving with coolness and vigour in the action at Melle, July 9, 1745; served at Laffeldt as Colonel, 12th Dragoons. In 1758 he commanded one of the miserable buccaneering expeditions to the French coast, which served only to exasperate the enemy. On this occasion our troops were driven off with greater loss than usual in the Bay of St Cast, near St Malo. Public feeling in England ran so strongly against Bligh that he resigned his commission and sank into obscurity.

******

The following infantry regiments were engaged:—

1st Foot Guards (Grenadier Guards).
2nd Foot Guards (Coldstream Regiment).
3rd Foot Guards (Scots Guards).
Royal Scots (1st, Lothian Regiment).
Lieut.-General Howard's (3rd, The Buffs).
Onslow's (8th, The King's Liverpool Regiment).
Sowle's (11th, Devonshire).
Duroure's (12th, Suffolk).
Pulteney's (13th, Somerset Light Infantry).
Major-General Howard's (19th, Yorkshire).
Bligh's (20th, Lancashire Fusiliers).
Campbell's (21st, Royal Scots Fusiliers).
Royal Welsh Fusiliers (23rd).
Earl of Rothes' (25th, King's Own Scottish Borderers).
Bragg's (28th, 1st Batt. Gloucestershire Regiment).
Late Handyside's (31st, 1st Batt. East Surrey Regiment).
Skelton's (32nd, Duke of Cornwall's Light Infantry).
Johnson's (33rd, 1st Batt. Duke of Wellingtons, West Riding Regiment).
Cholmondeley's (34th, 1st Batt. Border Regiment).
Lord Sempill's (42nd, Royal Highlanders, Black Watch).

The British Artillery was to march in the army's rear, escorted by an infantry battalion. It consisted of a heavy 6-pounder, serving as a "flag gun," drawn by nine horses; nine other 6-pounders, drawn by seven; four 8-inch howitzers—always styled *haubitzer* in despatches—with teams of five horses; twenty-seven 3-pounders and six 1½-pounders on galloping carriages. The whole forty-seven were under Colonel Lewis's command. (Duncan, *History of the Royal Artillery,* chap. xi.)

Louis XV. watched every movement of the powerful coalition which sought to crush him, and strove to parry the impending blow. On December 23, 1744, the Marquis d'Argenson, his Foreign Minister, sent the Powers a circular outlining peace conditions. It is probable that this unjust and unnecessary war would have ended then and there but for an event which encouraged his enemies to prolong it. The titular Emperor Charles VII. died in poverty on January 20, 1745. Francis of Lorraine was now the only candidate for the crown of Germany, and his election became a foregone conclusion. Maria Theresa haughtily refused the professed olive-branch, and spurred her generals to renewed efforts.

In March 1745, an Austrian Army overran Bavaria and drove the new Elector, Maximilian Joseph, from his capital. The young prince took his father's fate to heart. He concluded peace with Austria at Füssen (April 15, 1745), undertaking to vote for Francis of Lorraine, and to disarm his French auxiliaries. This defection left no excuse whatever for further intervention in German affairs, and would, of course, transfer the theatre of war to Flanders. Louis XV. knew that he could not reckon on Frederick of Prussia, who consistently fought for his own hand, and that he would be left to contend unaided against Austria and the Maritime Powers for a cause in which French interests were in no way concerned.

He therefore humbled himself so far as to sue for peace. Finding his overtures rejected, he set his back against the wall and summoned to his councils the only man who could avert the consequence of senseless ambition. At such a crisis, the voice of court cabals was hushed; and the "carpet generals" of Versailles ventured not a word of protest when their hated rival, Maurice de Saxe, was appointed Commander in Chief of the French armies in Flanders. With a chivalry, which recalls that of Outram before Lucknow, the old Duc de Noailles volunteered to serve under a leader whom he regarded as his pupil.

The general relief which came when patriotic Frenchmen knew that their destiny was in such capable hands was dashed by the news of the hero's serious illness. On April 23 Cumberland, informed Lord

Harrington that the marshal was "in so low a state that his death is dayly expected." He was not misinformed, for Saxe was paying the penalty for his prolonged excesses in an attack of dropsy, which brought him to the brink of the grave. Louis XV. was in despair, and all France shared in his poignant anxiety. But the prospect of glory raised that indomitable soul far above physical suffering. Voltaire met the sick man on the eve of his departure for the front, and asked what he could do in so miserable a plight. "It is not a question of living," was the reply, "but of leaving." (Voltaire, *Siècle de Louis XV*.)

On April 20, he reached the base of operations at Maubeuge, and placed himself under the care of a medical canon of Cambrai, whose prescription and regimen soon restored him to comparative health. (Barbier, *Journal*, vol. ii., he says that the chapter of Cambrai always included a canon who was versed in medicine).

He was now able to review his available field forces, consisting of 90 regular and 10 militia battalions with 160 squadrons—in other words, 69,000 infantry and 25,600 cavalry. The initial tactics of 1744 were repeated, and the campaign opened with a siege. But Saxe was kept posted in every movement in the Allies' camp. Knowing that they would take the offensive, he resolved to deceive them as to his real aims. A strong detachment under Lieuts.-General D'Estrées and Du Chayla was despatched towards Mons by way of St Ghislain, while on April 26 Saxe led the bulk of his forces to Tournai. The Duc d'Harcourt invested that city on the right bank of the Scheldt, while the Marquis de Dreux-Brézé completed the circle of trenches on the left bank. Communication between the besieging forces was established by pontoon bridges above and below the city.

✶✶✶✶✶✶

L. C. C. Letellier, Marquis de Courtenvaux, Comte D'Estrées, born 1697, fought under Belle Isle 1743-44, proved himself to be an honest and capable general in Flanders. Marshal of France 1757, and beat Cumberland at Hastenbeck in the same year. Compelled by a base court intrigue to resign command to the Duc de Richelieu. Created Duke 1763. Died *sine prole* 1774.
François, eldest son of Henri d'Harcourt, Marshal of France, born 1689, entered the Mousquetaires at fourteen; fought at Ramillies (1706); Lieutenant-General 1744; served under Belle Isle 1743 and 1746; in Flanders 1744-45; Marshal 1746; died 1750.

✶✶✶✶✶✶

Tournai, styled Doornyk in Flemish, was the capital of the Nervii, who offered so stubborn a resistance to Caesar. In 1667 it was captured after a few days' siege by Louis XIV., and Vauban's utmost skill was lavished on its new fortifications. The deep and rapid Scheldt, which traversed the *enceinte*, was utilised to fill the ditches. A system of advanced works, and a pentagonal citadel on rising ground at the southern extremity, placed Tournai in the first rank of European fortresses, while its position on the frontier made it the key of Western Flanders.

The Dutch garrison consisted of 12 battalions and 3 squadrons—at least 7000 men. One thing was wanting, however, to render Tournai impregnable—vigour in the generals who were responsible for its defence. Baron van Dort, who commanded the city, and Van Brakel, who was in charge of the citadel, had left their best days behind them, and neglected obvious precautions. Their eyes were fixed on Mons as a certain French objective, and Saxe's sudden appearance was a thunderbolt for the bewildered garrison.

On the night of April 30, 1745, Count Löwendahl, who was in charge of the siege operations, opened his trenches in front of two hornworks protecting the gates of Seven Fountains and of Lille, on the city's north-east and south-west. On May 1, the first parallel was completed, and work was pushed with such vigour that three days later a second parallel, with connecting zigzags, encircled the defences. Then 7 batteries, armed with 60 siege-guns and mortars, began to hail projectiles on Tournai.

The garrison was paralysed by this lightning speed of attack, and such defensive power as it possessed was reduced to zero by treachery. Löwendahl contrived to win over the Dutch engineer-in-chief by bribery, and a sorry tale of incompetence was disclosed by the *commandant's* despatches after his ignominious surrender:—

> We found it impossible to attempt a sortie, because Engineer Hertslet had omitted to place sixty barriers in their positions, which had been ordered last year but were still in magazine. We could not reach the glacis without breaking through the palisade. He must have been aware that other shortcomings would be brought to light, for on May 9 he quitted Tournai, apparently for the French camp.
>
> Soon after his flight we discovered that there were no banquettes protecting the palisade; that the traverses in the covered way had not been repaired; the counterscarp of the citadel had

no traverses at its sallying or retreating angles; and that the covered way could be enfiladed at every point. Further, the day before the engineer's escape he directed Sluice-master Schmidt, who followed him in flight, to remove six planks from every sluice on the side facing Hainault (east), so that the ditches were nearly dry. He left the great sluice below Tournai open, and the water fell three feet, enabling the enemy to construct bridges of communication with ease.

Then a great disaster occurred. On Friday night, May 7, the citadel powder-magazine was exploded, probably by a mine dug by some traitor, destroying our barracks and the brewery, with the whole stock of beer in store. . . . We daily disinterred the corpses of men, women, and children from the ruins. All this, coupled with the fact that two of our sappers have not been seen since the explosion, leads to a surmise that premeditated treachery has been at work.

Albeit that the garrison were frightened and demoralised from fear of further catastrophes, we all did our best to remedy our evil plight. But we could not make much use of the weapons in the arsenal, for many muskets burst at the first discharge, and their stocks were quite rotten. After capturing the hornwork which defended the gate of Seven Fountains the enemy began to batter both sides of the bastion in breach.—General van Dort to the States-General of Holland, May 23, 1745.

The Allies were completely deceived by Saxe's feint on St Ghislain and Mons, and all doubt vanished when they learnt from the governors of the latter fortress that 40 French squadrons, supported by infantry, had appeared on the heights commanding it. (The Prince of Hesse Philipsthal and Count Nava, governors of Mons, to Marshal Königsegg, April 22, 1745).

In transmitting the news to Harrington, Cumberland wrote (April 23):

By all the intelligence I have from different parts, the real design of the enemy is to besiege Mons.

The English Cabinet, however, were sceptical. Harrington replied (April 30):—

His Majesty is extremely pleased to see that you had drawn your forces together, as I will be impatient to know whether the true design of the French shall prove to be the siege of Mons, which is looked upon here as a very desperate enterprise, in sight almost of such an army as your Royal Highness will have under your command in the field.

At length, the allied generals obtained an inkling of Saxe's true design. On April 28 Sir Everard Fawkener wrote to Harrington:—

After a good deal of variety and contradiction, our advices for two or three days past agree that the enemy's army is before Tournai, and that place is so far invested that the post, which should have come in yesterday, does not appear. So it is taken for granted that all communication is stopt. The accounts of their numbers is not to be depended on. A person's computation, who said that he came from the army yesterday, makes them about 15,000 on our side of the town, and 40,000 on the other. But this is not a force for undertaking the siege of Tournai in the face of an army which might probably prove stronger upon equal trial.

Bad intelligence was among the causes of the Allies' discomfiture. Fawkener's estimate of the enemy's strength was at least fifty *per cent* too low. A week was wasted in indecision, and it was not until April 29 that a council of war determined to advance southwards on the morrow. Even then there remained a lingering suspicion that Mons might be the French objective. A glance at the map will show that the direct road from Brussels to Tournai runs through Enghien, Ath, and Leuze, and is 45 miles in length. The route taken by the allied army, by way of Soignies, trends towards Mons, and measures 50 miles.

On April 30, the army marched in two columns for Halle, 8 miles south of Brussels. After halting there for a couple of days it advanced to Soignies, a march of 14 miles. Here it was joined by 6 Dutch battalions and 2 Austrian squadrons from Mons, which was obviously no longer threatened by the French, with some hussars and Free Companies, (irregular troops, formed on a French model in 1744), who had been watching the frontiers. That an iron discipline was maintained in the British camp is proved by Cumberland's

General Orders:—

> Camp of Soignies, May 2.
> Parole, *St Georges et Londres.*

As H.R.H. intends to show all reasonable indulgence imaginable to his army, and as the pay of the British forces exceeds yet of any other troops, he expects they should observe strict discipline, being determined to show no mercy in case of misbehaviour. ... All morouders brought to ye provost this day to be tryed tomorrow by a general court marstial.

> May 4.
> Parole, *St Gudule et Bruxelles.*

A reserve guard of a subaltern and 40 men of the foot to mount constantly at ye headquarters to send centrys to the houses where provisions and liquors are sold, to prevent disorder, and to send centrys to ye magazines, and parties into the neighbourhood, where necessary, upon application from the country people that any soldiers are marouding. The Grand Guard is to patrole, and to take up all men they find stroling beyond y e Grand Guard, and carry them prisoners to ye regiments, they belong to, where a court marshal is immediately to be held at ye head of ye standard or collours, and the punishment adjudged to be instantly put into execution.

The army was detained by excessively wet weather at Soignies until May 5, when it shifted camp nine miles to Cambron. Thence Cumberland wrote to the Secretary of State:—

The Marshal Königsegg is in very good health, and much more active than is common at his years on horseback. He is quite young, and the day of the march from Halle to Soignies he was on horseback several hours, both in the morning and afternoon, in bad weather, without showing any signs of weariness. He leapt a ditch when one was in his way as readily as the youngest man in the company, so that I don't apprehend any inconvenience from his infirmity.—Cumberland to Harrington, May 6, 1745.

A three days' halt was called at Cambron, to give time for the roads to dry; for beyond the limits of the paved highway the whole country was a quagmire. As the danger zone looms nearer, orders show an increasing strictness:—

May 6. It is strictly ordered by H.R.H. that none presume to shoot or hunt, whether officers, private men, or officers or huntsmen—this to be a standing order. Besides the going out of the provost, there are 50 hussars ordered to patrole in ye front and rear of y e camp, and so cut down every man they meet beyond ye limits of the camp.

Here occurred the first brush with the enemy. Learning that 4000 French cavalry occupied Leuze, on the left front, Cumberland detached the Highland battalion (Black Watch) and other troops under the Hanoverian General Moltke, with instructions to drive them from that position. On May 7 the army broke camp at Cambron and marched to Moulbaix, 7½ miles. The duke's intelligence was still at fault, and he cherished delusions destined to be rudely dispelled.

I heard on my arrival that the body of troops the enemy had posted at Leuze had retired very precipitately on the first notice that we were advancing. I intended to have drawn nearer the enemy today, but the weather is so very wet that the marshal and I have thought it more advisable not to move till to-morrow, when I hope to be within two leagues of Tournai and one short league from the enemy. . . . For my own part, I cannot bring myself to believe the enemy will wait for us, notwithstanding it is assured that the French king has arrived at Lille, if not at the army.

My reasons are that they might have disputed our passage hither with great advantage of ground; that they have withdrawn the baggage over the Scheldt, and have not thrown up earth to form a circumvallation. However, I cannot say that everybody is of my opinion that the enemy will retire. I cannot come to any certain knowledge of the enemy's numbers, but I have concurring information the body on this side the Scheldt does not exceed 31 battalions and 32 squadrons. The weather is bad; heavy and constant rains all day, and still continues.—Cumberland to Harrington, May 8, 1745.

The General Orders prove that Cumberland's severity towards his men was not uncalled for:—

Château de Moulbaix, May 7.
The duke hopes that the three examples which have been made this morning will be a warning to the rest, for he is resolved to keep discipline and have orders obeyed, which will contribute to plenty in the camp, whereas the enormities committed by some bad men will cause but distress and scarcity.

In their march between Soignies and Moulbaix the Allies were reinforced by 2 Hanoverian and 4 Dutch battalions, including a portion of the garrison of Ath. The army which fought at Fontenoy was now complete, and was thus composed:—

	Battalions.	Men.	Squadrons.	Men.	Total.
Right wing, English, Hanoverians, and Austrians, under the Duke of Cumberland and Marshal Königsegg	25	16,500	45	6,750	23,250
Left wing, Dutch, commanded by the Prince of Waldeck	27	17,550	40	6,000	23,550
Grand total	52	34,050	85	12,750	46,800

Analysing the right wing, we find it consisting of—

	Battalions.	Men.	Squadrons.	Men.	Total.
British	20	13,000	26	3,900	16,900
Hanoverians	5	3,250	8	1,200	4,450
Austrians	...	...	8	1,200	1,200
Hussars	...	...	3	450	450
Two Free Companies	...	250	...	...	250
Total	25	16,500	45	6,750	23,250

The artillery numbered 80 guns, of calibres ranging from 1½- to 6-pounders.

On the evening of May 9, the last stage of this tiresome march was reached. The Allies encamped between Maubrai and Baugnies, almost within musket-shot of the enemy's advanced posts. Bruffoel, in the rear, served as Cumberland's headquarters, and a base for hospitals and baggage. Eleven days had been occupied in covering forty-eight miles, albeit that the generals knew full well that despatch was called for. Cumberland's official report of the battle begins thus:—

> The enemy opened their trenches before Tournai the 30th April, and as they employed a very great and unusual number of workmen, the siege advanced so fast that no time was to be lost,

but whatever was to be done towards obliging the enemy to raise it, was necessary to be put into execution immediately.—Cumberland to Harrington, Lessines, May 17, 1745.

The army was doomed to linger for thirty-six hours more before offering battle—a respite which gave Saxe time to compass its defeat. How startling is the contrast between this snail-pace advance and the movements of our unequalled Light Division during the Peninsular War. It reached Talavera in July 1809, after marching sixty-two miles in twenty-six hours, with only seventeen stragglers.

The Allies' camp was pitched on rising ground which commanded a splendid view of the French positions. Tournai, the goal on which such ardent hopes were fixed, lay six miles to the north-west. The quadruple spires of its noble cathedral and the adjacent belfry tower stood outlined against the horizon by a setting sun, and the boom of cannon proved that its garrison were in sore need of succour. Westwards rose the slender tower of the Prince de Ligne's castle, marking the site of Antoing. In the near foreground, the spire of Vezon Church emerged from a dense mass of foliage. Beyond that village there was an extensive plain which afforded an ideal battlefield. A gentle slope led upwards to the arena, whose entrance was narrowed on the left by the village of Fontenoy, on the right by Barri Wood.

Late as it was, the allied leaders rode forward to reconnoitre, escorted by twelve squadrons. The Duke of Cumberland is described as:

> A large man, with the fair round face and large eyes of his family, clad in the wide-sleeved scarlet coat of the lines, and a small three-cornered hat hardly covering a comely white periwig. In common with most of his friends, the duke wore the large, horseman's jack-boots, in which Charles XII. seemed to take such pride.—Picken, *History of the Black Watch*.

He was mounted on the same grey charger as he afterwards bestrode at Culloden. Beside him rode dark-featured Königsegg, wearing a round helmet of burnished brass, white body-coat, and tightfitting pantaloons, and the young Prince of Waldeck, whose short square figure was buttoned tightly in a dark-blue coat turned up with white. This trio found that Vezon was an outpost held by the enemy, and that Fontenoy was strongly fortified. The French camp on the plain beyond was masked by flying squadrons of cavalry.

On May 10, the allied generals met in council at Cumberland's headquarters. It was clear that the foe's position could be reached only through Vezon, which was thickly wooded and scored by ravines. They resolved to clear the ground in front for an immediate advance. At ten o'clock 6 battalions and 12 squadrons from the right wing, with 500 pioneers, 6 galloper 3-pounders, and 2 howitzers from the British train, paraded under Lord Crawford and Brigadier Roseberg of the Hanoverian contingent. (British troops engaged were the 1st Foot Guards, 3rd Buffs, 8th, 11th, and 42nd Foot, and one squadron from each cavalry regiment). This force advanced on Vezon and Fontenoy. After exchanging shots, the enemy evacuated Vezon, and burnt a hamlet south-east of Fontenoy which they had fortified. Cumberland took possession of Vezon and established his headquarters there. He neglected Lord Crawford's advice that the wood of Barri should be occupied. This was an amazing oversight, and bulked largely among the causes of our defeat.

This preliminary skirmish boded well for the future, and the Allies were in high spirits as they formed in order of battle, concealed from the enemy's ken by the woods of Vezon. On the extreme right the Black Watch were posted, with two Free Companies, facing the angle of Barri Wood. A gap of 200 yards separated them from the Guards, on whose left stood Ponsonby's and Onslow's brigades. The second line was formed by Howard's, Bland's, and Skelton's brigades. On the British left the Hanoverian infantry took position under General Zastrow, with their cavalry in the rear.

The British cavalry, under James Campbell and Lord Crawford, were drawn up on the right flank. Leftwise the Dutch extended in similar formation from the Hanoverians to Peronne, with their cavalry on the extreme left. In those days, manoeuvres were slow and punctiliously carried out. Twilight came ere the last battalion and squadron had reached their assigned posts. After reconnoitring the enemy's position, our generals resolved to defer battle until the morrow. The troops bivouacked on their arms at the spot assigned to each unit, while a council of war met to discuss a plan of battle.

Prince Waldeck, with a light heart, undertook to carry Fontenoy and Antoing on the left front, while the British and Hanoverians attacked the right of Fontenoy and made for the French camp through a gap between that village and Barri Wood. It was intended that the Anglo-Hanoverian cavalry should work round the wood and fall upon the French left. Some of Waldeck's hussars, however, who were sent forward to reconnoitre, were received by a discharge of cannon and musketry from its edge. Their repulse led to the abandonment of a movement which might have turned the scale of battle in our favour. The council of war finally agreed that fifteen squadrons of the right wing, under Sir James Campbell, should extend into the plain beyond Vezon to cover the formation of our infantry on the morrow.

★★★★★★

During the brief night before Fontenoy two Scots officers on the French side stole into the British camp to spend a merry hour with Lewis Grant of Achterblair and other friends. They met next day in mortal strife. One of them was John Roy (Red) Stewart of Kincardine, styled in *Tales of a Grandfather* "a most excellent partisan officer." He had served as lieutenant and quartermaster of the Scots Greys, and applied for a commission in the Black Watch on its first formation in 1730. Meeting with a rebuff, he crossed the Channel and joined Lord John Drummond's regiment in the French line.

During "The "45" he was one of Prince Charles Edward's right-hand men, but could not stomach the overbearing manner of Lord George Murray. John Roy's adventures after Culloden were as romantic as his master's, whom he joined on board the French vessel which carried both to lifelong exile. "By this means," adds Grant in his *Statistical Account of Abernethy* (1792), "his talents were lost to himself and his country. He had education without being educated; his address and figure showed his talents to great advantage. He was a good poet in English and Gaelic." Died 1752. (See also Forsyth, *In the Shadow of Cairngorm*, 1900, chap. xx.)

★★★★★★

While his enemies were toiling through the mud of Flanders to reach him, Marshal Saxe's brain was working to defeat their enterprise. He had ample intelligence of their movements, for parties of hussars and mounted *Grassins* scoured the country and reported details of every march and halting-place. The Allies had three routes open to them. They might advance by their right between Mont de Trinité and Barri Wood. This, he thought, would expose their left too much to be adopted; but he posted two brigades with some hussars, 15,000 men in all, between the range of hills and Barri. Then they might select the Leuze road, although it would entangle them in a densely wooded country seamed with ravines.

Saxe considered this line of advance impracticable, and contented himself with ordering light cavalry to patrol the whole country on his left. The third route was by the Allies' left, along the old Mons road, skirting Barri Wood and ending at Antoing. That townlet crowned the right bank of the Scheldt five miles from Tournai, and the river's overflow formed an impenetrable barrier southwards.

When, on May 9, Cumberland's army marched by its left after leaving Moulbaix, Saxe at once saw that it would approach him by the Mons road. He now cast about him for a spot wherein he might await attack with comparative security. The only possible battlefield was traversed by the highway five miles S.W. of Tournai. It was a cultivated plain, 1900 yards deep, with a maximum breadth of 3000. The base rested on Bon Secours Wood, the Scheldt, and Antoing. Its right was defined by a ridge sloping downwards towards Perrone and ending at the village of Fontenoy, which was the key of Saxe's position.

Between Fontenoy and the angle of Barri Wood there stretched a ridge 620 yards wide, whence the ground dipped gently towards Vezon, 900 yards southwards. One of Saxe's fixed ideas was that French infantry could not be relied on to meet a hostile charge in line, and the issue of Dettingen served to corroborate this view. He therefore put into practice a theory broached in chapter viii. of his *Rêveries*, and resolved to convert the battle arena into an improvised citadel by means of a chain of redoubts.

Louis XV. again, took the field in person, but left his bevy of mistresses at Versailles. On reaching Douai (May 7) with the *Dauphin*, he received despatches from Saxe announcing the enemy's approach. (Louis, Dauphin de France; 1729-65, predeceased his father. His abilities were mediocre; he was inclined to bigotry, and is chiefly remembered as the father of Louis XVI., Louis XVIII., and Charles X.) After ordering the garrisons of Valenciennes and Douai to reinforce his army before Tournai, he hurried onwards to Pont-à-Chin, a *château* on the edge of the northern attack. The sovereign's presence gave new vigour to the besiegers, who established themselves in the covered way.

On May 9 Louis removed to the Château de Calonne, between Tournai and Antoing. The saturnine silence which characterised him was dispelled for the nonce by the electricity of approaching battle. He busied himself with inspecting the camp magazines and hospitals, tasted ammunition-bread, and broth prepared for sick men. Then he discussed the situation in a council of war. When Saxe broached his scheme of field fortifications he was met by loud protests from the swarm of carpet generals, who maintained that Frenchmen were well able to deal with their foes in open ground.

******

Five days after Fontenoy Philip Yorke wrote thus to H. Walpole the elder: "We may thank Count Saxe for our misfortunes. It was he who advised them to throw up entrenchments along part of the line, against the opinion of the rest of the council of war, who were for giving us battle *en rase campagne*."—Quoted in Appendix to Stanhope's *History of England*, vol. iii.

******

Louis XV. imposed silence on these armchair critics by thus addressing Saxe:

> In confiding to you the command of my army I intend that everyone shall obey you, and I will be the first to set an example of obedience.

Secure in a free hand, the marshal prepared his plan of battle. The Marquis de Dreux-Brézé was left with 21,550 men in the trenches, and ordered to contain the garrison of Tournai at all costs. The bulk of his army—66 battalions and 129 squadrons, equivalent to 66,000 men—were to be drawn up athwart the Mons and Leuze roads, facing eastwards. Retreat, in case of disaster, was secured by fortified bridges thrown across the Scheldt at Calonne and Vaulx, in the rear. Then he set to work with zest on his scheme of field fortifications.

Fontenoy became the apex of a triangle whose base stretched between Antoing and the angle of Barri Wood. That hamlet was strongly entrenched, full advantage being taken of sunken roads on its north and east. The walls of its houses were cut through with the pickaxe, bringing down the roofs, and cannon were mounted on the heaps of rubbish thus formed. Fontenoy was held, by the Brigade Dauphin, consisting of 2 battalions of Le Roi and 1 of Diesbach's Switzers.

Three redoubts were run up on the ridge between Fontenoy and Antoing, and garrisoned by Swiss from Diesbach's and Bettens' regiments. Antoing itself was fortified with especial care. Its defence was assigned to 4 battalions of Piedmont and 1 of Royal Marine. The left front was covered by Barri Wood. At its extremity, facing Fontenoy, which was 620 yards distant, two redoubts were erected. The fieldwork nearest Fontenoy was held by a battalion of the Eu regiment, and played a great part in the battle as the "*Redoubt d'Eu.*" The wood was cleared in its proximity, and defended by an abatis of trees. The edge was lined with the irregular troops termed Grassins, who had given Marshal Wade so much trouble. This system of temporary fortifications was garnished with 100 cannon, and 2 battalions of Diesbach were detailed to assist in working them. Six 12-pounders were mounted on the high bank of the Scheldt facing Antoing, to play on the left flank of a force attacking in that quarter.

No one who visits the scene of this memorable encounter can fail to render justice to the skill and foresight shown by these marvellous works, which were carried out on May 9 and 10. A naturally strong position was rendered almost impregnable. One weak spot was left in Saxe's defensive system. A sixth redoubt should have crowned the ridge between the Redoubt d'Eu and Fontenoy. Saxe admitted that this oversight very nearly lost the battle; but he could not believe that any troops in the world would attempt to force a passage at that point.

Saxe's next step was to distribute his mobile forces over the fortified area. He had 60 battalions and 110 squadrons, or 59,000 men, at his disposal. A prudent general always secures his lines of retreat. Three battalions of the *Gardes Françaises* and Swiss regiments, numbering 6000, were thrown into the *têtes de pont* at Calonne and Vaulx. Including the garrisons of the redoubts and entrenchments, there remained 53,000 men to take part in the impending battle. These were disposed in three lines: the first of infantry, with cavalry in the rear. The gap between Fontenoy and the Redoubt d'Eu, facing Vezon, was a point of special danger. Picked troops were told off to defend it. Resting on Fontenoy stood 3 battalions of Le Roi; on their left was a battalion of Aubeterre, then 3 battalions of Courten. Next in order came 4 battalions of *Gardes Françaises* and 2 of *Gardes Suisses*, with 12 guns on their front. Six hundred yards to the rear of this first line the cavalry regiments were posted in a formation four ranks deep, and behind them the Household Cavalry.

On the right flank, between Antoing and Fontenoy, stood 3 battalions of Crillon Infantry and 1 of Biron. In their rear the three dragoon regiments, Royal, Bauffremont, and Mestre-de-Camp, were stationed *en potence*. ("Gallows-shape." These engines of punishment were conspicuous objects in eighteenth-century landscapes).

Saxe's reserves occupied the left flank, covered by Barri Wood. In the first line stood the Irish Brigade, consisting of the regiments Clare, Ruth, Lally, Berwick, Dillon, and Bulkeley—3870 men in all. On their left was Royal Corse and Normandy, which came up after the battle had begun. On their right, connecting reserves with fighting line, were Royal Vaisseaux, with 4 guns in their front. In the Irish Brigade's rear were the regiments Hainault, *Royal Infanterie*, Soissonnais, and La Couronne, and behind them again two lines of cavalry regiments, the extreme left being occupied by the *Carabiniers*.

On May 10, these operations were interrupted by the enemy's reconnaissance, which drove Saxe's outposts from Vezon, compelling him to evacuate and burn an outlying hamlet of Fontenoy. Some squadrons of Dutch cavalry also deployed on the French right flank, and remained throughout the day in position, their right resting on Vezon. Before night fell every unit was in its assigned position. The king and *dauphin* rode down the lines, greeted by shouts, *Vive le Roi!* which to many thousands were the *Ave Caesar, morituri te salutant*, of the Roman arena. Louis XV. passed the night at Calonne. Contrary to his wont, he was in high spirits.

After supper, the talk ran on battles in which his predecessors had taken part. Poictiers (September 19, 1356) was the last, and the French had never yet beaten their hereditary foes. Louis gaily expressed a hope that he would be the first king of France to break the record of defeat. The man who had organised a victory claimed in anticipation by his worthless master, retired, utterly worn out with toil and sickness, to his bivouac between the first and second lines. At ten o'clock all was still in a field which was soon to be filled with the uproar of a pitched battle.

Chapter 5

Fontenoy

Our troops enjoyed but little sleep on the night before Fontenoy, for they were under orders to march at 2 a.m. on that fateful morrow. Men's hearts beat wildly at the thought of the coming fray, and death lost its terrors in the anticipation of glory. At the appointed hour, the whole camp was astir, and long before dawn each unit was under arms and in its assigned position. At 4 a.m. Cumberland rode down the line to the extreme right, where his Guards Brigade had lain on their arms. There he learnt for the first time that a fieldwork, famous in history as the Redoubt d'Eu, guarded the edge of Barri Wood on his right front. This obstacle would take the right wing in flank as they advanced up the slope from Vezon.

A change of plans was called for, and the allied generals met in hurried consultation. They agreed that a special brigade from the right wing should assail this redoubt, while the Dutch advanced against Fontenoy and Antoing. When all three had been carried, the British and Hanoverian infantry were to press forward through the gap between Fontenoy and Barri Wood. These simple tactics depended for success on the two flank movements. Cumberland intrusted the command of the right attack to Colonel James Ingoldsby of the 1st Guards, who had a high reputation, and was in his chief's special favour. ("The idea of attacking the fort near the wood was wholly H.R.H.'s, and he had chosen for that service Brigadier Ingoldsby as a man in whom he had confidence"—Ligonier to Harrington, May 14, 1745).

To him was assigned a brigade, consisting of Duroure's (12th Foot), Pulteney's (13th), the Black Watch, and Böschlanger's Hanoverian regiment. What followed had so decisive an effect on the fortune of war that Ingoldsby's movements must be stated in some detail from the records of the court-martial which afterwards tried him for disobedience to orders. (Minutes of a court-martial on Brigadier Ingoldsby, held at camp, Dieghem, July 13, 1745, Lieut.-General the Earl of Dunmore presiding). He had explicit orders from the duke "to march up to the French battery, not to fire, but to seize on the cannon, if possible." A detachment from the train was to accompany his brigade, "to turn the cannon, if they could, on the enemy, and if not, to spike them." (Evidence of Captain Boscawen).

Ingoldsby started with his brigade at 6 a.m., but halted in front of Vezon, on the left of a hollow lane which trended leftwise towards the edge of Barri Wood, half a mile distant. After reconnoitring the ground in front, Ingoldsby sent Brigade Major Bernard to ask the duke for cannon. While waiting for them he assembled his commanding officers and asked their opinion as to the best method of attacking. Colonel Sir Robert Munro of Foulis commanding the Black Watch was prompt to reply.

The captain of one of the Free Companies had explored Barri Wood at his request, and reported its extremity to be lined with the enemy, and defended by an abatis and cannon. Sir Robert advised that the brigade should form on the right of the hollow lane and advance, while his Highlanders cleared the wood. Ingoldsby accepted this plan of action, but took no steps to carry it out. (Evidence of Lieutenant-Colonel Sir Robert Munro, Bart, of Foulis). His demand for cannon was immediately met by Cumberland, who sent Captain Mitchelson of the Artillery with three 6-pounders, under Major Bernard's guidance.

Mitchelson found the brigade still halted on the left of the lane, and asked Ingoldsby for orders. The reply was, "I cannot tell," or words to that effect. Happily, Cumberland himself followed the guns to see how they fared, and Mitchelson got leave from him to ply the enemy lining the wood with grape. He then advanced his guns to the front of Duroure's, and opened fire. (Evidence of Captain Mitchelson, R.A.) It was answered by several shots from the redoubt, which, however, was not visible from Ingoldsby's position. (Evidence of Sir Robert Munro). Meanwhile the brigadier wheeled his regiments back by platoons; the grenadier companies moved along the sunken lane, while the rest formed on its right side. Duroure's and the Black Watch were in front, behind them Pulteney's and the Hanoverians. (Evidence of Captain Mackenzie of Pulteney's). Ingoldsby ordered them to incline to the left, and a slow advance began.

After watching these movements, Cumberland rode off, satisfied that his orders were being obeyed. But Ingoldsby was perturbed by the sight of Grassins massed at the edge of Barri Wood, and believed that it was held in great strength. He again halted, and sent Captain Crawford of Pulteney's for further instructions. Cumberland "expressed great astonishment" at the brigade's inaction, and sent Ingoldsby some instructions. There is some doubt as to their precise nature. According to Crawford, Ingoldsby "was to defend himself if attacked, but by all means to see and attack the enemy." Major Balfour, B.A., who was standing close to the Commander-in-Chief, heard him tell Crawford that the brigadier was "to attack the battery in the wood, and to maintain himself if he could; if not, to make the best of his way off." (Evidence of Captain Crawford and Major Balfour). That this disastrous delay was partly due to Cumberland's contradictory orders admits of no doubt.

At 6.30 Sir James Campbell began to defile by the Mons road through Vezon with 15 squadrons, destined to cover the formation of the British and Hanoverian infantry. Thinking that he had better await the success of the right attack before exposing his men to cannon fire from the wood, he sent Captain Forbes of the Scots Greys to report Ingoldsby's progress. Forbes found the brigade still clinging to the hollow lane, threequarters of an hour after the start. (Evidence of Captain John Forbes of the Royal North British Dragoons).

As the advance of the right wing could not begin until Ingoldsby had carried out orders, Cumberland grew impatient, and despatched Lord Bury for news of him. Ingoldsby told this *aide-de-camp* that he saw some troops in the wood, but could not guess their number. He had consulted his officers, who considered it impracticable (!). What, he asked, was Lord Bury's opinion? This appeal was evaded, on the plea that Bury was on duty which admitted of no delay. (Evidence of Lord Bury, A.D.C.)

On learning that the brigade was still inactive, Cumberland "expressed a good deal of surprise," and, pausing, said that he would go to Ingoldsby himself. (Evidence of Captain Fitzwilliam and Lieut.-Colonel Yorke). He found the entire force crowded in the sunken lane, while their leader was on horseback at the head of Duroure's. Mitchelson's 6-pounders were still in front, playing on the edge of the wood. After a consultation between Cumberland and Ingoldsby, the troops returned to their old position on the left of the lane.

It was now 7 a.m., and the general advance could no longer be delayed. On a signal, given by four cannon fired in quick succession, the

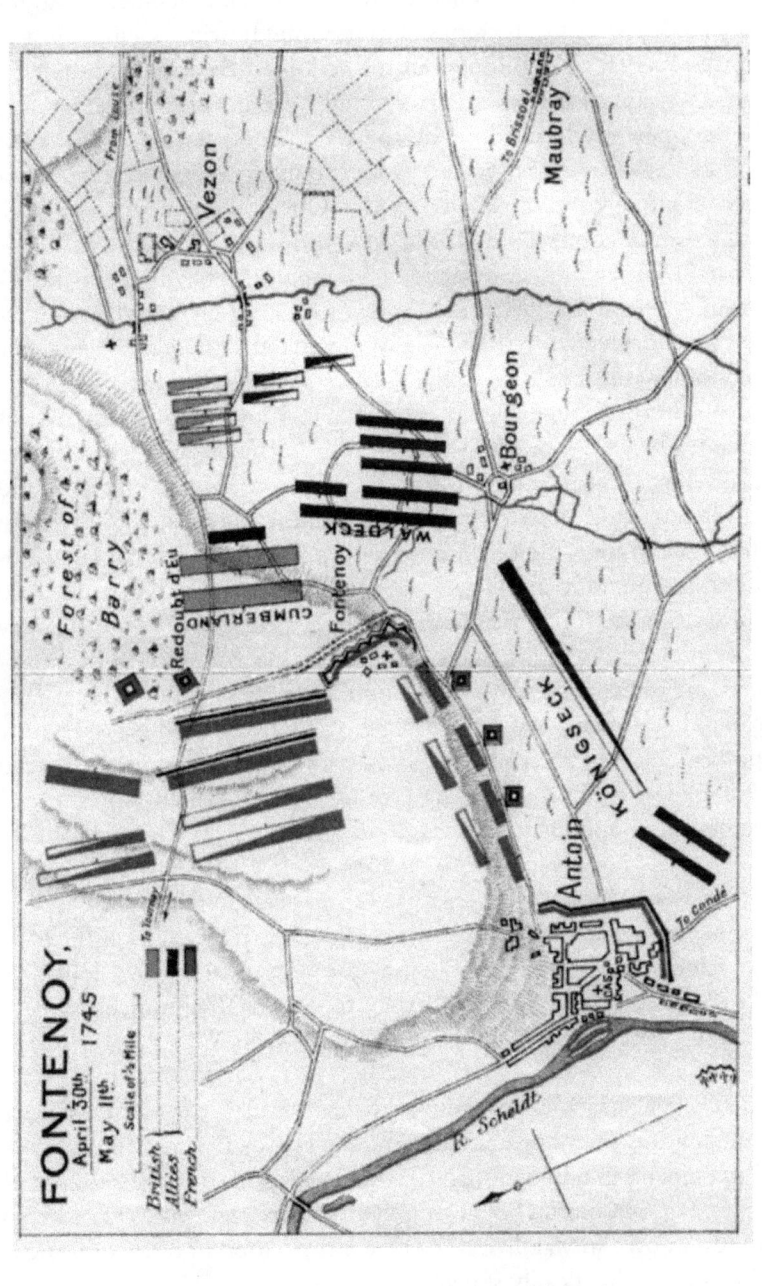

Dutch cavalry moved in two columns towards Fontenoy and Antoing. They were met by a tremendous fire from the entrenchments, and retired, unmasking two batteries of cannon and howitzers, which played on the French right throughout the action. At the same moment Sir James Campbell led his cavalry through Vezon, in view of extending in the open between Fontenoy and Barri Wood. As soon as they left the shelter of trees and houses they encountered a hail of round-shot from Fontenoy and the Redoubt d'Eu. One of these projectiles struck the gallant Campbell's thigh. He was borne dying from the field, and his men, left without a leader, rejoined the main body in the infantry's rear. Command of the cavalry devolved on Lord Crawford and Hawley, who formed them in the rear of the infantry. There they remained, motionless, until the fate of the day was virtually decided.

Nothing daunted by this mishap, Sir John Ligonier ordered his infantry to push through Vezon. As each regiment debouched on the plain beyond, it halted until the succeeding corps had emerged, and covered it while deploying. Then the regiments wheeled to the right and left and took their appointed places. The ground sloped upwards towards Fontenoy and the Redoubt d'Eu, which were barely 400 yards from the foremost battalions. From these defences our infantry sustained a murderous cannonade, while the complicated manoeuvres preliminary to battle formation were carried out with parade ground accuracy. They were also galled by divers small galloper guns, pushed closer to their serried ranks, until Cumberland ordered seven 3-pounders to the front of the Guards' Brigade, which soon silenced their punier opponents.

******

In 1743 Marshal Saxe borrowed from Sweden the idea of giving each line battalion two light guns, drawn by teams of three. Such was the germ of our field artillery. But these gallopers were a source of infinite anxiety to commanding officers, and they were withdrawn during the Seven Years' War.

******

Their first victim was the man whose rashness had lost Dettingen. The Duc de Gramont, commanding the French Guards, was slain by a 3-pounder ball while in the act of embracing his uncle, Marshal Noailles. For two mortal hours were our infantry exposed to the severest ordeal known in war. It was 9 a.m. ere they stood in order of battle at the edge of that deadly slope.

Meanwhile the fortune of battle still hung on the right attack. At

Battle of Fontenoy

8 a.m. Cumberland again galloped up to Ingoldsby's brigade, which he found motionless in its old position. He held a hurried colloquy with their leader. What passed between them will never be known, for Lieut.-Colonel Napier, who is our only authority for this episode, tactfully withdrew out of earshot. (Evidence of Lieut.-Colonel Robert Napier, A.D.C.) Its purport may be guessed from the harassed brigadier's rejoinder to a message sent him by Sir John Ligonier, who had lost all patience with his loitering. In delivering it to Ingoldsby, Captain Amherst said:

> The general bids me tell you that he wonders you have not advanced; and it is his order that you advance and attack!—Evidence of Captain Amherst, A.D.C. to Sir John Ligonier.

"Be pleased to tell General Ligonier," was the reply, "that I have received the duke's orders to advance in line with that line"—pointing to the first line of British infantry on his left.

Human patience has its limits, and our infantry had been for six hours on their legs. Ligonier sent word to Cumberland that he was ready to advance as soon as the left wing had carried out their promised attack on Fontenoy and Antoing. The Dutch, therefore, rushed forward. One dense column made for Fontenoy by a road connecting it with Vezon, under cover of a cloud of cavalry which deployed on its flanks.

The Prince of Waldeck had not taken the trouble to reconnoitre his objectives, and was quite unaware of their immense strength. His men were welcomed with a terrific discharge of grape and musketry. They faced about, taking cover behind the hamlet which Saxe had burnt on the previous day. A second Dutch column, with cavalry in its rear, advanced on Antoing by the Condé road. Encountering a storm of projectiles from the three redoubts, they wavered, and their discomfiture was completed by a flanking fire from the heavy guns across the Scheldt.

The Dutchmen's stomach for fighting disappeared. Their cavalry went about; and while the bulk of them halted within cannon-shot, facing the French right flank, a minority anticipated one of the incidents of Waterloo. Colonel Appius rode off with his regiment to Ath, whence he sent word to the States-General that their army had been cut to pieces, with the sole exception of the corps which his prudence had preserved. (Stanhope, *History of England*, vol. iii.)

After the failure of the left attack, Cumberland resolved to capture the terrible Redoubt d'Eu at all costs. At a moment of stress the ties of blood appeal with tenfold force. He bethought him of Böschlanger's Hanoverians under Ingoldsby's command. They, at least, might be trusted. He sent an *aide-de-camp* to their colonel with injunctions to attack the redoubt "sword in hand." Then, without waiting for this movement to develop, Cumberland again changed his mind.

★★★★★★

Evidence of Lieut.-Colonel Robert Napier, A.D.C. "Two or three hours after the brigade had marched, the duke, coming from the left of the army, saw the brigadier still halted on the left of the hollow way. He said, 'Why has not Ingoldsby advanced?' on which witness went to the brigadier and told him what the duke had said. The brigadier was about to give him some reason when the duke came up close behind. Witness left them together. Soon after this he was sent by the duke to a Hanoverian battalion, which was a little in the rear of the British regiments of the brigade, with orders to attack the fort sword in hand. The Commanding Officer not understanding, witness explained, 'Bayonets fixed,' on which the C. O. said, 'Very well, march!'

★★★★★★

In point of fact, the leaders of the right wing were in a terrible dilemma. It was 11 a.m.: both flank attacks had failed miserably, and their longsuffering infantry had stood for five hours in the open under a galling cannonade. Cumberland and Königsegg saw that they must either beat an ignominious retreat or advance through a crossfire to meet the French Army, advantageously posted. They adopted the second alternative. It has hitherto been assumed that Cumberland was alone to blame for its fatal issue. A well-informed French writer credits the old Marshal with the idea of penetrating the gap between Fontenoy and the Redoubt d'Eu. (*Grand Dictionnaire Universel du XIX Siècle*. Paris: 1872. Art. "Fontenoy.") This theory receives strong corroboration in the attitude subsequently adopted by Königsegg. He was well content to share responsibility for all that occurred with his colleague.

★★★★★★

Lieut.-General Lord Dunmore, who joined the army after Fontenoy, wrote to Harrington, May 23: "It gives me the greatest satisfaction to hear the attack was made in concurrence with the Field-Marshal's opinion." (The writer, John, Earl of Dun-

PLAN DE LA BATAILLE DE FONTENOY
PAR L'ARMÉE FRANÇOISE
Sur Celle des Alliez sous les
Dédié au Roy par son très humble très obéissant Serviteur et

EXPLICATIONS
BRIGADES BATAILLONS,
ET RENVOIS.

INFANTERIE.

1 Les deux Redoutes du Bois de Bary défendues par le Régiment d'EU.
2 Le Village, Eglise & Cimetière de Fontenoy, défendu par la Brigade de DAUPHIN & d'un Bataillon de BEAUVOISIS ; à la Brigade de DAUPHIN s'est joint pendant l'Action un Bataillon du Régiment du ROY, fait en tout 5
3 Redoutes entre Fontenoy & Anthoin soutenues par des Détachements de DIESBACK & de BETHENS 1
4 Retranchemens d'ANTHOIN.
5 La Brigade de PIEMONT composée de quatre Bataillons de PIEMONT & un de ROYAL LA MARINE, gardoient les Retranchemens d'Anthoin.
6 Bataillon de BILON qui avoit été placé derrière la Brigade de PIEMONT, a été porté dès le commencement de l'Action en ligne entre Fontenoy & Anthoin, à la droite de CRILLON . 1
7 NORMANDIE ; il n'arriva que pour les dernières charges que les Troupes du Roy ont faites ; cette Brigade eut encore assez de temps pour s'y distinguer avec honneur 3
8 ROYAL CORSE
   Deux autres Bataillons étoient dans le Château d'Elmont

9 BUKLEY
10 DILLON   } Brigades Irlandoises
11 BERWICK   } de chacune un Bataillon.
12 LALLY
13 ROOTH
14 CLARE

15 ROYAL VAISSEAUX 1
16 HAINAUT 1
17 ROYAL 1
18 SOISSONNOIS ayant LA COURONNE pour Chef de Brigade.
19 LA COURONNE 1
20 GARDES-SUISSES 1
   Deux autres Bataillons étoient aux Retranchemens du Pont de Vaux.
21 GARDES-FRANÇOISES
   Deux autres Bataillons étoient aux Retranchemens du Pont de Vaux, & dès le commencement de l'Action, deux Bataillons passèrent encore aux mêmes Retranchemens.
22 COURTEN
23 AUBETERRE, Chef de Brigade de COURTEN
24 DU ROY
   Deux autres Bataillons indiqués sous le même Nº étoient dans les Retranchemens du Village de Fontenoy.
25 DIESBACK
   Deux autres Bataillons étoient, l'un au service de l'Artillerie, & l'autre dans les trois Redoutes entre Fontenoy & Anthoin.
26 BETHENS
   Les Bataillons de BETHENS & de DIEBACK faisoient la gauche de la Ligne formée entre Anthoin & Fontenoy.
27 CRILLON avança jusqu'à la deuxième Redoute
28 Troupes qui se portèrent au centre pendant l'Action aux chiffres 16, 17, 18 & 19 ; sont l'on y verra HAINAUT, ROYAL, SOISSONNOIS & la COURONNE.

a ROYAL LA MARINE
  Aux Retranchemens d'Anthoin 1

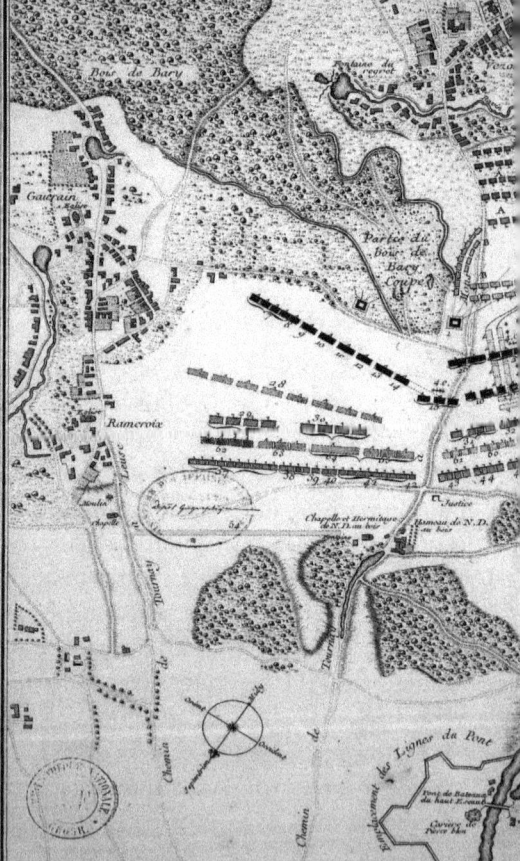

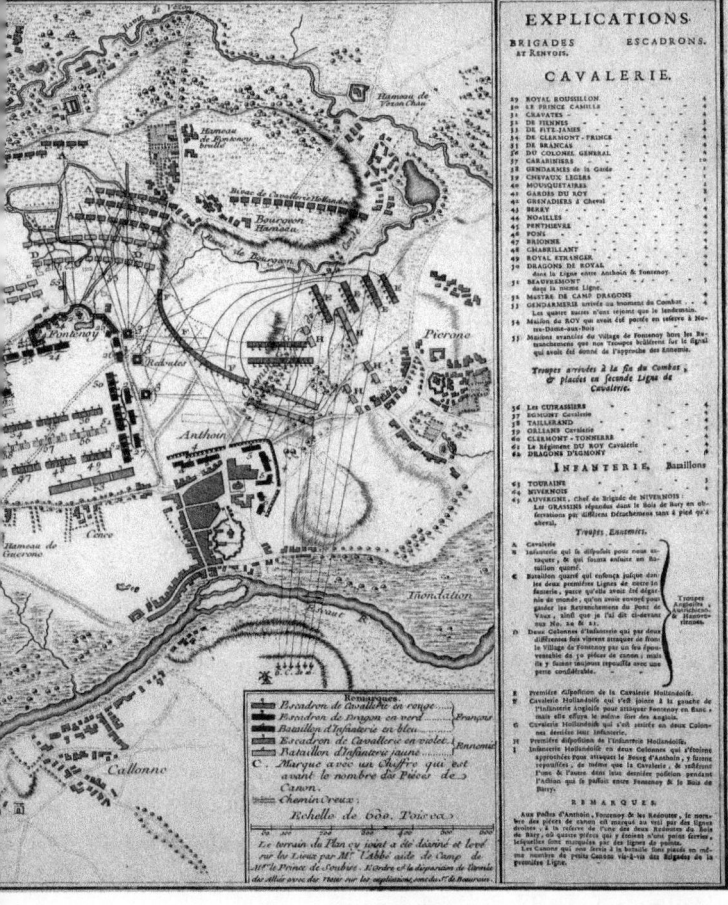

more, had been colonel of the 3rd Foot since 1713. He died, 1752, General and Governor of Plymouth.)

★★★★★★

According to this new plan of action, the Dutch were to make a second attempt on Fontenoy with a stiffening of British infantry, while the right wing assailed the centre of the French position. Colonel Napier was sent back to Ingoldsby's brigade with orders to detach the Black Watch in support of the second left attack. (Evidence of Lieut.-Colonel Napier). At this moment Ingoldsby was slightly wounded, and carried to the rear. His command devolved on the Hanoverian General Zastrow, who ordered Pulteney's and Böschlanger's regiments to fall in with Skelton's brigade. The right attack was definitely abandoned.

Did Duroure's (12th Foot) take part in the second attack on Fontenoy? Its subsequent movements are not traceable in the records of Ingoldsby's court martial. The official report, however, states that the Dutch were supported by two English battalions; and the fact that Duroure's lost nearly half its strength leads to a surmise that it was engaged in that unhappy enterprise. We have ample evidence of the glorious share taken by the Black Watch. Our Highlanders lay under the imputation of lukewarmness towards the Hanoverian cause. (General Stewart, *Sketches of Highlanders*, vol. i.)

Such unworthy suspicions were not shared by the future victor of Culloden. Sir Robert Munro enjoyed his entire confidence, and had obtained permission for his men to fight in their own fashions with broadsword and target. (Doddridge, *Life of Colonel Gardiner*, Appendix II.; contemporary pamphlet, *The Conduct of the Officers at Fontenoy Considered*).

Heartily sick of this long inaction, the Highlanders doubled to the left, and assailed Fontenoy without waiting for the lagging Dutch. The Brigade Dauphin's nerves were terribly shaken by the irruption of these "Highland furies, who rushed upon us with more violence than ever sea did when driven by a tempest." (A French account of Fontenoy, published at Paris, May 26, 1745). When the yelling mass of tartan and flashing" broadswords came within musket shot of Fontenoy entrenchments, they flung themselves to the ground, while the enemies' bullets whistled harmlessly above.

Stout-hearted Sir Robert Munro, however, disdained such means of safety. He stood erect near the colours, amid a hail of shot. Then, pouring in a volley at close range, the Black Watch swarmed into the entrenchments. So terrible was the fire from the enemy, disposed in five lines, that the brave Highlanders were compelled to retreat. The colonel was so bulky that no horse could carry him. He stuck fast in the trenches, and would have been made prisoner had not his men carried him out of danger to the ruined hamlet of Fontenoy. One of them wrote:

> Here, we were obliged to skulk behind houses and hedges for about an hour and a half, waiting for the Dutch, who, when they came up, behaved but so so. Our regiment being in some disorder, I wanted to draw them up in the rear of the Dutch, which their general would scarce allow of; but at last I did, and soon marched them again to the front. In half an hour after that the Dutch quite gave way, and Sir Robert Munro thought proper that we should retire. . . . We had orders to march with all expedition to assist the Hanoverians.—Captain J. Munro to Lord-President Forbes of Culloden; *Culloden Papers.* The writer was promoted lieutenant-colonel of the Black Watch, July 25, 1745, superseding a major and three captains, for special gallantry at Fontenoy, Sir James Munro obtaining the colonelcy of the 37th Regiment; Stewart's *Sketches of Highlanders,* vol. i.

This second failure took all the heart out of the Dutchmen, whose discomfiture was completed by a charge of French dragoons drawn up *en potence* on their right flank. They retired out of range, and remained impassive spectators of the main attack.

The movement had begun simultaneously with that on the left. Despite his colleagues' entreaties that he should not incur unnecessary risks, Cumberland took his place at the head of the first line and gave orders to advance on the French position.

★★★★★★

The official report of May 17 runs: "When our lines were drawn up in good order, with the cavalry behind them, H.R.H. put himself at their head and gave orders to march directly on the enemy. Prince Waldeck moved at the same time to attack Fontenoy, which the left wing did but *faintly,* and during their march there was a most terrible fire of cannon." The despatch as published substituted "without effect" for "faintly," in order to spare Dutch susceptibilities.

★★★★★★

16,000 men sprang forward, dragging twelve 6 pounders with

FONTENOY FROM THE FRENCH POSITION

their own stalwart arms. The formation, at starting, was identical with the battle order of the previous day. The Hanoverian regiments occupied the left flank, but the ground in front was so narrow that they were compressed into a third line. We who live in an age of khaki and long ranges can form no conception of the splendour of that scarlet-clad multitude, bristling with gorgeous flags. In this array they slowly mounted the slope crowned by Fontenoy and the Redoubt d'Eu, which poured forth a tremendous flanking fire. Whole ranks were swept away, but still they pressed forward over heaps of dead and dying, their sergeants dressing the ranks with long halberds.

On attaining the summit of the ridge, our heroes suddenly found themselves face to face with the French Army. On its right, resting on the Redoubt d'Eu, stood the French and Swiss Guards; then came Aubeterre, the line ending with Le Roi, flanked by the batteries of Fontenoy. The improvised glacis held by these picked troops was traversed by a sunken road, which concealed the enemy from view until the assailants were within point-blank range.

******

The enemy were all along upon the height with their different batteries, the whole length of which ran a hollow way which they had made a very good entrenchment."—Letter of Lieut. Forbes, *Culloden Papers.*

******

They were equally startled by the appearance of the guns which preceded our line. Some of their officers pressed forward, shouting, "Let us take these English cannon!" They found themselves confronted by an army at a distance of thirty paces! We halted instinctively. During this awful pause an incident occurred which infuses a touch of grim humour into the tale of slaughter. The Guards' Brigade, on the right of the first line, found themselves opposite the French Household Infantry. Lord Charles Hay, a fiery young officer of the First Guards, stepped to the front of his battalion and saluted with his hat. Then he took out a pocket-flask and ironically drank to their health, shouting, "We are the English Guards, and we hope you will stand till we come up to you, and not swim the Scheldt as you did the Main at Dettingen!" Then, turning to his men, he called for three cheers, which were given with a will.

******

Lord Charles Hay was the second son of the Marquis of Tweeddale. Of him Walpole said that "he had more parts of an Irish-

French Guards at Fontenoy

man than of a Scot "(Horace Walpole to Mann, November 26, 1744). He was severely wounded at Fontenoy, and reported as killed; but he recovered, to receive formal letters complimenting him from the officers and men (Hamilton, *History of the Grenadier Guards*, vol. ii., chap. xv.) In 1757 he served as brigade-major to Lord Loudoun in the expedition which captured Louisbourg, Cape Breton. Impatient at his chief's procrastination, he preferrred a charge of cowardice against him. Sent home in disgrace, he escaped the consequences of a court-martial by dying of a broken heart (1760).

******

The French officers were dumb foundered by such eccentric proceedings. The Duc de Biron, Count d'Auteroche, and others hurried to the front, returned Lord Charles's salute, and called for counter-cheers, which were very feebly rendered. Then a volley rang out from the French line.

******

Voltaire's version of this famous episode has become proverbial. It is quoted by some writers as an instance of misplaced chivalry; by others as a blind adherence to the dogma that the side which fired first was *ipso facto* beaten. He wrote: "The English officers saluted the French by doffing their hats. The Comtes de Chabannes and Auteroche, and the Duc de Biron, who had come forward, as well as all the officers of the French, returned the greeting. My Lord Charles Hai, captain in the English Guards, cried, 'Gentlemen of the French Guards, fire!'
The Comte d'Auteroche, then lieutenant of Grenadiers, shouted, 'Gentlemen, we never fire first; fire yourselves'" (*Voltaire, Siècle de Louis XV,* vol. i., chap. xxiv.) The writer, however, was not above distorting facts in order to serve his interests at court or score a point. His legend is scattered to the winds by a letter from Lord Charles Hay to his brother, the Marquis of Tweeddale, written not three weeks after the battle.
This narrative has been followed in the text. It was first unearthed by Carlyle, and is quoted in Hayward's *Essays*, vol. i., chap. xxiv. Moreover, Cumberland's official report declares that "We advanced, nevertheless, to the enemy, and received their discharge at a distance of 30 paces before we fired" (Cumberland to Harrington, May 17). And Sir John Ligonier uses almost the same words in writing to the Secretary of State (May 14),

"We got up to the enemy, however, and received their discharge at 30 paces without firing a shot" (see Carlyle, Frederick the Great, bk. xv.)

✶✶✶✶✶✶

Now came the turn of our gallant fellows. A deadly discharge was poured in by the First (Grenadier) and Third (Scots) Guards, and then the Second (Coldstream) Regiment fired while their comrades reloaded. The line regiments in flank took up the tale, while the majors coolly levelled the pieces with their spontoons. Tremendous was the effect of the hail of lead at so close a range. It swept away the entire front rank, killing and wounding 700 officers and men. The other three looked behind them for support, and seeing nothing nearer than the cavalry, which was 600 yards in the rear, they broke and fled in confusion.

At this crisis the Third Guards were thrown into momentary disorder by the fearful flanking fire from the Redoubt d'Eu; but Lord Panmure coolly rallied the unbroken companies, and the methodical advance continued. The dense mass scattered all before it like chaff by a sustained musketry fire. Thus they penetrated 300 yards beyond the flanking batteries, and stood proudly in the centre of the French position, masters of the battlefield. Let us leave them to enjoy a short-lived triumph to follow the fortunes of war from the French side.

On the morning of Fontenoy Louis XV rose at 4 a.m. and awoke the Minister of War, who attended him throughout the campaigns. Then he crossed the Scheldt at Calonne, and took up the post assigned to him at the battlefield's western edge.

✶✶✶✶✶✶

Le Voyer de Paulmy, Comte d'Argenson (1696-1764), and his brother, the Marquis d'Argenson (Minister of Foreign Affairs), played a great part at this epoch. The Comte d'Argenson was an old official adept in every species of chicane. He was Saxe's secret but inveterate foe. He fell out with the all-powerful Marquise de Pompadour and was exiled from court in 1757.

✶✶✶✶✶✶

This point of vantage served as a Gallows Hill. It was styled "*Notre Dame de Justice*," and is still visible at the intersection of the old Mons road and that leading from Ramecroix to Antoing. In his rear the chapel and hermitage of Notre Dame aux Bois emerged from a grove of trees, which were packed with spectators eager to witness a pitched battle. A tent was pitched for his accommodation, and he was

Austrian–Prussian Cuirassiers

attended by the *Dauphin*, Noailles, Richelieu, and d'Argenson, while two squadrons of Horse Guards were drawn up in the rear. In case of disaster an easy retreat lay open by Calonne bridge. The presence of the sovereign did much to inspirit subjects who were fighting under his very eyes. But Saxe soon discovered that nothing is more embarrassing in a day of battle than a king who can neither direct nor supervise the execution of manoeuvres.

The marshal had spent a night of physical torture, and when dawn broke he was too weak to sit his charger. The weight of a *cuirass* was insupportable, and he donned a buckler of quilted taffetas. Then he was drawn by grenadiers in a wicker chair to the left, where he took position at the Redoubt d'Eu.

At 5 a.m. Vezon in front was hidden in mist. When it lifted, Saxe perceived the enemy's cavalry emerging from Vezon. Orders had been passed round to fire on anything that approached. The guns spoke out, and after watching their effect on the left he mounted and rode to the other flank, where he witnessed the repulse of the first Dutch attack on Fontenoy and Antoing. Deeming his right adequately protected, he was returning to the Redoubt d'Eu when he was startled by encountering the musketry-fire of a dense mass of infantry in front. In violation of every rule of war, the enemy had pierced the one weak joint in his defensive armour! His first line had melted into a mob of fugitives.

Saxe threw aside the buckler which impeded his movements and galloped back to rally the cavalry, compelled to move leftwise by the crowd of flying foot soldiers.

It was necessary to reassure the king, whose retreat would have caused a *sauve qui peut*. Saxe found him calmer than his courtiers. Old Noailles was convinced that all was over, and implored his master to seek safety while there was yet time. Louis replied, "I am sure that the marshal will do all he can, but I am going to stay where I am!"

On Saxes approach the king asked him whether the battle was really lost. "What coward, sire, has told you that?" was the reply, accompanied by an energetic oath. "We must all conquer or die together. Permit me to act alone." Then he galloped off to restore order in front.

Meanwhile the Anglo Hanoverian line pushed slowly forward, firing by divisions as coolly as on the parade-ground. Aubeterre endeavoured to bar the way. They were pulverised by a tremendous volley. Now the British infantry, finding their front comparatively free, formed in squares of battalions, in view of breaking the French centre and enveloping both Fontenoy and the redoubt. This was a hazardous movement, for the flanking fire redoubled, causing temporary disorder. Saxe, perceiving their hesitation, ordered an attack on both sides. Le Roi assailed the British right. Our Coldstream regiment sallied forth from the mass, poured in a crushing volley, and returned in triumph to their comrades. The left attack was delivered by infantry from the reserves. Royal Vaisseaux, Hainault, Royal Infanterie, Soissonnais, and La Couronne charged furiously up to the British squares. All were repulsed with hideous slaughter. But their self-sacrifice was not in vain. The official report states—

> We found ourselves between cross-fires of small arms and cannon, and were likewise exposed to that from the front, so that we found it necessary to retire to the height of Fontenoy and the fort by the wood, from which there was likewise a continual fire which occasioned some confusion. But by the attention of H.R.H. and the marshal it was stopped.

After a brief interval devoted to restoring order in the ranks, Cumberland and Königsegg formed their troops into a hollow square, with guns in the centre and front towards the foe. Then a second advance began. Saxe endeavoured to shake the invincible phalanx by repeated cavalry charges, directing his colonels to press home until their horses' breasts were in contact with the square. But what could cavalry effect against a mass so highly disciplined and so intrepid? One regiment after another recoiled in flight, and the king and *dauphin* were for a moment separated by a mob of stampeding horsemen. Like Napoleon at Waterloo, Saxe incurred censure for needless sacrifice of life in futile attacks. He justified these tactics in a conversation long afterwards with D'Espagnac.

> While Fontenoy remained untaken, the enemy's success in the centre was disadvantageous to them, for they had no pivot (*point d'appui*). The farther they penetrated the more were they exposed to the fire of our troops and batteries in their rear. It was essential to distract their attention by repeated cavalry charges, which were, it is true, unable to produce a decisive effect, but gave us time to organise the general attack on which all depended.—D'Espagnac, vol. ii.

While confusion on the French side was at its height, the brigade of Household Cavalry in the rear, four squadrons of *Gendarmerie* who had just arrived from Douai, and the far-famed *Carabiniers*, all charged in a solid mass. They were driven back with fearful slaughter, the *Carabiniers* alone having twenty-seven officers killed and wounded. Nor were renewed attacks by the infantry a better result. Vaisseaux had whole ranks swept away by our pitiless musketry under the eyes of Saxe, who exclaimed, "Is it possible that such troops should not be victorious?" Their fate was shared by Hainault and Normandie, who returned to the charge with undiminished ardour. Dillon's Irishmen threw themselves with Celtic fury on our left flank. Their heroism was unavailing, and the brave colonel was wounded. Our infantry were careful to husband their ammunition. After destroying one wave of foemen which beat against them, they reloaded to await the next.

At one o'clock Saxe again crossed the British front and made for the Fontenoy entrenchments. He found the cannon firing blank cartridge. Their whole provision of round-shot and grape was spent! Even his stubborn spirit sank. He begged the Duc d'Harcourt, whom he met, to conjure their master to cross the Scheldt while yet there was time. He sent troops from Antoing to the Bridge of Calonne, and ordered the cannon to be removed thither from the entrenchments. This was the psychological moment for a general advance. Voltaire admits that:

> If the Dutch had but put themselves in movement and joined hands with the English, there would have been no resource, nay, no retreat, for the French Army, nor, in all probability, for the king and his son.—*Siècle de Louis XV*, chap. xv.

On the other hand, Cumberland seems to have given no orders to the left wing after his second attack began. He was indeed as completely isolated in the centre of his gigantic square as was Nelson while the *Victory* was locked in a death embrace with the *Rédoutable*. Then the Dutchmen remained quiescent on the left. Nor did the garrison of Tournai make a sign. They were effectually contained by the strong force manning the trenches, and attempted no sortie, which might have proved an effectual diversion in the French rear.

Now it was that Cumberland tardily bethought him of his splendid cavalry, which had stood unwilling spectators of their comrades' exertions. He sent Lord Crawford orders to charge. The ground in front was not less suited to cavalry than the rolling plains of Waterloo, but the cross-fire from Fontenoy and the redoubt was a more serious obstacle. However, bugles rang out, the British regiments trotted up

BRITISH CAVALRY AT THE CHARGE

the slope, while some Austrian and Dutch squadrons advanced on their left. Cumberland himself rode back to bring up the Ligoniers (7th Dragoon Guards), and Lord Crawford headed the Horse Guards. Running the gauntlet of Fontenoy and the Redoubt D'Eu, they were advancing to the rescue of their hard-pressed comrades when they were involved in the backward surge of a mass of Dutch and Austrian fugitives.

The immense strength of Crawford's charger alone saved him from being trampled to death. He rallied the broken squadrons, but they were again hurled back by a tide of runaways. Two squadrons of the Blues were got together, and were joined by the North British Dragoons (Scots Greys) and Hawley's (1st Royal Dragoons), which charged in alternate squadrons. But the hour for useful cooperation was past, and the cavalry effected little in support of their comrades' advance. It must be admitted that until the general retreat they were very poorly handled. Shock tactics were invented by Frederick the Great at a later period, and the true role of cavalry was not grasped by leaders of 1745. But Cumberland's neglect to employ these fine regiments until the very eve of retreat must be reckoned among his sins of omission at Fontenoy.

It was now past 1.30 p.m. The hollow square had again advanced several hundred yards beyond the flanking batteries, sweeping all before it by sheer force of impetus. Its frontal breadth was undiminished; and the farther it pushed the more readily were losses repaired by line regiments, which joined it without orders. In point of fact, it was rapidly melting away under the awful flanking fire, and had already lost a third of its strength. The mighty *phalanx* was evidently without guidance. It swayed to and fro in indecision; but each man kept a proud mien, as though he were conscious of standing a master of the battlefield.

These oscillations did not escape Count Löwendahl. Meeting his perplexed chief, he exclaimed, "Marshal, this is a great day for the king: these people will never be able to escape him!" The pair galloped back to Gallows Hill, which was only 500 yards from the British square. A tumultuous council raged round Louis XV.; but all agreed that nothing had succeeded hitherto because nothing had been done in concert. From the French side Fontenoy had been but "an affair of outposts." It was resolved to unite all the forces available in a final effort to roll back the tide of victory.

Before this could be effected it was necessary to pulverise the en-

The British Advance

emy with grape-shot, to which they could not reply, their own artillery being within the square. Voltaire has stooped so low as to falsify history in order to credit the all-powerful Duc de Richelieu with this masterstroke. (*Siècle de Louis XV*, chap. xiv.) A note preserved in the French War Ministry proves that it was prompted by a Captain Isnard of the Touraine regiment, whose great service was recompensed with the Cross of St Louis. Observing four cannon unemployed on the field, and as many more which could readily be brought up, Isnard suggested that they should be dragged within point-blank range of the enemy's square. This was immediately done, and a salvo of grape-shot cut lanes in the solid mass of human flesh. Our ranks closed up; but endurance has its bounds, and some confusion was caused by the awful carnage.

Saxe watched the effect of his artillery-fire, while he mustered every available man for the final effort. As the Dutch remained motionless, he was able to withdraw all the troops posted to repel an attack on his right flank. He rallied the broken infantry regiments, especially Vaisseaux and Normandie, which had returned again and again to the charge with admirable spirit. Count Lally-Tollendal ran from rank to rank imploring his chiefs to employ the brave Irishmen. His appeal was answered. The remains of Dillon's, and the other regiments of the Irish Brigade, flung themselves on the British right flank.

A simultaneous attack was made on its left by all the regiments which had been posted between Fontenoy and Antoing. The French and Swiss Guards, eager to revenge their repulse, assailed the front, and exchanged volleys, muzzle to muzzle. While Saxe and Löwendahl were leading the infantry against the foe, Biron, D'Estrées, and Richelieu brought up the whole Household Cavalry to charge the British front. In seven or eight minutes our victory was converted into defeat. Deserted by their allies, and assailed by overwhelming forces, our magnificent infantry were pressed slowly back. With heavy hearts did Cumberland and Königsegg give orders for a general retreat.

For twelve hours our men, still numbering 11,000, had been without food or rest. It was inevitable that some disorder should have attended their first retrograde steps. But the rigid discipline of those days shone brightly in an hour of mortal stress. Each battalion rallied round its colours, and compact formation was speedily restored. The *Carabiniers* and Noailles' regiment attempted to break our rear. They were received by the Guards and Zastrow's Hanoverians with a fire so withering that they were well-nigh destroyed. The line battalions

First Foot Guards at Fontenoy

faced about every hundred paces, and held pursuers in awe.

Cumberland exposed his life freely in order to keep the men together, and Ligonier rode coolly off to collect scattered units. He found Lieut.-General Howard's (The Buffs) still advancing in line, with drums beating, against the enemy in front, in the very midst of French tents and camp-kettles.

"Howard," he shouted, "cease beating your drums, face your regiment about, and retire as quickly as you can, for the army is defeated!" (*Historical Record of the 3rd Regiment*). He then made provision for covering the retreat through Vezon. Skelton's (32nd Foot) and Cholmondeley's (34th) were told off as a rear-guard. Howard's (The Buffs) were ordered to hold the churchyard, while hedges and ravines were lined with the Black Watch. On either flank the cavalry closed in to form a screen for the retiring army. In this hazardous service the Royal Horse Guards especially distinguished themselves. ("The behaviour of the Blue Guards is highly to be commended."—Official Report).

When the last battalion had passed the zone of danger Lord Crawford saluted his horsemen, remarking that "they had gained as much honour in covering so great a retreat as if they had won the battle." Sir John Ligonier was almost the last on the field. When praised for his fine retreat, he modestly replied that "if it were praiseworthy no part of it belonged to him, for it was contrived and executed by Lord Crawford." The latter styled Ligonier "an extreme good officer." It is pleasant to find these knights without fear and without reproach exchanging compliments. (Maclachlan, *W.A., Duke of Cumberland*).

The twelve field-guns which accompanied the infantry were perforce left behind, for the teams, supplied by contractors, had galloped off to Brussels at the first check. The French made few prisoners except the wounded men, who were left at Bruffoel on the strength of the Frankfort cartel.

> We lost no colours, standards, or kettledrums, but have taken one standard.

So, runs Cumberland's official report. On the other hand, O'Callaghan, the historian of the Irish Brigade, declares that a pair of colours were wrested from the Coldstream Guards by Bulkeley's Irish regiment. (*History of the Irish Brigade*, bk. vii.) Moreover, the Duke of Wellington's Supplementary Despatches contain a letter of August 25, 1815, from Lord Bathurst to the Iron Duke, who commanded our army of occupation, which runs—

Field-Marshal Earl Ligonier

> I understand that there are at Paris—at the École *Militaire*, if I am not mistaken—several English colours, particularly one belonging to the Coldstream regiment, taken at Fontenoy. I hope your Grace will make inquiries about these trophies, and that you will take the proper measures for their restoration.—*The Supplementary Despatches of the Duke of Wellington*, 1864,. xi.

The result of this demand is not recorded. Again, Captain G. Bowles wrote during the occupation of Paris:—

> We are proceeding on more liberal principles, and do not talk of requiring anything except some old colours now hung up at the Hotel des Invalides, which were, I believe, taken at the battle of Fontenoy.—*Malmesbury Correspondence*, vol. ii.

Per contra we have the official denial of Cumberland himself, who, with all his failings, was scrupulously truthful. The Coldstream regiment has no record of the alleged loss, which could not have been long concealed, even had the officers been capable of conspiring to suppress it. In view of the extraordinary staunchness of the Guards Brigade, which had not a single unwounded survivor missing at roll-call on the morrow, and the immense importance then attaching to colours, I am inclined to return a verdict of "Not proven" on this much-debated issue.

The army re-formed in the rear of Vezon, and after collecting the impedimenta of all kinds, resumed their retreat on Ath. This thirteen miles' march, after as many hours of incessant exertion, must have strained their endurance to the utmost. Cumberland rode with the rear-guard, encouraging his weary men by precept and example, and it was 3 a.m. on the morrow ere he reached Ath. Königsegg had been severely shaken by a fall from his horse, and was carried thither on a litter.

✶✶✶✶✶✶

Philip Yorke told Horace Walpole the elder, on May 16, that the marshal "was run over and bruised by the Dutch cavalry in their flight." His position between the first and second lines of our infantry attack renders this very unlikely. A man of over seventy, racked by gout, would probably be unable to sit his horse for twelve hours.

✶✶✶✶✶✶

Marshal Saxe was blamed by "carpet generals" for not turning the defeat into a rout. Hayward, who has studied the question fully, remarks:—

FIRST FOOT GUARDS AT FONTENOY

Seeing the English cavalry advancing to support their infantry, he halted his troops 100 yards from the battlefield. His words were:

> As we had enough of it, I thought only of restoring order among the troops engaged in the charge.—Hayward's *Essays*, 2nd series, "Marshal Saxe," vol. i.

It cannot be denied that his tactics frequently led to a suspicion that he was loath to strike a blow which might end operations in the field. War could alone give scope to his redundant energy: he loved its excitement, revelled in the unlimited power which it confers on a commander-in-chief, and knew that his best qualities suffered atrophy in piping times of peace. But he is not open to such imputations for having called off his weary troopers at the edge of Vezon. The enemy was defeated but not dismayed, for discipline and morale were intact, and their cavalry was admirably handled. To push his men into a very *daedalus* of ravines and woods was to court disaster. The Dutch contingent, 20,000 strong, was a standing menace to his right flank. Saxe, therefore, contented himself with launching the Grassins in pursuit of the retiring columns, while he concentrated the rest of his forces on the field of battle.

When order had been restored, Louis XV. rode from regiment to regiment, greeted by shouts of *Vive le Roi! Victoire!* Hats were flung into the air, bullet-torn standards frantically waved, men and officers embraced each other. The king was perfectly calm. To every leader he gave a few words of commendation, and strictly enjoined that the enemy's wounded should receive the same care as his own.

The young *dauphin* had borne his baptism of fire with courage, and sought in vain for leave to head one of the desperate charges of cavalry. When victory came, he was prodigal of congratulations and sympathy. Seeing Lally-Tollendal sitting on a drum, amid the shattered remains of his regiment, he promised special rewards from the sovereign. "*Monseigneur*," replied Lally, pointing to the heaps of dead and dying, "the king's favours are like those of the Gospel—they fall upon the halt and the blind." When twilight shrouded that scene of carnage, Louis XV. led his son into the midst of the plain strewn with corpses, and said:

> My son, meditate on this awful sight; learn not to sport with your subjects' lives, or pour out their blood in unjust wars.

Happy would it have been for Louis and for the world had the impressions of Fontenoy proved durable. It was the one great day in a career which has left an indelible blot on our civilisation.

Marshal Saxe was not present at this memorable scene. He suffered agonies from thirst, and was compelled to retire to his tent for the purpose of being tapped. Thence he was carried in his wicker chair to the royal presence. He found strength enough to clasp the king's knees and murmur, "Sire, I have lived long enough. I ardently wished to see this day, and your Majesty victorious." Then, pointing to the field bestrewn with corpses, he remarked, "You see what a battle means!"

Louis raised him up, embraced him tenderly, and spoke with warmth of his great services. The hero replied modestly:

> Sire, I have a fault to acknowledge. I ought to have placed one more redoubt between Barri Wood and Fontenoy, but I could not believe that any general would dare to hazard an attack at that point.

Fontenoy ranks among the most murderous battles of the eighteenth century. Saxe's chosen arena had very narrow limits, and resembled those medieval lists wherein bands of combatants fought to the death. But Count Pajol justly observes:—

> What made the contest so deadly was the strife with the British column, which is without parallel in the annals of war. The momentum of that *phalanx* was irresistible. It was, so to speak, a rock which required mining.—*Guerres sous Louis XV*, vol. iii.

Voltaire's estimate of French casualties was, he said, "based on an exact account"; Pajol's on returns submitted to the Ministry of War. They are compared in the following table:—

	Voltaire.	Pajol.
Infantry killed—		
Officers	53	53
Men	1681	1662
Total	1734	1715
Infantry wounded—		
Officers	321	336
Men	3282	3110
Total	3603	3446
Infantry casualties	5337	5161
Cavalry casualties	1800	...
Grand total	7137	...

The percentage to the number engaged was 12.2. Among the wounded were Colonels Dillon and Clare of the Irish Brigade; and fifteen other superior officers were killed on the spot or died of their injuries. Maurice de Saxe deserves the lion's share of credit for breaking the long record of French defeats sustained at the hands of their island foes. His intelligence was so admirably organised, that every movement in the hostile camp was reported with the utmost speed possible in those days. His choice of a battlefield was as consummate as Wellington's, and he showed even greater foresight in extracting every advantage from an admirable position. If the ridge in front of Mont St Jean had been defended by redoubts, our losses at Waterloo would have been comparatively insignificant. Disregarding physical pain and weakness, he was ubiquitous on the battlefield, and issued his orders with calmness at a time when the nerves of lesser men gave way.

Equally conspicuous was his modesty in the hour of triumph. Among his lieutenants, Löwendahl alone approached his master in generalship. The others displayed that *furia francese* which impressed Italians in 1859, and one and all did their duty well. Among French infantry regiments those of the Irish Brigade stood first. Their desperate valour was a factor of great importance in our disaster. Aubeterre, Vaisseaux, Normandie, and one battalion of Eu were undismayed by repeated checks. Turning to cavalry regiments, we find the *Carabiniers, Gendarmerie*, and Household showing themselves worthy of great traditions; but all were staunch under artillery-fire, and reckless of their lives in attack.

The Allies' loss at Fontenoy was 7545 officers and men. Our infantry of the right wing bore all the burden and heat of that awful day. The British regiments returned 1237 killed and 2425 wounded; the Hanoverians 432 and 978 respectively. Then our infantry casualties were 5072, or 32 *per cent* of the numbers engaged. Some of the regiments lost half their strength. The following figures tell a tale more eloquent than words:—

Regiment.	Killed.	Wounded.	Missing.	Total.
Royal Welsh Fusiliers	189	86	47	322
Duroure's (12th Foot)	159	159	3	321
Campbell's (21st)	5	152	129	286
Late Handyside's (31st)	133	141	12	286
Third Guards	109	138	nil	247
First Guards	89	151	nil	240
Second Guards	114	125	nil	239
Sowle's (11th Foot)	53	124	47	224

N.B.—The grenadier company above, (late Handyside's), went into action seventy-five strong, and brought only eleven unwounded men to Ath. Both subalterns were killed.—*Hist. Record of the 31st Regiment.*

Nearly all who were reported as missing were afterwards accounted for as killed or wounded.

The returns for Hanoverian regiments prove that our German fellow subjects were equally steadfast:—

Regiment.	Killed.	Wounded.	Missing.	Total.
Böschlanger's	156	201	20	377
Zastrow's	90	209	...	299
Spörken's	65	214	...	279
Oberg's	54	155	28	237
Campen's	67	141	2	210

The sister arm suffered less severely. Its casualties were—killed, 168; wounded and missing, 483; or 651 in all, giving a percentage of 10. Those of the British regiments were 340. The heaviest were incurred by the Royal Horse Guards, who had 11 killed, 49 wounded, and 7 missing. The Hanoverian cavalry, numbering 1200 sabres, returned 311 casualties, or more than 25 *per cent*. The Anglo-German artillery lost 58 of all ranks, from lieutenant to "*matross*"—nearly 10 *per cent*. The returns sent to England contain no reference to Austrian losses. At 10 *per cent* they would amount to 120. On the left wing 1544 officers and men were put out of action.

The fact that our Dutch allies were deprived of only 6.5 *per cent* of their strength is sufficient evidence of their lukewarmness. In the light of more recent experience our loss in officers was not excessive. Lieut.-General Sir James Campbell, commanding the cavalry, and Major-General Hon. H. Ponsonby were killed; Lord Albemarle, Brigadiers Churchill and Ingoldsby, and Major-General Hon. Charles Howard were wounded—the latter in four places. The Guards lost Colonel Carpenter, commanding the brigade as senior field officer, and Lieut. Colonel Hon. Robert Douglas. In the line five colonels or lieutenant-colonels were numbered with the slain. Among the wounded was Lord George Sackville, commanding the 28th Regiment, afterwards charged with misconduct at Minden.

As might have been expected, the heaviest tale of slaughter occurred among infantry officers. On the British side 193 were killed or wounded, the Royal Welsh Fusiliers losing 22 and Duroure's (12th Foot) 19, including its colonel and lieutenant-colonel.

******

In the cloister of Westminster Abbey there is a monument "to preserve and unite the memory of two affectionate brothers, valiant soldiers and sincere Christians." One of them was Scipio Aurore—like Ligonier, of Huguenot descent. He was Adjutant-General and Colonel of the 12th Foot, and "after forty-one years of faithful service was mortally wounded at the battle of Fontenoy, aged 56 years, and lies interred on the ramparts of Arth, in the Low Countries."

******

Our cavalry had only 3 officers killed and 27 wounded. Philip Yorke wrote five days after the battle:

> The Duke of Cumberland's behaviour, was by all accounts the most heroic and gallant imaginable. He was the whole day in the thickest of the fire. When he saw the ranks breaking, he rode up and encouraged the soldiers in the most moving and expressive terms; called them countrymen; that it was his highest glory to be at their head; that he scorned to expose them to more danger than he would be in himself; put them in mind of Blenheim and Ramillies. In short, I am convinced that his presence and intrepidity contributed to our coming off so well. ... H.R.H. seems determined to keep up strict discipline, and drew out a pistol on an officer whom he saw running away, (see mention of incident in next chapter)—This letter was addressed to Horace Walpole the elder, and is quoted in Stanhope, vol. iii., Appendix.

Sir John Ligonier's testimony to his young chief's valour is equally emphatic.

> The marshal is surprised at the genius for the profession of arms which he finds displayed by the prince, and has taken him into particular affection. A solid judgment, coolness rare on occasions when the loss of life is one of the least evils one has to fear, an intrepidity without equal, the most brilliant valour,—such are the qualities which I have remarked in this young prince. In a word, he has all the attributes of the great Condé except ferocity. It is a pity he will not display them long, for Heaven is not called on to work miracles every day.—Ligonier to Harrington, May 14, 1745.

Some of the most stirring episodes of the battle occurred under Cumberland's eye. Private Thomas Stevenson of Ligonier's Horse (7th Dragoon Guards), after losing his charger, got leave from the officers of the Royal Welsh Fusiliers to carry a firelock in their grenadier company. Cumberland saw the brave fellow fighting in his heavy jackboots, and gave him a money reward. But when Stevenson rejoined his corps at Ath on the morrow, he was refused admission to the lines until his absence was explained. He demanded a regimental court-martial, at which Lieut. Izard of the Fusiliers corroborated his story, adding that the trooper behaved with great intrepidity, and was one of nine grenadiers who came out of action unscathed. The prisoner was honourably acquitted, and Cumberland procured him a lieutenant's commission in the Welsh regiment. (*Historical Records of the 7th Dragoon Guards*).

A private of the Black Watch, whose name has not been preserved, slew nine Frenchmen with his broadsword, and was in the act of disposing of a tenth when his arm was carried off by a cannonball. Cumberland witnessed the catastrophe, and promised the man something which would compensate him for the loss of his limb. The praise of this regiment and of its colonel was echoed throughout Europe. (Doddridge, *Life of Colonel Gardiner*, vol. i.) So infectious is enthusiasm that the chaplain forgot that he was a man of peace.

When Sir Robert Munro paraded his men at early dawn, he observed their minister in the ranks with drawn broadsword, and ordered him to the rear on pain of losing his commission. "D—n my commission!" exclaimed the fiery cleric; and he was foremost in the fray throughout.

******

This was the well-known Adam Ferguson (1723-1816), afterwards Professor of Moral Philosophy at Edinburgh University. He was the author of several well-known works, and a grand old man in every sense. At his house occurred the memorable meeting between Walter Scott and Robert Burns.

******

The Black Watch was singled out for special praise in Cumberland's report. In token of his high appreciation, he invited the corps collectively to ask any favour they pleased. The response was worthy of a heroic age. The Highlanders unanimously begged a free pardon for two comrades who were under sentence of flogging for having allowed some French prisoners to escape, because its infliction would

The Black Watch at Fontenoy

disgrace the regiment and the culprits' families.

Other incidents of the encounter deserve record. General Ponsonby, according to the official report:

> Was slain at the head of the First Foot Guards, which remained the whole day without being once put into confusion, though they lost many brave officers as well as privates. (Among the slain were Captains Harvey, Berckeley (sic), and Brereton, and Ensign Sir Alex. Cockburn, Bart.)

When Ponsonby was laid low, he was in the act of giving his watch and ring to his grandson and *aide-de-camp*, Brabazon Ponsonby. It is a curious coincidence that his kinsman, Sir William Ponsonby, at Waterloo delivered his watch and a miniature to his *aide-de-camp*, with instructions to deliver them to his family; and both officers were immediately slain by some Polish lancers. (Booth, *Battle of Waterloo*. 1817. Vol. i.)

Colonel Erskine, commanding the Royal North British Dragoons (Scots Greys), tied the regimental standard round his son's leg and said, "Go, and take good care of your charge. If you return alive from the field, you must produce that standard!"

When all was over, his parental heart was gladdened by the appearance of the cornet, who rode up and pointed to his precious charge intact.

While we credit William Augustus, Duke of Cumberland, with great physical courage, and admit that he saved a defeat from degenerating into a rout, we must hold him responsible for the fatal issue of Fontenoy. His intelligence was inexcusably bad; his slow advance on Tournai gave Saxe ample time to prepare the death-trap into which the Allies blundered. On May 10 Barri Wood might easily have been cleared of the Grassins, and the Redoubt d'Eu would then have become untenable. Saxe had no reserves available to recapture any of his field works.

Favouritism was Cumberland's bane throughout life. It prompted the selection of Ingoldsby for the duty of storming this redoubt. The brigadier may have been the "brave and honest man" of Sir John Ligonier's despatch, (Ligonier to Harrington, May 14, 1745), but numerous allusions to his doings in the Chequers Court Papers lead to a suspicion that he shared the hard-drinking customs of those days. At 7 a.m. on May 11 Cumberland ought to have discovered that it was not a "fighting day" for Ingoldsby, and should have remorselessly superseded him for disobedience. He added to the wretched man's hesitation by giving him conflicting orders. Another blunder on the right attack was Cumberland's withdrawal of the Black Watch to support the second Dutch attempt on Fontenoy. No one can doubt that, if Sir Robert Munro's advice had been acted upon, his Highlanders would have made short work of the Grassins, and stormed the chief obstacle to our advance.

******

A contemporary writer hit the mark when he said that Ingoldsby "smelt too long at the physic to have any inclination to swallow it" (Campbell Maclachlan's *Life of Cumberland*). Carlyle's version of this episode in his *Frederick the Great,* bk. xv., chap. viii., is inaccurate in every detail: "Ingoldsby, speed imperative on him, pushed into the wood; found French light troops (God knows how many of them!) prowling about there; found the redoubt a terribly strong thing, with ditch, drawbridge, what not; spent some thirty or forty of his Highlanders in some frantic attempt on it by rule of thumb; and found he would 'need artillery' and other things." The records of Ingoldsby's court-martial, and Captain J. Munro's letter to Lord-President Forbes (*Culloden Papers*), already quoted, prove that the 136 casualties reported by the Black Watch occurred during and after the second left attack.

******

Turning to the left attack, we see the same evils of divided command which had made Marshal Wade's campaign the laughing-stock of Europe. The Dutch regiments ought to have had a stiffening of British and Hanoverians at first. The experiment was made on a small scale in the eleven o'clock attack on Fontenoy, which very nearly succeeded. Cumberland, too, should have seen that obstacles on his left front were properly reconnoitred. Had this been done, he would have recognised that the left attack would be more arduous than that assigned to the right wing. It is impossible to study the ground without arriving at the conclusion that Saxe's redoubts and entrenchments between Fontenoy and Antoing were too hard a nut to crack for mercenaries whose hearts were not in the cause. They were held by a superior force; there was no cover for assailants, who were also exposed to artillery-fire from heavy guns beyond their reach.

A further count against Cumberland is his inferior handling of the splendid cavalry force on the right wing. The first council of war held at Bruffoel decided to dispatch it, by the outskirts of Barri Wood, to fall on the enemy's left. This idea was abandoned when a party of Waldeck's hussars, sent forward to reconnoitre, were greeted with grapeshot from the two redoubts. A "Stonewall" Jackson would probably have carried out this movement with crushing effect. In 1745, however, no cavalry leader could be trusted to act in broken ground with abundant cover. A graver charge is the neglect to employ cavalry as a screen for the infantry formation prior to the main attack. Cumberland pleads guilty to this count in his official report:—

> Lieutenant-General Campbell was ordered to cover the infantry of the right wing, whilst it should be forming, with fifteen squadrons, by extending himself along the plain from the wood towards the village of Fontenoy. But General Campbell having lost his leg by a cannon-shot, the disposition which had been entrusted to him did not take effect. However, General Ligonier formed the two lines of infantry quite exposed, without any interruption from the enemy than a brisk cannonade, which did great execution.

Our cavalry regiments were fully equal in quality to those on the French side; and the ground in front of Vezon was well adapted to manoeuvring. Yet Cumberland was so absorbed in the infantry attack that he left his horse regiments idle in the rear until the time for useful action had gone by.

Lastly, we have the oft-repeated assertion that the main or frontal attack on the French camp was a violation of all the rules of war. The self-same charge was brought against Napoleon by Austrian generals of the old school; and such parrot-cries will always be heard from men whose native common-sense has been smothered by prejudice and routine. The best justification of the desperate resolve taken by Cumberland and Königsegg is, that the attempt to storm Saxe's main position twice nearly succeeded. *Audace, toujours de l'audace*, spells victory.

Would Tournai have been relieved if the French Army had been driven pell-mell across the Scheldt? Such questions have a purely academic interest. It is impossible to avoid a conviction that the enemy's vast superiority in numbers and military skill would then have involved us in worse disaster. The Allies might have been themselves besieged on the Fontenoy plateau. Their communications would have been cut by a cavalry force far superior to their own, and no co-operation would have been received from the garrison of Tournai.

It will be admitted on all sides that Cumberland did his duty on that day according to his narrow lights. The blame for a serious reverse—which was repeated in the same arena half a century later—does not rest on his shoulders. It must be borne by a system which rated the accident of birth far above personal merit, and placed our country's honour in the hands of a man unfitted for the sacred trust by youth, temperament, and inexperience.

Full justice is rendered in Cumberland's official report of the battle to all his colleagues:—

> The honour gained by the infantry is in great measure owing to the conduct and bravery of Lieut.-General Ligonier. Major-General Zastrow *of the Hanoverian troops* and Lord Albemarle did all that could be expected from brave and experienced officers. (The words in italics appear in the draft despatch of May 17, but were deleted by the Cabinet, in order to avoid exciting British jealousy).

Königsegg fought between the first and second lines of infantry. He "was present on horseback during the whole action, and gave his orders with great calmness." (*Ibid*). Prince Waldeck comes in for a meed of praise, despite his failure to second the right wing, but the services rendered by Lord Crawford in covering the retreat were never recognised. Whatever doubts beset us in weighing the leader's conduct, there can be none as to that of our unrivalled infantry. Their firmness and discipline extorted admiration from the foe.—

> The British behaved well, and were excelled in ardour by none of our officers. . . . I cannot say as much for the other auxiliaries, some of whom seemed as if they had no great concern in the matter, whichever way it went. In short, we gained the victory, but may I never see such another!—*An Account of Fontenoy*. Paris: May 26, 1745.

Still weightier testimony comes from the *Traité des Légions*, which was inspired, if not written, by Saxe himself:—

> I do not know whether many of our generals would have dared to push infantry into open ground in the teeth of a great body of cavalry, and imagine that they could maintain 12 or 20 battalions for many hours in the midst of a hostile army as the English did at Fontenoy. And this without being once shaken by cavalry charges or once relaxing their discharge of musketry.

Such exploits we have seen; but our self-esteem forbids us to dwell upon them, for we know full well that we are not in a condition to imitate them.—*Traité des Légions*, 4th edition. The Hague: 1757. The author is generally supposed to have been Saxe himself, but this treatise was probably written by his friend, Baron d'Espagnac.

Cumberland singles out the Brigade of Guards, the 12th, 31st, and 42nd Foot for special praise; but every infantry regiment did its duty nobly. Fontenoy should be borne on the colours of all who shared in the glory of that day. May our country have defenders as staunch in the time of stress which is surely approaching!

A hundred and sixty years have wrought little change in the battlefield. The woods of Barri and Bon Secours have indeed been pushed back by cultivation, just as the forest of Soignies has receded far from Mont St Jean and Waterloo itself. The old Mons highway, which was the line of our main attack, still serves for country carts. Fontenoy's humble spire and cluster of cottages remain intact. Taking a sunken track which crosses the fatal ridge between that village and Barri Wood, we see on its right the only memorial of the battle. This is a cemetery in which the hecatombs of the slain were buried. Its wall facing Tournai displays a vulgar inscription commemorating the valour of the Irish Brigade.

Following this road, which ran along the front of the position held by Saxe's first line, we reach the Mons road, and can still identify the site of the Redoubt d'Eu at the intersection of the two. Every foot of the well-tilled slope which descends eastwards was drenched with British blood. At its base Vezon's white houses, still peep from thick foliage, and one of them bears the date 1737 in variegated brickwork. While the actual field of Fontenoy has suffered less change than that of Waterloo, its environs have been sorely disfigured.

The face of nature between Ramecroix and Tournai is seamed with stupendous quarries, and the Scheldt's once pleasant banks, from Antoing to the plateau formerly crowned by Tournai's citadel, are defiled by innumerable cement works. These unlovely creations of an age of "mechanickal arts and merchandize," as Bacon has it, are creeping slowly towards the arena of Fontenoy. A time when mutual hatred has yielded to sympathy and fuller knowledge seems opportune for united action between descendants of the men who fought and died there, to secure the scene of such splendid heroism from desecration.

CHAPTER 6

The Allies' Retreat

Tidings of Fontenoy were received with resignation at home. The voice of public opinion was echoed by Philip Yorke when he wrote—

The best that can be said of it, now it is all over, is that our Johns love fighting for their money, and that there was no other chance of raising the siege.—Philip Yorke to Horace Walpole the elder, May 27, 1745, quoted in an appendix to Stanhope's *History of England.*

National grief was mitigated by the accounts received from all quarters of the heroism of our troops. Sir Everard Fawkener was, of course, first in the field:—

Nothing, by the testimony of the whole army, could exceed the resolution which H.R.H. shewed during an action which lasted eight hours, during six of which he was in as hot a fire as ever was known. He was in the hottest of it, encouraging, rallying, leading, observing, and disposing everything that could promise advantage. He did not come hither till about three in the morning, after having had all possible attention to everything. The marshall told me he was astonisht at the prodigies of valour shown by that young prince—these were his words.—Fawkener to Harrington, Ath, May 12, 1745.

On the same day Cumberland gave the Foreign Secretary his own first impressions of the battle:—

I marcht yesterday from the camp at Bruffoel with the whole army, about two in the morning, to attack that of the enemy near Tournai, which was posted between the Chaussée d'Ath and the Scheldt; but I am sorry to say it was not with the success I hoped for. My infantry was formed in two lines before the enemy's camp between three and four; but as the horse that was to support them had some demies to pass, they could not be in readiness so soon, so that the whole army did not move to the attack until about seven, and in this interval the infantry was exposed to a furious cannonade.

The right wing, however, advanced with great resolution, and gained ground of the enemy; but being continually galled by the fire of batterys and redoubts on the flanks, and also of a very smart and continued discharge of small arms, and the left wing not advancing equally with them, they could not maintain the ground they had got, but were obliged to retire.

They were twice rallied, but without effect, so it was judged necessary, about one of the clock, that the army should retreat, and it was done with so good order and countenance that the enemy did not give us any disturbance; and the army with its baggage is now encampt under the guns of Ath. I don't know of any colours or standards taken, but we have taken one standard.... In filling the vacant commands I hope that regard will be paid to those who have been so much exposed and have behaved so well.—Cumberland to Harrington, Ath, May 12.

Five days later the duke sent home:

> A relation of the action between the allied army and that of France near Tournai, the 11th May 1745, n.s."

This official narrative was of Fawkener's drafting.

> In drawing up the account of the action, I kept exactly to orders. Praise or blame could not come from me, for I saw not anything.—Fawkener to Newcastle, May 26).

In forwarding it Cumberland wrote:—

> I hope His Majesty will have the goodness to give me leave to recommend to the vacant commissions. It will be a great encouragement to the troops that exact justice should be done on so memorable an occasion.... I am very well pleased to find from Mr Trevor's letter that the alarm first taken at The Hague subsided a good deal on recceipt of my letter. If this accident should put the States upon taking the state of the army into se-

rious consideration, it would be a good effect of this loss, which would more than compensate for their share of it. A little firmness and vigour shown immediately, and some present succour, as well from the king as the States, would put us into as good a condition as ever; for we are yet in spirits, especially the right wing.—Cumberland to Harrington, May 15.

The Fontenoy despatches were supplemented by a private letter from Fawkener:—

> The duke would not allow anything to be said of him in the relation made, but certainly nothing but his presence and example could have establisht that order with which the retreat was made. There was hardly any confusion, even with the baggage. We who marcht with it came within a league of the field of battle two hours after it was over, and kept at a foot's pace to Ath. His Royal Highness is reserved for great things, but must give himself time; for if he will do so much, so great, repeated dangers may at last reach him. It is too much to do, as well as to direct. There was nothing of that vehement impetuosity for which the late King of Sweden was distinguished in his behaviour, for he saw, and examined, and gave his orders with the utmost calmness and precision.—Fawkener to Harrington, May 17.

The Fontenoy despatches had much the same effect on the British Ministry as tidings of Ramillies on Louis XIV.'s courtiers. They found consolation in reflecting that the king was in perfect health, which, after all, was the most important point. Newcastle craved Cumberland's leave:

> With a heart full of duty and concern, to assure your Royal Highness that, next to your miraculous preservation in the midst of so many dangers, nothing has given such real joy to your faithful servants, which is to all his Majesty's subjects, as the concurrent testimony which every one, as well from our own army as from the Austrians and Dutch, gives of your Royal Highness's intrepidity, conduct, temper, and humanity throughout the whole action; ... and this is our only comfort under so heavy a loss of so many brave officers and soldiers. We natter ourselves that Providence has preserved your Royal Highness to be a great and, I hope, an immediate instrument of honour

and advantage to your country and all Europe.—Newcastle to Cumberland, May 18.

George II. was on his way to Hanover when the despatches arrived. He received them while windbound at Harwich, and ordered the Lords-Justices of Regency to send out reinforcements at once. (Newcastle to Fawkener, May 18 and 21). His own opinion of the battle was not vouchsafed until a month later:—

> The king attributes the miscarriage of the attack upon the French lines at Tournai (which he has always considered as a well-concerted attempt for the preservation of Tournai) solely to the misbehaviour of the left wing, which we hope may upon future occasions be zealous to recover the reputation they have lost.—Harrington to Cumberland, June 22.

Newcastle duly announced the dispatch of three line regiments to Flanders, with drafts of fifteen men per company of the four Guards' battalions.

★★★★★★

These three were Price's (14th Foot), Mordaunt's (18th), and Handysides, which I have not been able to identify. It was not the "Late Handyside's (31st)" of the Fontenoy despatches which suffered so terribly in the battle.

★★★★★★

He added—

> Their Lordships have thought proper, in publishing the account, to soften a little some few expressions with regard to the behaviour of the Dutch troops, which they hope his Royal Highness will approve. For though it was extremely right that the relation of the action, which was for His Majesty's aprobation and that of the Council, should convey exactly the facts without any regard for persons or States, yet in an account to be published by authority it will be thought better to avoid anything that might create any uneasiness in so ticklish and so necessary an ally as the Republic is at present.—Newcastle to Fawkener, May 18.

The knowledge that he was still esteemed a brave and steadfast leader at home was balm to Cumberland's wounded spirit. He replied:

> It is a matter of the greatest consolation to me that my conduct

has the aprobation of the king and his ministers. I had, before, that of having acted with the steadiest view to the glory of His Majesty's arms, the honour and interest of my country, and the good of the common cause, all of which I shall pursue with the greatest alacrity, as my endeavours are so favourably interpreted and so cordially accepted. . . . The relation I sent home of the action of the 11th was designed solely for the use of His Majesty and his Ministers. They were, therefore, certainly in the right to soften or leave out whatever they might think fit before the publication of it. I am very sensible of the caution which ought to be used towards our very good allies. But things are spoke much more plainly at The Hague.—Cumberland to Newcastle, May 26.

While the young commander-in-chief was engaged in the painful task of explaining his reverse, the Allies showed a bold front to the foe. They tarried for five days round Ath while the shattered regiments were reorganised. No sign of panic is seen in the General Orders, which call for returns of killed, wounded, and missing, direct the sale of dead men's effects and the dispatch of their widows to London. They proclaimed a tariff of rewards for the recovery of weapons dropped during the retreat. Casualties among the horses were to be reported to Sir John Hawley, who recorded 629. As is invariably the case with a defeated army, the spy mania raged with fury. An order of May 13 runs thus.—

> The duke having been informed that several officers have taken French deserters as servants, H.R.H. does not approve of that practice, therefore orders that they provide themselves with other servants in a week's time, after which those men must have passes from the duke's secretary to go to Brussels; and if any such are found in the army after that time, they will be immediately hanged as spies.

Again, on May 28—

> There is a tall man come from Bavaria, and is suspected of being a spy. All those soldiers who have returned from the French service are to come to the headquarters this afternoon, with a sergeant from each regiment, at 4 o'clock, in order to be examined by Major-General Bland.

This poor wretch, Patrick Crowe by name, was duly hanged at the head of the line on the following Monday.

On May 15 Captain Watts of the King's Regiment of Horse (7th Dragoon Guards) was tried for cowardice during the retreat from Fontenoy. The charge was quaintly set forth in one of the few autograph orders which have been preserved:—

> The reason of my ordering a court-martial to examine into the conduct of Captain Watts was, towards the end of the attack we made upon the French camp near Tournai on the 11th of May last, I ordered the 1st and 3rd squadrons of the King's Regiment of Horse to form at about 600 yards from the defile, while I went back to form the foot, which were going through the said defile; that whilst I was employed in so doing, the said squadrons came galloping back in great disorder, and that the foremost man of them was Captain Watts, at whose head I was obliged to clap a pistol in order to make him return.
>
> William.

Fortunately for Watts' professional future, he was able to prove that he had been swept away by a cavalry stampede, and thus secured an honourable acquittal.

Ath was too near the enemy's position to serve as a rallying-point. Its environs were haunted by swarms of light troops, who cut up stragglers and intercepted convoys. On May 14 Cumberland found it necessary to detach 200 troopers and 600 foot, under Brigadier Skelton, in order to "prevent French Pandours and Grassins from infesting the edge of the camp." On May 16, the Allies retreated five miles northwards to Lessines, a position of some natural strength, and watered by the Denain, over which they threw pontoon bridges.

Hence Duroure's (12th Foot), Campbell's (21st), and the Royal Welsh Fusiliers, which had been terribly punished at Fontenoy, were sent into garrison. Their places were taken by troops which had escaped the carnage. Barrell's (4th Foot) joined the army at Lessines, and Captain Wolfe was appointed Brigade-Major. (Note in Wright's *Life of James Wolfe*, chap. iv.) Other reliefs were—Fleming's (36th Foot), from Audenarde; Ponsonby's (37th), from Bruges; Lord Henry Beauclerk's (31st) and Ligonier's (48th), from Ostend. Nor were the States-General of Holland backward in repairing the wreck caused by Fontenoy. Cumberland did full justice to their spirit, while he hinted at divergence in views as to the army's movements.

> I do not consider it possible to secure Mons and cover Flanders.

The Dutch want to keep on this side and preserve Mons, where there are four battalions in garrison. But the marshal and I agree that, if pressed, we ought not to expose all Flanders to be overrun; and we have too near an interest in the preservation of the coast. I hope that the measures taken by His Majesty and the States-General for recruiting this army will not leave us under so disagreeable an alternative.

The States received the news of our disappointment with great composure, and fell immediately upon deliberating and repairing the breach made in our strength by the accident, of which their letter to Marshal Königsegg is very honourable testimony. (The letter referred to announced the dispatch of five reserve battalions, to reinforce the left wing under Prince Waldeck). By the great precautions (we are told) the enemy are using before Tournai, it looks as if their present views were altogether fixed upon making sure of that conquest.

This will give time.... Though recruiting is in the main a work of time, yet in the present exigency that may be shortened by compleating the battalions of Guards by draughts from those at home, allowing the captains of those companies from which drafts are made £3 for every man drafted.—Cumberland to Harrington, May 22.

Great Britain was then very sparsely peopled, and her militia force had been grossly neglected. In the dearth of recruits the Cabinet was compelled to adopt Sir John Ligonier's suggestion to draw upon German sources, (see chapter 4).

On June 7, 1745, a convention was signed by Maria Theresa by which she ceded us 6 battalions of Austrian infantry and 12 companies of hussars for an annual sum of £81,070, 19s. 1d., or £10 per head, all expenses included. Among the many advantages of compulsory military service is its economy to the State; for an army which does not compete with other forms of industry in the labour market pays its troops on a scale which secures the necessaries of life and no more. The Austrian army is still the cheapest in Europe, but the budget for 1905 provides for 382,416 officers and men at a cost of 308,996,000 crowns, (*Almanack de Gotha*), equivalent to £33.7 per head. The low value of human life was a direct incentive to war during the eighteenth century. Under this agreement 5600 Austrians, out of 8000 promised, joined the allied army in June. (Cumberland to

Harrington, June 7 and 12). Ligonier was not satisfied. He wrote to Harrington on June 7—

> I hope, my lord, you will send us something from the Rhine. *Je veux dire des troupes d'Hanovre ou d'Autriche.* We can fight, my lord, but there must be some proportion in numbers. The French have put 13 battalions of their militia in Tournai, so that their army remains in force. Your lordship knows that the day of the Battle of Fontenoi the duke's army was but 46 battalions and 79 squadrons, and the enemy's more than double that number. And yet, *si la gauche avait secondé*—but no more of that!

Further reinforcements poured in. On June 16 the Landgrave of Hesse placed 6000 of his troops at our disposal for a substantial consideration. In the Dutch contingent no effort was made to restore morale or discipline, (Fawkener to Harrington, June 14), but Cumberland's salutary strictness soon brought the right wing into perfect working order. On June 11 it numbered 16,094 bayonets and 4262 sabres, and the allied army—on paper—reached a total of 70,000. Marshal Königsegg summed up the situation with some ability in a despatch to Harrington of June 26:—

> We have, it is true, received from England and Holland reinforcements replacing our losses at Fontenoy, and have put the army on the same footing as it was prior to our attack. Taking the enemy's losses into account, then and since, before Tournai, we should not be so unequally matched were it not for the resources at their disposal—I mean the French militia, drafts from which have filled up the gaps in their regiments. They have at present 133 battalions and 204 squadrons, and being more than twice as strong as we, they can undertake any enterprise without hindrance from ourselves. We shall have the disheartening spectacle of the capture of strong places in succession without the possibility of affording them relief, because we are numerically the weaker, and our forces include elements on which we could not rely in case of emergency.
> We attempted to save Tournai on unimpeachable grounds; a portion of the hostile army being occupied in the siege and cut off from the rest by a river. The standard of valour and firmness was at least as high in our own troops; and if the left wing had but seconded the ardour of the right, we should have gained a complete victory over an enemy whom we had already driv-

en back in confusion. This unhappy experience has prompted greater circumspection, especially as we do not perceive the possibility of succour in case of the slightest check.

At the Hague they promised me a force of 80,000 men, but in point of fact we opened the campaign with only 47 battalions and 83 squadrons, besides about 12 of dragoons, hussars, and free lances in the service of the queen, my mistress. The whole barely totalled 40,000, partly because the English contingent was incomplete and partly owing to the fact that a large number of Dutch regiments was locked up in garrison. In spite of this inferiority, if we had only been able to muster our forces fifteen days earlier, as I represented at the Hague, we should have prevented the enemy from laying siege to Tournai.

I venture to remark parenthetically that, had the same efforts been made in England and Holland at the outset of the campaign as have since been made to repair our losses, affairs would have taken a very different course. The defensive policy which we have perforce adopted presents insurmountable difficulties. Flanders, between Mons, Namur, and the sea, has not a single fortress in a state of defence, and each of these strongholds must have a garrison of 10,000 men.

Thus, we must choose between neglecting frontier defence and fatally weakening our field forces. In short, my lord, in the absence of some striking success in Germany which would compel the French to send a strong detachment thither, we are not in a position to hamper the enemy's operations during the remaining four or five months of the campaign.

France was plunged in a delirium of joy by the first great victory snatched from her hereditary foes. A *Te Deum*, sung at Notre Dame on May 20, 1745, to celebrate the success was attended by forty bishops and the flower of the French aristocracy. Every city broke out into fireworks and illuminations on an unprecedented scale. Voltaire seized the occasion with the instinct of a born journalist. He obtained the salient facts of Fontenoy from Comte d'Argenson, and threw them into the form of an epic poem. *Fontenoy* was published on May 17, and 21,000 copies were sold in a few days. Within ten months it had run into eight editions. *Fontenoy* is overloaded with mythology, and its diction seems absurdly stilted to modern readers. It is hardly fair to judge a literary work conceived in hot haste on an occasion so extraordinary by the ordinary canons of criticism. *Fontenoy* was a rhymed bulletin, and it was eagerly read by thousands whose instinctive craving for news was not catered for by war telegrams. In the preface to his eighth edition Voltaire told the critics that he "laboured less as a poet than a citizen."

On the morrow of Fontenoy Louis XV. addressed a rescript to Marshal Saxe, which assumes a lion's share of the credit, and classes the leader's exploits with those of certain favoured regiments.

> My cousin, however great were the successes which it has pleased God to bestow on my arms during the last campaign, I have now received a more marked token of His mighty protection in the victory which I have just gained over my enemies. If I owe it to the valour of my troops, and especially my Household and *Carabiniers*, you have none the less contributed to it by your courage, counsel, and foresight.

More substantial rewards poured in on the man whom the King delighted to honour. He was created Governor of Alsace, with a salary of 120,000 *livres*.

Meanwhile Saxe focussed all his efforts on the siege of Tournai, and desired nothing more than to be left in undisturbed possession of the battlefield. His field force remained there under the protection of a chain of redoubts and entrenchments. (Advices for the camp before Tournai of May 20). At daybreak on May 12 he launched the Grassins in pursuit of the retreating foe. They captured twelve cannon, and vast quantities of military stores, which had proved too heavy for transport. A detachment under D'Estrées pushed as far as Leuze, picking up 3000 stragglers. A party of Grassins overran the Château of Bruffoel, where 1200 of the Allies' wounded had been left at the enemy's mercy. They stripped the poor creatures, and robbed the surgeons of their instruments and medical comforts. These atrocities stirred Cumberland to fury.

On May 15 he hurled a remonstrance at Saxe, couched in vigorous if ungrammatical French. The Cartel of Frankfort, regulating the treatment of wounded men and the exchange of prisoners, was invoked, and reprisals were threatened. The marshal's rejoinder was conciliatory. He wrote from the camp before Tournai, May 16:—

> You are aware, *Monseigneur*, that, in a day of battle and the heat of pursuit, disorders must occur which it is impossible to prevent or remedy. The general officer whom I sent in advance to

gather up prisoners did all in his power to assist your wounded men by removing them from the different places where they were lying exposed to the rapacity of our troops, who stole from the camp after nightfall in search of booty. After providing for their safety he sent them into hospitals, where they are receiving exactly the same treatment as our wounded. Such were the king's orders, given me on the battlefield.

Saxe assured the duke that his surgeons were released as soon as their status was known, and undertook to return any property which they might have lost in the confusion. But he declared that the King of England had infringed the Cartel of Frankfort by detaining Marshal Belle-Isle and his brother as prisoners of war. (They had been captured in Hanoverian territory, February 20, 1744, and taken to London). That treaty was now null and void. He concluded with a suggestion that Cumberland should send *commissaires* to ascertain the treatment which his wounded men were receiving.

The Belle-Isle case was, indeed, an awkward precedent, and the duke determined to ignore it. Lords Albemarle and Crawford were sent to the French camp as *commissaires* under the Frankfort Cartel, but they found Saxe obdurate. Charges of inhumanity and foul play are invariably made in war-time. The *Gentleman's Magazine* of July 1747 quotes a contemporary letter from a person of distinction at The Hague, whose style could only be Lord Chesterfield's:—

> In what *Gazette* do you think we should ever have read that English officers, made prisoners of war when wounded, were refused necessaries for their money and the assistance of surgeons, so that wounds in themselves not mortal or dangerous were suffered to become both by this kind of usage, notwithstanding the warmest remonstrances? ... Do you really fancy that there is a person at Paris mad enough, I won't say to tell the world, but to whisper to his wife, that notwithstanding the kind, the tender, the charitable orders that his Most Christian Majesty was heard to give with regard to the unhappy brave men that, after being admired for their valour and intrepidity, were by the fortune of war left wounded in the field of battle, his soldiers should knock out the brains of the English with the butt-end of their muskets with such expressions as these in their mouths—"Ha! dog, are not you dead yet?"
>
> The fact is strange and inhuman; altogether inconsistent with

humanity or the rules of war; quite irreconcilable with the boasted valour and, to speak the truth, with the usual practice of the French nation. But here lies the mischief after all, that, notwithstanding these exaggerations, in spite of these improbabilities, it is still a fact, a certain and indubitable fact.

Further testimony is found in *The Scots Magazine* of July 1745:—

> We surgeons, sent to take care of the wounded when carried from the field of battle, were made prisoners of war, and treated in a very merciless way; for not only we, but about one thousand more, were stripped of everything valuable we had—*viz.*, watches, swords, money, cloaths; and not only so, but our very instruments were taken from us, although the barbarians saw hundreds daily imploring our assistance. In this unprecedented way we remained three days, numbers dying every hour because we had nothing to dress them with, when they were slung in waggons and drove along the causeway to Lille, Valenciennes, &c. In this jolting journey you may easily conceive the misery of these poor wretches, most with their legs, arms, &c, shattered to pieces.

Cumberland's wrath at finding the Frankfort Cartel set at nought found issue in an attempt to arouse public indignation at home. He ordered brigade-majors to collect all the grape-shot, irregular balls, and pieces of metal found in wounds. (General Order, May 18). Moreover:

> A trumpet from the allied army carried the king a coffer, sealed with the arms of the Duke of Cumberland, Generals Count Königsegg, Prince Waldeck, and Baron Wendt, filled with pieces of thick glass, brass and iron buttons ... that were taken from the wounds of Lieut.-General Campbell and of other officers and soldiers.—*Scots Magazine*, August.

The Dum-Dum bullets, of which we heard so much during the Boer War, were, after all, a faint echo of Fontenoy. On the other side we have the statement of Voltaire:—

> Hospitals had been made ready in neighbouring towns, especially Lille; and not merely succour, but every luxury was placed at the disposal of the French and Allies' wounded. Indeed, they were well-nigh killed with kindness, and the surgeons had to

check the excessive goodwill of the populace. In a word, the hospitals were so well organised that wounded men preferred them to lodgings in private houses. Such things had never been seen previously.—*Siècle de Louis XV,* chap. xvi

The truth, of course, lies between extremes. There can be no doubt that the Grassins indulged their love of plundering to the full; and our wounded must have suffered torments during transport to hospital in carts innocent of springs. But there was no ground for a charge of deliberate cruelty, or even neglect.

Graver events were brewing which destroyed the Allies' hope of regaining lost ground. They had lingered within striking distance of Tournai in the belief that its resistance would paralyse French activity. Löwendahl, however, pushed the siege with redoubled vigour. During the throes of Fontenoy the French occupied the rest of the covered way, and concentrated their fire on a hornwork which defended the gate of Seven Fountains. It was carried on May 15, and three days later a practicable breach was made in an adjacent bastion. Subsequent developments are told in a letter from the imbecile governor of Tournai:—

> A general assault was inevitable, which we might have awaited had there been ground enough for a retrenchment behind the breach. But the *terre pleine* at that point was too narrow to accommodate more than fifteen men abreast. Thus the assault would have entailed heavy losses, without postponing the surrender for more than a day or two. We could expect no relief from the allied army, whose attack on the enemy's camp on May 11 had been unfortunately repulsed. We therefore thought proper, after weighing *pros* and *cons*, to beat the *chamade* in order to save the garrison. This was done yesterday (May 22), and we sent two colonels to the French camp with terms of capitulation, receiving two officers of equal rank in return to serve as hostages.—General Baron Van Dort, Governor of Tournai, to the States-General of Holland, May 23.

The reply was a summons to surrender. Marshal Saxe wrote:

> The king's intention, is that the Lille Gate shall be placed in his hands tomorrow morning.

Van Dort called a council of war, which asked for a delay of eight days to admit of a reference to the States-General. Saxe granted this respite, with a proviso that the garrison should forthwith surrender Tournai and retire to the citadel. Thereon another council of war was held, which considered that:

> As we had only four months' provisions for our effective strength, it would be an unpardonable blunder to risk the lives of so fine a body of troops, consisting of 12 battalions and 3 squadrons, which might be employed elsewhere on the State's service. We therefore resolved, with the sole exception of Lieut.-General Leuwe, to give up the town at 2 p.m. tomorrow and retreat to the citadel, provided that His Majesty granted us eight days' delay in order to obtain your High Mightiness' orders with regard to a complete surrender.—General Baron Van Dort, Governor of Tournai, to the States-General of Holland, May 23.

In forwarding this distressing letter to Marshal Königsegg, the States-General wrote:—

> We observe, on the one hand, that the citadel cannot accommodate the entire garrison, especially if the three squadrons, women, children, and servants, are to be quartered there. They cannot possibly hold out much longer. Would it not be better to surrender the citadel and employ the garrison of 7000 men elsewhere in support of the common cause? On the other hand, there is the chance of raising the siege, should the citadel hold out. The French may undertake some important enterprise in another direction if they be not detained at Tournai.
> We have therefore drawn up two sets of instructions in alternative for Governor Van Dort. The first, marked (1), authorises him to surrender the citadel on the best terms he can secure, after consulting a council of war; the second, (2) enjoins him to defend it as long as possible. We enclose copies for your information, and are giving the originals to Colonel Lintelo, who starts for Ghent early tomorrow, and will wait there for written orders from you, which he will deliver to Van Dort. He will stay at Ghent until midnight on May 30, in order to reach Tournai before June 1. Please send him any instructions you think proper under the circumstances.—States-General to Marshal Königsegg, May 26.

Königsegg's rejoinder expressed a satisfaction which he could hardly have felt at this ingenious attempt to shift responsibility to his shoulders. Being still confined to bed by gout, he had summoned the other generals to his quarters. They were unanimous in condemning Van Dort's lukewarmness, which was probably due to his advanced age, but were equally resolved to sustain his flagging energy. Instructions had gone to Lintelo at Ghent to deliver the order marked (2), and:

> To insist on a vigorous defence. Do not receive your wounded men or any other impedimenta in the citadel. Far better leave them at the enemy's mercy. As for your cavalry, they might surely make a dash for Audenarde on a dark night, or if that is impossible, you might eat the horses. It is absolutely necessary to detain the French, and make your citadel cost them as dearly as you can. You must not think of sparing the garrison—make frequent sorties, &c.

These were counsels of perfection for the superannuated governor. Far better would it have been to supersede him by Ligonier or Lord Crawford. The rest of an ignominious story was told by General Van Brakel, to whom Van Dort resigned command on the plea of sickness. After acknowledging receipt of Königsegg's orders to hold out, he wrote—

> At 9.30 a.m. on June 1 the enemy began to bombard us with 60 mortars, afterwards increased to 90, from batteries opposite the Valenciennes and St Martin's Gates. The tremendous fire with that of 28 siege-guns, 24pounders and upwards, reduced the citadel to a heap of ruins, and killed or wounded many of the garrison. On June 9 the French began battering the left face of the Orleans bastion, and on the 19th, despite our heavy return fire, a breach was made large enough to admit 30 or 40 men abreast. All our defences were destroyed; the parapet was swept away, exposing our troops to an incessant discharge of small-arms. We had 1170 sick and wounded.
>
> The men were lodged in damp and unwholesome galleries, which were so overcrowded that many were obliged to stand in an open ditch. Besides, our shells were expended, and many of our muskets were unserviceable. I called a council of war, which resolved *nem. con.* that we were not in a condition to sustain a general assault, and that if we wished to obtain terms, it was high time to hang out the white flag. This was done between 3 and 4 p.m. on June 19. We sent articles of capitulation

by Colonels Fagel d'Assenfeldt and De Lancy, who served as hostages, receiving in exchange Colonels the Earl of Perth of Fitz-James' regiment and La Serre of the Royal Vaisseaux. At 9 a.m. yesterday the Marquis de Vaudreuil brought us the king's marginal notes on each article. The third, disqualifying us from military service until January 1, 1747, seemed unnecessarily severe, and contrary to the State's interests.

We therefore sent deputies to the marquis, imploring him to obtain some modification of these terms. He assured us, on his word of honour, that the king would not make the slightest change, and that if we sent him a deputation it would not be received. Our council of war was convinced that further defence was not to be thought of, and decided by a majority of voices to acquiesce in the king's conditions. Thereon the capitulation was signed and exchanged on June 20, 1745.—Baron Van Brakel to Königsegg, June 21.

In announcing this catastrophe to the Regency at home, Cumberland remarked—

A very small sense of honour would have put such a garrison out of the reach of so mortifying a capitulation, What the articles of it call the "honours of war" must, after such a defence, be lookt upon as an insult, and be called—if it had its right name—the mean hire of treachery and cowardice. The garrison of Tournai have, by their own ill-behaviour, put schakles upon themselves at a time when they are most wanted, and are become a dead expense. If, therefore, they are all broke, except any part of them who may have distinguished themselves from the rest, the States might save expense. The garrison marcht out yesterday; they are to be conducted in three marches to Ghent. Before they evacuated the citadel the French King made a publick entry into the town.—Cumberland to Harrington, June 25.

Ever since Fontenoy, strained relations had prevailed between the right and left wings, and all hope of cordial co-operation vanished with the surrender of Tournai. British and Dutch soldiers fought fiercely when they met, and mutual animosity reached such a pitch that no Dutchman was allowed to enter Ghent citadel with side-arms, or remain after tattoo. (General Order, July 1).

The one obstacle to an advance removed, the French were in a position to take the offensive. On June 30 Saxe ordered Clermont-

Gallerande, to occupy Binche, midway between Mons and Charleroi, with 3 battalions and 34 squadrons.

✶✶✶✶✶✶

P.-G., Marquis de Clermont-Gallerande (1682-1756), began his military career in the *Mousquetaires*, and rose to Lieutenant-General in 1738. He was an active soldier, but prone to insubordination, and a secret enemy of Saxe.

✶✶✶✶✶✶

This move was a menace to two strongholds of vast importance in Dutch eyes. Despite all that Cumberland could urge, 8 battalions from the left wing were thrown into Mons, 6 were sent to Namur, while Charleroi and Ath were proportionately strengthened. There remained only 40,865 men available for field operations. (Returns of July 7, 1745). The Dutch generals pronounced Lessines untenable with so small a force, and on June 30 Cumberland unwillingly shifted camp to Grammont. This retrograde movement excited keen dissatisfaction at home, which was voiced by a contemporary writer:—

> Our situation there (Lessines) was such as would have kept the French behind the Scheldt, or obliged them to fight us on ground of our own choosing, and on a plain where our cavalry could have acted. This was evident to the meanest soldier in the English troops. . . . But, to the amazement of all Europe, an ignominious, precipitate retreat was resolved on, and urged in such a manner by the generals of our Allies as demonstrated it to be agreeable to the inclinations, if not in consequence of the orders, of their masters. The French could scarcely believe their own good fortune, and even the people of Brussels hooted and hissed at our troops as they passed along.—Campbell Maclachlan, W. A., Duke of Cumberland.

Cumberland's stout heart did not forsake him. He could still reckon on an army 40,000 strong, half of which was British and Hanoverian. Assembling a council of war, he proposed to intermingle the troops of the four allied nations and attack the enemy. Though he pledged his word that the issue would be very different from that of Fontenoy, the sullen Dutch were obdurate. A dispute arose which was kept within bounds only by Königsegg s tact and good temper.

The French now prepared for a general advance. After demolishing Vauban's fortifications encircling Tournai, they marched in six columns to Leuze. The Grassins pushed onwards to Lessines, threatening the Allies' rear. In Cumberland's words—

> The next day after changing our camp the French came into the plains of Lessines so thick that our hussars were forced to quit it before they could be sustained. The day following the whole French Army advanced to within a short league of Grammont, and even seemed as if they intended to attack us, upon which we threw seven English battalions into Grammont, which, with twelve pieces of cannon, made it a very good position. This morning, about 4 a.m., the whole French army put itself in motion, upon which we stood to arms. They marcht and countermarcht about ten hours, and at last they encampt about the town of Grammont, on the other side of the river, at about a league's distance every way.
>
> I think while we are in this camp we are in no danger; yet on the other hand I see we are driven to the fatal choice of either abandoning Flanders or Brussels. But that we may do what we can towards saving Ghent, and yet remain in this camp, we have detached Lieut.-General Moltke with ten squadrons and three battalions to take possession of Alost, and observe the enemy's motions, in order to throw himself into Ghent if necessary. I am sorry to be constrained to be so short on this occasion, but the truth is I have not been fairly in bed since three nights, and have had but little quiet or repose since I came from Lessines.— Cumberland to Harrington, Grammont, July 6.

Moltke's aim was to secure Ghent, which held immense stores of warlike material. His column, 4000 strong, included Rich's Dragoons (4th Hussars), five squadrons of Hanoverian and as many of Dutch cavalry, the Royals (1st Foot), Bligh's (20th), and Handyside's. Alost was occupied on July 8. But on the same day Saxe sent Du Chayla towards Ghent with 15,000 men and orders to reconnoitre the Allies' base. His *Grassins* extended eastwards and entrenched themselves in the Château de Massenem, eight miles from Alost.

General Moltke, on learning that these dreaded troops were on his front, dispatched the Royals to dislodge them (July 9). Finding himself hemmed in on all sides, Colonel de Grassin called for volunteers to carry news of his danger to Du Chayla. Fifteen men made a dash through the Royals, five of whom succeeded in reaching the French camp. (Barbier, *Journal*, vol. ii. These brave men received a reward of 100 *louis d'or* each). Du Chayla promptly threw his division across the Ghent *chaussée*, and awaited the British approach towards Ghent. Meantime the Royals, failing to make any impression on Massenem *Château* in the absence of artillery, rejoined the main body.

Moltke held by the letter of his instructions. His little force took the road for Ghent, the Royals leading, the rear brought up by five squadrons of Dutch cavalry. Nothing was seen of the enemy until the head of his column reached Melle Priory, where the Crillon Infantry brigade was encountered drawn up athwart the causeway. Hedges and houses on either side were lined with French troops, while a battery of twelve cannon was planted forty yards to the left.

Nothing daunted, the Royals charged the enemy in front, and scattered them in all directions. Then they wheeled to the left and captured the French guns. But Du Chayla's pontoons, drawn up behind the artillery, gave cover for an attack by two other French brigades—Normandie and Royal Étranger. While the infantry were exchanging volleys, Rich's Dragoons and the Hanoverian cavalry made a dash for Ghent. That goal would have been reached but for the self-devotion of Captain St Sauveur of Berry Cavalry, who held the Allies' horse at bay with a mere handful of his own until the arrival of the Normandie brigade.

Moltke was now outnumbered by nearly three to one. He made for Ghent with the Royals, Rich's Dragoons, and the Hanoverians. They were greeted by a tremendous musketry-fire from either side of the causeway, and reached their destination with a loss of one-third of their numbers. The first news of this reverse was a hurried scrawl received by Cumberland from Moltke at Ghent on May 10:—

> I encountered the whole right wing of the French Army, which was posted on the *chaussée*, in the priory, in houses, and hedged gardens. Although I cleared my front, I could not proceed, because everything buzzed with people and all the houses were full of infantry. Learning that 10,000 French were posted at the extremity of Melle, I made the Royals, who have behaved like lions, keep up a musketry-fire, in order to gain time to get my cavalry through. This I managed to effect, despite masses of infantry, and ditches wherein many men and horses broke their necks, so that I have lost many people.
>
> I know not whether Brigadier Bligh, commanding my left wing, has been as lucky as I myself, who reached Ghent at 10 o'clock this night. God Himself inspired me not to waste time

by sparring with the Grassins, or my whole force must have been destroyed. This is no country for cavalry, which is sacrificed and repulsed. It cannot act with any effect, and is apt to throw infantry into confusion.—Lieut.-General Moltke to the Duke of Cumberland, Ghent, July 9, 1745.

Brigadier Bligh was more fortunate. Mustering his own regiment, Handyside's, and the Dutch cavalry, he fell back on Alost through woods and narrow lanes. The Grassins closed in on his rear, capturing tents and baggage. He retreated from Alost to Termonde, whence he reported 292 of the two British regiments as killed, wounded, or missing. (Bligh to Cumberland, Termonde, July 10). Du Chayla took 1500 prisoners and an immense booty. 500 of the Allies were killed or wounded, and despatches destined for England were intercepted which told all Cumberland's weakness and discouragement. The French loss was nearly 1000.

Our defeat at Melle placed Ghent beyond reach of succour. Marshal Saxe reinforced Du Chayla by 15,000 men under Löwendahl, who invested Ghent, while Saxe himself watched the Allies' movements. On July 11 Löwendahl summoned the garrison to surrender. At the same time his dragoons swam across the moat unopposed, while two grenadier battalions seized the Bruges Gate and established themselves on the glacis. The turbulent populace were quiescent, for they cordially detested the British troops. The Dutch garrison, 2200 strong, retired to the citadel, followed by our Royal Welsh Fusiliers, whom Cumberland had thrown into Ghent, and the wreck of Moltke's relieving force. But before investment was complete the luckless general escaped with the Hanoverian cavalry. He reached Sluys at nightfall, and thus related his reception at the Dutch stronghold:—

> On arriving there I sent an officer to the commandant for his permission to pass and make my way to Antwerp. He refused to admit us, on the plea that it was too late to open the gates. Next morning I renewed all sorts of remonstrances, which I have no desire to repeat, being so spent with fatigue that I can scarcely breathe. He was again obdurate. I thought to do him honour by sending Colonel De Chiga, of the queen's service, with an earnest prayer to afford us such refuge as the King of Sweden obtained from the Turks. All was useless.

Finding retreat to Antwerp impossible, Moltke led his weary troopers to Ostend. He gave Cumberland a most disheartening account of that naval base, which was more important to the Allies than all the rest of Flanders. Its garrison of 1200 was insufficient to man a vast enceinte, which was in very bad repair. He concluded with a truly piteous appeal:—

> I humbly beseech your Royal Highness to order me hence by way of Holland, with my cavalry, which still consists of 450 rank and file. I would rather again fight a much superior enemy than remain here. I will not interfere in any way in the defences of Ostend. Besides, like all my officers, I am destitute of a shift of clothes, and do not possess a *sou*. All these trials would be endurable if one enjoyed good health, and were able to do something, however little, for the service's good. It is, and will ever be, a satisfaction to me that no one can accuse me of being deaf to the call of duty. *Nee Hercules contra Deos*: the force opposed to us was too great.—Moltke to Cumberland, Ostend, July 14.

Löwendahl opened trenches before Ghent citadel on the night of July 14, and pushed his sap up to the walls without interruption. When siege artillery and mortars were about to speak, the Dutch governor's heart failed him. At 6 a.m. on the morrow he surrendered the citadel, with an immense accumulation of stores. Besides the Dutch garrison, the Royal Welsh Fusiliers, the Royals, and most of Rich's Dragoons became prisoners of war. But after the capitulation Quartermaster Kelly of Rich's contrived to smuggle out 4 cornets and 160 troopers by a sally-port. He piloted them safely through the French lines to Antwerp, and on reaching Cumberland's camp was rewarded with a cornetcy.—Cumberland to Harrington, July 19.

The fall of Ghent was a prelude to that of Bruges, which was an open town and offered no resistance to the French. Audenarde was next attacked. Its magazines were defended by Lord Henry Beauclerk's regiment (48th Foot) and a Dutch battalion. After a two days' siege the latter mutinied and hung out the white flag (July 19, 1745). Of this surrender Fawkener wrote:—

> The Dutch part of the garrison was in as much haste to capitulate as their countrymen have been elsewhere, and the governor not coming into the measure, they refused doing any more duty... It shows the spirit of indolent timidity is generally spread, and it is a mighty fall of what was once lookt upon as the best infantry of Europe.—Fawkener to Newcastle, July 26.

While Löwendahl was capturing fortresses in rapid succession, his chief swept Cumberland's army before him. Clermont-Gallerande advanced to Chievres, threatening Mons, and laid Austrian Hainault under contribution. The Allies' position at Grammont was clearly untenable. On June 10 they retreated to Meerbeek, near Ninove. There Cumberland learnt the capture of Ghent, and was forced to fall back on Brussels. He retired to Dieghem, five miles east of the capital, on July 14, whence he wrote in low spirits to the Secretary of State:—

> What motions the French Army may make I cannot pretend to give any account of, for they detach and recall detachments so often that it is impossible, without better means of intelligence than we possess, to come at any knowledge of what they are doing.—Cumberland to Harrington, Dieghem, July 19.

On reaching Dieghem he brought Brigadier Ingoldsby before a general court-martial on charges of disobedience to orders at Fontenoy. This unpleasant step was, doubtless, suggested by a despatch from Hanover, where Harrington was in attendance on George II.

> As His Majesty has been pleased, for the encouragement of the army, to dispose of almost every vacant commission to officers who were present at the late action, I am expressly commanded to signify the king's pleasure to your Royal Highness that the strictest enquiry should be made into the conduct of such as are accused of having misbehaved therein, and those who lye under that imputation should be brought to tryal, and punished if found guilty. This His Majesty looks upon to be absolutely necessary for preserving the discipline of the army, and preventing future faults of the same kind. Besides that, it may be well apprehended that, if no care is taken to examine into the conduct of particular people, and to punish as well as to reward, a parliamentary enquiry may be set on foot the next session, which could not fail to be attended with very disagreeable consequences.—Harrington to Cumberland, June 9.

On July 15, therefore, a court-martial, consisting of Lord Dunmore and eleven other general officers, tried Brigadier James Ingoldsby on the charge:

> That he received orders from the duke to attack a redoubt or battery in the last action near Fontenoy, which orders he did not execute.

The case for the prosecution has been summarised in chapter 5. It is so incoherent and involved that the court must have had great difficulty in sifting truth from masses of irrelevant matter. Moreover, a very material witness, in the person of Cumberland himself, was not examined. In his defence the prisoner adduced a surgeon who had attended Colonel Duroure, to prove that, in the dying man's opinion:

> Brigadier Ingoldsby had behaved in an exceeding pretty manner the whole day.

Sir Robert Munro, too, swore that the prisoner had:

> Given his orders as became an officer who understood his business, and was capable to execute it.

The written defence put into court is worth quoting:—

> Sir Robert Munro hath given you an account of the dispositions I had made to perform the duty I was set upon, which I was ready to put into execution, and had begun it when it was altered by H.R.H.'s order, which made me apprehend I was no longer to pursue it, but march in line with the Foot of the first line, which I did till I was wounded and carried off. There only remains for me to say that if any misconduct has been on my part, I can safely lay my hand to my heart and aver that it has in no shape proceeded either from want of obedience to undertake what was commanded me or resolution to perform it; and if any unhappy mistake has been made by me, I hope you will impute it to no other cause than to misapprehension, and not clearly understanding the orders that were given me. It is an unspeakable grief to me that, after near forty years' service without any reproach, I should be treated as I have been.

The court found the charge of disobedience to orders proved, and held that Ingoldsby's delays before ordering his brigade to advance were highly prejudicial to the king's service. Inasmuch as his failure arose from an error of judgment, and not from want of courage, it suspended him during the duke's pleasure. (Sentence of court-martial, dated July 17, 1745).

Cumberland probably felt some qualms of conscience in dealing with this painful case, for the prisoner's contention that he had been harassed by inconsistent orders was amply borne out by the evidence. In reporting the sentence for orders, he wrote:—

> My personal thoughts are that the best way will be to permit him to sell out, for, after such a slur as this, he will never be able to serve with honour or dignity.—Cumberland to Harrington, July 29.

In the end Ingoldsby was suspended for three months. He was permitted to sell his company in the First Guards but not his majority, in which he was superseded (November 20) by Lieut.-Colonel John Laforey. (Harrington to Cumberland, Hanover, August 13).

From Dieghem Cumberland indited one of the few autograph despatches which have come down to us. Hitherto he had relied on Fawkener's facile pen, but the nature of this communication was so confidential that he was compelled to rely on his own powers of composition.

> My lord, I am sorry to be obliged to trouble you at a time when you have so many other afairs in your hands; but as you have shown yourself so willing to serve all my friends here that you are sensible how much it is for the good of the service to get rid of useless, worn-out officers, I desire your advice which way you think it best to get the king's consent for two worn-out colonells who are of no use to us. One is Major-General Johnson, and the other Sowl, who is now in a madhouse.
>
> As they are utterly useless, the king would reap a double advantage from their retirement, as it would give His Majesty the oportunity of rewarding young people of quallity, who have the same obligation to the king when they buy as if it (a regiment) was given them. If this were possible, the method I could wish would be to have Colonel Ligonier to succeed Sowl, and Conway to Ligonier, and Johnson's to Lord Bury. (Francis Ligonier was a brother of the famous Sir John, whom he succeeded in command of the 7th Dragoon Guards. He died of exhaustion after the Battle of Falkirk, 1746, and was buried in Westminster Abbey). They are both young, but I believe there are few in the army who would be less at a loss to behave in any difficult comand or detachment than they. This, my lord, I leave to your consideration and advice as well as help, in which afair could I succeed it would add greatly to the obligations I have to you for the success and despatch my recommendations have met with this campaign.—I remain, your affectionate friend,
> William. (Cumberland to Harrington, July 20, 1745).

The veterans who were thus to be superseded by a brace of *aides-de-camp* commanded the regiments afterwards numbered 33 and 11; but this little job did not recommend itself to George II. Two months later Cumberland jogged his father's memory in a second autograph despatch:—

> As to the affairs of Sowle's and Johnson's regiments, I do not yet give over hopeing that His Majesty may be convinced that two young men of quality who have a great application to their trade, and have shown both conduct and courage in three campaigns, are more usefull than two elder officers who are incapacitated from doing the king any service whatever. But this I leave to your thought, and hope that if you should see ocasion, you will attempt or else put me in the most likely method of succeeding with the king on that point.—Cumberland to Harrington, September 26.

On July 24, the French Army, under Louis XV. in person, advanced to Oordeghem. This movement threatened Cumberland's communications with England by way of Antwerp, and compelled him to retire (July 26) to Saventhem, on the south eastern outskirts of Brussels. Hence he wrote a despatch which reflects the Allies' despondency:—

> There is reason to apprehend the entire loss of the country. All I have to keep the field with is about 34,000 men; and the enemy has, in the king's camp alone, 70,000, and Comte de Clermont-Gallerande has another corps of about 8000. Should we lose Brussels, the queen's whole government would be overthrown; and on the other hand, should we lose Antwerp we should be unable to subsist ourselves or keep communications with Holland. So that the Marshal and I both joyn in opinion to prefer the securing of Antwerp to Brussels, whenever the fatal choice shall be thrown upon us.
> I have thought it my duty to inform as well His Majesty at Hanover, as the Lords-Justices, of the violent situation of H.M.'s affairs and those of his allys in this country. They may rest assured that, on my part,, nothing shall be wanting to make the best use of our diminutive army. I have still the pleasure and comfort left that every man on the right wing is heartily disposed to do his duty for his king and country.—Cumberland to Newcastle, July 26.

The English Council of Regency took alarm at Cumberland's account of the parlous condition of Ostend. They dispatched Major General Braddock to examine its defences, and poured in supplies of all kinds.

✶✶✶✶✶✶

Edward Braddock (1695-1755) was a typical British officer—brave, intemperate, headstrong, and punctilious. In 1755 he commanded an expedition against the French in North America, which was cut to pieces near the site of Pittsburgh (Pa.) His defeat and death were due to his own stubbornness in rejecting the advice of George Washington, second in command.

✶✶✶✶✶✶

But worse was to follow. Our consul at Ostend sent word that Count Kaunitz, Austrian Minister in Flanders, had vetoed a resolution of the council of war to lay the environs under water by cutting the dykes. (Wenzelius, afterwards Prinz von Kaunitz, 1711-94), was an eighteenth century Metternich, with equal vanity but far greater honesty of purpose).

Newcastle sent a vigorous remonstrance to Brussels, suggesting at the same time the supersession of the decrepid governor, General O'Connor. Kaunitz proving obdurate, the Regency tardily undertook to defend a naval base of priceless importance.

While despatches from Flanders were a dreary record of retreat and reverses, news came from another hemisphere which filled the nation's heart with joy. Under the Treaty of Utrecht (1713) Great Britain was confirmed in the possession of Nova Scotia and Newfoundland, though France retained ill-defined rights of fishery, which have been a perennial source of friction ever since. France was also given the island of Cape Breton, commanding the Gulf of St Lawrence. Here she established a naval base at Louisbourg, on the north-east of the island.

It became a port of call for homeward-bound Indiamen, and a magazine for vessels engaged in the lucrative cod fishery. Louisbourg, with its citadel and vast enceinte of forts and batteries, cost £1,000,000 to the French Exchequer, and was the strongest place in North America. When war broke out in 1743 the governor sent two expeditions to attack our Nova Scotian settlements. Though both ended in failure, these raids deepened the sense of insecurity which distracted our American colonies. They were stirred to action by a memorial drawn up by Robert Auchmuty, who presided over the local Court of Admiralty.

This admirable State paper painted the results of seizing Louisbourg in glowing colours, and suggested common-sense methods of raising troops and organising a campaign for its reduction. Auchmuty found a powerful ally in Governor Shirley of Massachusetts Bay.

******

William Shirley (1694-1771) was the son of a London merchant. Finding a legal career distasteful, he emigrated to Boston, and after years of intrigue and "lobbying" obtained the governorship of Massachusetts Bay. A lifelong enemy of French influence in America, he took for a motto "*Delenda est Canada!*"

******

Thanks to his eloquence, the scheme was adopted by the Assembly at Boston by a single vote. He then sent Auchmuty's memorial to the Secretary of State, with a suggestion that Commodore Warren, commanding the Leeward Islands Squadron, might be ordered to co-operate with the colonists. A better choice could not have been made. Peter Warren possessed a thorough knowledge of American waters, and had amassed great wealth by preying on French commerce with America and India. Wisdom was not conspicuous in British Cabinets of that day, but the advantages promised by Auchmuty's plan were so obvious that Warren was ordered to take his vessels northwards without delay.

The colonies of Massachusetts Bay, Connecticut, New Hampshire, and Rhode Island were largely peopled by descendants of Puritans driven from their native soil by persecution. Assured of the mother country's support, the old enthusiasm which had defied absolutism at home blazed forth anew. Funds were voted by the Boston Assembly; farmers, merchants, seamen vied with each other in enrolling and equipping volunteers. In a few weeks, New England possessed a workmanlike force of 3850 men. By universal consent command was given to William Pepperell of Piscataway, whose lack of military training was compensated by his natural aptitude and enthusiasm.

******

William Pepperell (1696-1759), "the hero of Louisbourg," was a wealthy merchant and shipowner, and the foremost man in Massachusetts. His baronetcy dated from November 1746, but he left no male issue to inherit it.

******

A remarkable feature in this well-planned enterprise was the secrecy which enshrouded it. No tidings reached Versailles of the storm cloud which was gathering.

The little army embarked at Boston, March 20, 1745, on eighty transports, with a convoy of eighteen small armed vessels. Cape Canso was made a fortnight later, and the troops encamped there to await Warren's arrival. A privateer was stationed off Louisbourg to watch French vessels entering the harbour. This was a lucky precaution, for they intercepted and beat off the *Rénommée*, which arrived from Brest with despatches. On April 23 Commodore Warrens squadron of four war vessels appeared in the offing. The army re-embarked, and steered for Gabarus Bay, four miles south of Louisbourg. On April 30, 2000 men landed there from boats. A feeble attempt was made to oppose them by the French governor. It was foiled by Pepperell, who drew the enemy from his real objective by a feint and put his men ashore two miles farther up the bay. When the enemy attacked, after a toilsome march over broken ground, they were repulsed, and their leader was captured.

The besiegers were puzzled by the French governor's inaction, which was not explained until Louisbourg was in their hands. Colonial service was highly unpopular in France, although one year spent abroad reckoned as two. The officers had but one object in expatriating themselves—to realise a fortune rapidly, without regard to the means employed. Now the home government had devoted large sums to repairing the fortifications of Louisbourg, but a mere pittance only had reached the hands which had toiled to render them nearly impregnable. On learning how grossly they had been cheated by their officers, the garrison rose in mutiny. For six months all duty had been suspended.

The appearance of an enemy kindled the ardent patriotism which lurked in every Frenchman's breast. The mutineers implored their officers to forget differences and lead them against the English. But men who were lost to a sense of honour were not stirred by so touching an appeal. The officers could not conceal their distrust of these overtures, and their sullen aloofness damped the enthusiasm of their men. With such leading as their comrades in Flanders enjoyed, the 1500 troops who garrisoned Louisbourg would have made short work of the raw colonial levies opposed to them.

Encouraged by this initial success, the besiegers proceeded to invest Louisbourg. They were assisted by engineers and sailors from Warren's ships, who displayed a degree of sympathy with citizen-soldiers which was very rare in those days. Trenches were opened, and batteries mounted with heavy guns from the squadron. After a few days' firing the French abandoned their principal battery without spiking the guns. Too late they perceived the fatal consequences of their supineness. An attempt to recapture this main defence was repulsed with heavy loss. On their side, the colonists failed in an attack on an island battery, but were in no wise cast down by this disappointment.

Versailles was thoroughly alarmed by the *Rénommée's* intelligence, and the only warship available was hurriedly fitted out to succour Louisbourg. She was the *Vigilante*, carrying 64 guns and 560 men. On May 19 she arrived off the harbour with vast supplies of warlike munitions. After a smart encounter with Warren's squadron, the *Vigilante* was overpowered and captured. Louisbourg's fate was now sealed. A general assault was planned, and Warren determined to push his largest ships into the harbour at point-blank range. This combined action was anticipated by the surrender of Louisbourg, June 27, 1745. The garrison, still numbering 900 men, became prisoners of war, but were conveyed to France under stipulation that they were not to serve for a year.

The advantages derived by Great Britain from this well-contrived affair did not end with the capitulation. Warren hoisted the French flag over the fortress, and kept his ships in harbour ready to slip their anchors as soon as an enemy's approach was signalled. Several rich Indiamen, homeward bound, sailed into the trap so cleverly laid. Thus prizes worth nearly a million sterling were taken in a few weeks. The squadron's return to England, laden with booty, provoked an outburst of exultation, and the spirits of our army in Flanders were raised by a *feu de joie*. (Fawkener to Harrington, Vilvorden, August 12). Rewards were granted with a lavish hand. Warren was promoted Rear-Admiral of the Blue, Pepperell obtained a baronetcy, and Parliament voted the reimbursement of all expenses incurred by the colonists. (See list below). Auchmuty alone had no reward, save the consciousness of having done his duty.

The loss of this great naval and fishing centre was a terrible blow for France. Barbier recorded that on its capture the price of sugar rose from 14 to 27 *sous* per lb.; coffee became 50 *per cent* dearer; and what salt cod reached Paris for consumption during Lent came by way of Holland. (*Journal*, vol. iii.)

✶✶✶✶✶✶

The cost of the Louisbourg expedition was not voted till 1748, when it figured thus in estimates:—

To Massachusetts Bay	£183,649
" New Hampshire	16,355
" Connecticut	28,860

| " Rhode Island | 6,632 |
| Besides smaller sums, amounting in all to | 255,746 |

Sir Peter Warren's keen business instinct prompted him to use this amount to the best advantage. Money was scarce in the colonies. He bought 650,000 ounces of foreign silver and 10 tons of copper, which were carried to Boston by H.M.S. *Mermaid*, July 1750. This timely supply enabled Massachusetts to redeem its load of inconvertible paper.

※※※※※※

From a British point of view, the reduction of Cape Breton was the one really creditable exploit of the war. Dettingen, with which it opened so auspiciously, was a happy accident; the naval successes, which lessened the sting of failure at its close, were won by greatly superior force. Englishmen could not avoid contrasting their generals' blunders in the Low Countries with the prompt decision and stout heart shown by their erstwhile neglected and despised colonists. For the first time in history the denizens of these islands had a vague intuition of their imperial destinies—a sense of solidarity with a new and vaster England across the sea. It was left to the next generation to alienate nascent forces which, had they but remained in unison, would have given peace and happiness to the world.

※※※※※※

It is much to be regretted that a graphic account of this expedition was not compiled while its memory was fresh. My authorities are—Beatson's *Naval and Military Memoirs*, vol. i.; Adelung, vol. v.; Gibson's *Journal of the Siege of Louisburg* (the estimates for 1748 provide £547, 15s. as a payment to him); a *Thanksgiving Sermon* by the Minister of the South Church, Boston, 1745; and Usher Parsons' *Life of Sir William Pepperell, Bart*. Boston, 1855.

※※※※※※

CHAPTER 7

The Scottish Rising

The Lords-Justices of Regency had special reasons for maintaining our communications with the Continent, for rumours were rife of another invasion. Fontenoy, in fact, served as a prelude to Prince Charles Edward's romantic effort to win England back to her old allegiance. He learned our defeat while visiting the young Duc de Bouillon in Normandy, and argued that he would never again have so many chances in his favour. The flower of the English Army was locked up in Flanders, whence reports came to him of its disorganisation and despair.

Barely 8000 regular troops were available for home defence. Charles Edward hastened to Paris in the hope of obtaining help from Louis XV.; but his enthusiasm received a cold douche from the king's advisers. Some of them wished to concentrate all available forces in an effort to crush the Allies in Flanders; others were influenced by Frederick of Prussia's remonstrances against supporting the Catholic party in England. Charles Edward perceived that he must rely on his own resources, and restore James III. to the throne by his subjects' aid.

Where should the hazardous enterprise begin? Memories of the abortive invasion of 1744 were too fresh to warrant a descent on the English coast. The descendant of Scottish kings turned with brighter hopes to his ancestral realm, now linked with England by a union which had not yet been consolidated by mutual advantage. The Highlands were then as remote from London as British Columbia in our day, and offered an ideal field for guerilla warfare. They were inhabited by warlike clans, whose chiefs' despotism had the sanction of immemorial usage, and was enhanced by heritable jurisdictions giving them powers of life and death. In Hobert Chambers' eloquent words—

The constitution of Highland society ... was strictly and simply patriarchal. The clans were families, each of which, bearing one name, occupied a well-defined tract of country, the property of which had been acquired long before the introduction of writs. Each clan was governed by its chief, whose native designation, *Kean Kinnhe*, "The Head of the Family," sufficiently indicated the grounds and nature of his powers. In almost every clan there were some subordinate chiefs called chieftains, being cadets of the principal family who had acquired a distinct territory and founded separate *septs*.

In every clan, moreover, there were two ranks of people—the *Doaine-uailse*, or gentlemen, who could clearly trace their derivation from the chiefs of former times, and assert their kinsmanship to the present; and a race of commoners, who could not tell how they came to belong to the clan, and who always acted in inferior offices. . . . The *Doaine-uailse* were, in every sense of the word, gentlemen—*poor* gentlemen perhaps, but yet fully entitled, by their feelings and acquirements, to that appellation.

On the contrary, the commoners, who yet generally believed themselves related to the chiefs, were a race of mere serfs, having no idea of a noble ancestry to nerve their exertion or elevate their conduct. The *Doaine-uailse* invariably formed the body upon which the chief depended in war; for they were inspired with notions of the most exalted heroism, by the well-remembered deeds of their forefathers, and always acted upon the supposition that their honour was a precious gift, which it was incumbent on them to deliver down unsullied to posterity. The commoners, on the contrary, were often left behind to perform the humble duties of agriculture and cow-driving; or, if admitted into the army of the clan, were put into the rear rank, and armed in an inferior manner.—Chambers, *History of the Rebellion*, chap. i.

Charles Edward had kept up a close correspondence with chieftains who were devoted to his cause, and believed that he would attract 15,000 armed adherents on raising the royal standard in the Western Highlands. He quitted Paris secretly, because there was some reason to fear a forcible detention should his designs leak out, and posted to Nantes. Here he had a devoted follower in the person of an

Irish privateer owner named Walsh. With this henchman's assistance he loaded the *Doutelle*, carrying 18 guns, with arms for 2000 men and £2000 in specie. On July 7, 1745, she sailed from St Nazaire, carrying the hope of Jacobite England and seven followers eager to stake their lives in his cause.

✶✶✶✶✶✶

"The seven men of Moidart," as they were styled, were the old Marquis of Tullibardine, *de jure* Duke of Atholl; Sir Thomas Sheridan, who had been the prince's tutor; Sir John Macdonald, in the Spanish service; an Irish clergyman named O'Kelly; James Strickland, the solitary English conspirator; Æneas Macdonald, who was a banker in. Paris; and Colonel O'Sullivan, of the French Army.

✶✶✶✶✶✶

This desperate scheme was executed without the knowledge of the French court; but Walsh procured instructions from the Ministry of Marine for the 64-gun ship *Elizabeth* to cruise off the Scottish coast, with an unavowed intention of utilising her as convoy. She joined her little consort off Belle Isle, and the pair steered northwest. Four days after starting they were chased by the 58-gun ship *Lion*, Captain Piercy Brett, which soon overhauled the *Elizabeth*, and engaged her at musket-shot until both were well-nigh knocked to pieces. But for the gentle force exerted by Walsh, who knew the vast interests at stake, Charles Edward would have plunged into the murderous conflict. At length, the *Elizabeth* had 205 killed and wounded, while her antagonist's losses were 162. They separated, each making the best of her way to port. This was a grievous blow, for the *Elizabeth* carried a full cargo of arms and munitions, besides 100 trained engineers and other officers.

The little *Doutelle* held on her course alone, and on July 19, 1745, she cast anchor in Loch Nanagh, an arm of the sea between Moidart and Arisaig. News of the prince's coming spread like wildfire; but first impressions were unfavourable. What could such puny forces effect against England? This pertinent question was asked by young Clanranald and Lochiel, who boarded the *Doutelle*. After much hesitation they were won over by Charles Edward's passionate appeals. Their adhesion turned the scale in his favour. The Western Highlands rose in arms. On August 30, 1745, the royal standard was raised at Glenfinan, near the head of Loch Shiel, and a proclamation of war was hurled against the Hanoverian usurper.

So imperfect were communications in those days that nearly a month elapsed ere the British Government became aware that its existence was threatened. Lord Harrington wrote from Hanover, where he was in attendance on George II.:—

> I prepared your Royal Highness in my last for the possibility of the French court's being induced by their late successes to meditate some attempt on His Majesty's British dominions. What we then only foresaw as a thing that might happen is now but too much verified, for the king has certain and infallible intelligence, and I am ordered to acquaint you in the utmost confidence that the resolution is actually formed at the Court of France to execute immediately such an invasion. . . . It is therefore the king's pleasure that your Royal Highness should lose no time in taking such measures that you may be sure of a communication with the sea, in order to throw over such a number of British troops as may be necessary for the defence of H.M.'s British dominions, with as little prejudice as possible to our interests on the Continent.—Harrington to Cumberland, July 26.

Cumberland was naturally impatient for news. His *fidus Achates* replied:—

> H.R.H. is under some surprise that he has not yet heard from England of the expedition of the Pretenders son, considering how long it has been talkt about abroad. The first intimation we had of it here was from an inquiry made on the subject of the Pretender of one of our trumpets by Mons. de Saxe's secretary; . . . and it has been advised from the French Army that the king said at table that he was landed in Scotland with some other persons.—Fawkener to Newcastle, August 9.

Louis XV. was better informed than the government which had so much at stake. On August 13 the Duke of Newcastle gave Cumberland a belated version of Charles Edward's movements:—

> Your Royal Highness will have heard that all accounts in France agree that the Pretender's son embarked at Nantes on the 15th past, N.S., and, as is confidently given out, for Scotland. We have not heard of his being landed there, but proper orders are sent to Sir John Cope and the rest of H.M.'s servants in Scotland on this advice. The Lords-Justices in Council yesterday ordered

a proclamation to be issued, offering a reward of £30,000 for apprehending the Pretender's son, in case he should land, or attempt to land, in any part of H.M.'s dominions.

******

Lieut.-General Sir John Cope (1690?-1760) entered the service in 1707, and commanded the troops sent to Flanders in 1742. He had just been appointed Commander-in-Chief in Scotland.

******

On the same day Lord Harrington wrote from Hanover:—

> His Majesty doubts not that the Lords-Justices will concert with you whatever they shall apprehend necessary to be performed on your Royal Highness's part towards disappointing the dangerous designs of his Majesty's foreign enemies and traitorous subjects who may be concerned in that expedition which the Court of France would have the world to believe that they have no share in, though the king has certain knowledge to the contrary.

At such a crisis Ostend was of priceless importance as a naval base, and England's sea power stood her in good stead. Newcastle wrote that the Lords-Justices of the Regency had:

> Ordered a small squadron to cruise off Ostend, and two or three small ships to lye constantly off Dunkirk and prevent any transport ships going into or coming out of that port. A strong squadron will be immediately assembled at the Downs or at Spithead under the command of Admiral Vernon; and notice is given to Vice-Admiral Martin, who is cruising with fifteen ships at the mouth of the Channel.—Newcastle to Cumberland, August 6.

Cumberland made frantic efforts to atone for past neglect. The garrison of Ostend was reinforced by the Royal Scots Fusiliers, under gallant, whimsical Sir Andrew Agnew, and Skelton's regiment (32nd Foot). General Chanclos of the Austrian service had been sent to examine the defences. While he endorsed Moltke's strictures, he thought that the place might sustain a siege with three additional battalions and more artillery. (Cumberland to Newcastle, July 29).

Chanclos' requirements were met by the dispatch of a combined battalion of Guards from London. But with the probability of an invasion before them, the colonels were loath to part with their best men, and the draughts were of exceedingly poor quality. That persistent meddler, Lord Stair, undertook to hold Ostend against all comers if he were given the command of two more Guards battalions. He met with a flat refusal from the Regency, who dared not lessen the slender force available for protecting London. On August 7, however, fourteen British and Dutch transports entered the harbour with abundant artillery and supplies of all kinds. Two days later Cumberland dispatched the Royal Irish regiment to Ostend by way of Antwerp.

These succours arrived at the nick of time, for, on August 9, 21,000 men, and 6000 led horses to carry fascines, appeared on the landward side. Löwendahl, who conducted the siege, summoned an outwork known as Fort Plassendael to surrender, and was promptly obeyed. (Fawkener to Harrington, August 9 and 12). Then he encamped in two lines, and made preparations for an investment. Count Kaunitz's refusal to allow the environs to be inundated was fatal to the defence. The enemy were able to erect batteries on the beach, which kept our cruisers at a respectful distance.

Meanwhile the Allies had shifted their headquarters from Saventhem to Vilvorden, an ancient townlet seven miles north of Brussels, on the canal connecting that city with Antwerp, "encamping the whole army in one line along the canal, which puts us somewhat nearer Antwerp without abandoning Brussels." (Cumberland to Newcastle, August 1). The duke established himself in Vilvorden Castle; the British and Hanoverians were posted northwards as far as the canal-head on the Rupel; while the Dutch extended in the other direction to Brussels. A corps of engineers was improvised; and great numbers of peasants were employed, on a daily wage of 4s. 2d,, in erecting a chain of redoubts and entrenchments along the line of the canal. (General Orders, Vilvorden, August 19).

The British soldier is rarely seen at his best during a continuous retreat, and demoralisation was rife, which called for severe examples. Between July 28 and 30 the General Orders were written in letters of blood:—

> All men found gathering peas and beans under pretence of rooting, to be hanged as morauders, without tryal.
> An officer and thirty men have orders to parade at the head of the Hanoverian cavalry, with whom the Provost is to make his rounds, and hang, upon the spot, those whom he finds morauding.

> George Rice, of Major-General Johnson's regiment (33rd Foot), to receive 800 lashes for mutinous expressions.
> John Almond, of Brigadier Mordaunt's (18th Foot), to receive 500 lashes for robing Corporal Yarborow, and to be put under stopages until satisfaction is made to ye corporal.
> Thos. Townsend, of Brigadier Cholmeley's (34th Foot), for insolent behaviour to his captain, to receive 800 lashes at ye head of ye regiment.

Draconian justice was the rule at Vilvorden.

> *August 15.* John Burridge, of Lieut. General Howard's (The Buffs), to be hanged imediatly without a court-martial for morauding.
> *September 10.* Mathew Colehoun, being tried for clipping, and condemned by ye sentence of a G. C.-martial to suffer death, to be hanged tomorrow at 8, near Port Crulé.

Tampering with the coin of the realm was rife in an army which contained a leaven of jail-birds. On August 15, a reward of ten *ducats*, or two guineas, and a free pardon were offered for information regarding a quantity of base money found in the rear of Major-General Howard's (19th Foot). The French Army was drawing nearer, and its Irish Brigade offered a warm welcome to deserters. Hence the following General Order:—

> Daniel White, tryed for endeavouring to seduce men to desert, to receive 1000 lashes at the head of every brigade of foot of ye Line, and never to appear in camp or garrison, on pain of being hanged. To begin tomorrow, and continued as ye provost shall find him able to bear it.

The army was kept constantly on the alert in its new position. Brussels was put out of bounds. Every officer and man was to join his colours on a signal given by firing three cannon.

> All guards and rear-guards to be loaded with running ball. In case of alarum, each regiment is to march without further orders to sustain their picquets, which must . . . be ready to turn out at the first notice; and in case of any alarum of ye enemy's appearing on ye side of ye canal, they are to march imediatly to the entrenchments along ye canal oposite to their several encampments.—G. O., August 6, 8, and 17.

These precautions were rendered necessary by the French advance. On August 6 Louis XV. and Marshal Saxe pushed their main forces to Alost, threatening Brussels and Antwerp. Their left extended to Termonde, which was defended by a Dutch garrison and Lord Henry Beauclerk's (48th Foot). On August 9 Fawkener relates another futile effort at relief:—

> H.R.H. attempted to throw a detachment into Dendermonde (Termonde), but was disappointed. 300 men from each army embarkt on boats from Antwerp, but about St Amand they found detachments of the enemy, and the river there being narrow, the tide slack, and wind contrary, there was no contending, and as many as could came back. The major who commanded the Dutch, a worthy, gallant officer, was killed.—Fawkener to Newcastle, August 9.

The siege of Termonde began on the morrow. Its environs had been laid under water, but Saxe had no difficulty in draining it into the Dender. Thus the principal defences were neutralised. Trenches were opened, and a concentrated fire began from mortars and heavy ordnance. After enduring this for twenty-four hours the garrison capitulated (August 13). Thus a park of artillery fell into the enemy's hands, which was promptly transferred to the trenches before Ostend.

Redoubled vigour was shown in the investment of that fortress. On August 14 Löwendahl completed the first parallel and began to trace the second. On the following night some British transports contrived to slip into the harbour. They landed reinforcements and stores, and took off the cavalry, which was worse than useless. But the French battery on the Dunes was completed on August 15, which enfiladed the harbour. Ostend was now cut off from succour, and its fate could not long be delayed. General Chanclos anticipated the worst when he wrote—

> The enemy commenced firing at 10 a.m. yesterday from 20 pieces of artillery and 10 or 12 mortars. This has continued the whole day and for part of the night. This morning their batteries have been augmented, and keep up a very heavy fire on our works and on all parts of the town, so that no one is safe. I dread its effect on the garrison, who have no place for a moment's repose. It is true that we have not lost many men, but the reason is discreditable. The labourers cannot be kept at work, and our artillerymen desert their batteries. A good deal of time

is thus wasted; and this fact, coupled with many others, leads to a fear that I may not be able to hold this place as long as I could have wished.—General Comte de Chanclos to Cumberland, Ostend, August 19.

The five British battalions shut up at Ostend were without a general. Somewhat late in the day Cumberland dispatched Lord Crawford and Brigadier Mordaunt to take command of these troops, "encourage them in their duty, and see General Chanclos' orders strictly obeyed." (Cumberland to Newcastle, Vilvorden, August 20). Unhappily the vessel which took them from Antwerp was kept at a distance by the French battery on the Dunes.

On August 14 Louis XV.'s army drew closer to the canal utilised by Cumberland for defending his position. The king established himself at Lippeloo, Marshal Saxe at Opdorp, and their right wing extended to Steinhuffel, covered by four dragoon regiments under the Duc de Chevreuse. (Fawkener to Newcastle, August 20). From this new position the marshal held a curious correspondence with Cumberland on the exchange of prisoners.

Several thousands had accumulated in French hands, and the dearth of men on our side rendered it essential to revive the Cartel of Frankfort. But Louis XV. persisted in declaring it nullified by the Belle-Isles' unjust detention in England. On August 19 Cumberland forwarded to Saxe a letter from Marshal Belle-Isle to Newcastle acknowledging their liberation. Anxiety to secure much-needed reinforcements prompted him to press for the renewal of the Cartel, in terms which were unusual—to say the least of it—in communication between hostile leaders. His letter was subscribed "Your affectionate friend, William."

The Belle-Isle brothers, in fact, landed at Calais on August 14, and a week later they arrived at Lippeloo. Louis XV. received them cordially, and the elder Belle-Isle won Saxe's heart by admitting that he owed liberty to his exploits. On the previous day the marshal had replied to Cumberland in a friendly strain:—

We have not yet heard, *monseigneur*, of their arrival in France; but the king, His Very Christian Majesty, to whom I communicated your Royal Highness's despatch, told me that as soon as he had cognisance thereof he would take steps to release his English and Hanoverian prisoners. In fact, the Convention of Frankfort will regain its force. I have much pleasure, *monsei-*

gneur, in repaying the courtesy and goodness with which your Royal Highness has deigned to honour me in your last letter. I am as fully sensible of these favours as I am eager to seek an opportunity of convincing you of my wish to deserve them, and to testify the profound respect with which I have the honour to be, *monseigneur*, &c,

Maurice de Saxe.

Charles Edward's triumphant progress through the Highlands compelled King George to quit his beloved Hanover. On August 24 Newcastle sent the commander-in-chief a despatch received from the Duke of Argyle, who was a pillar of the Hanoverian cause in Scotland:

> With an account of the Pretender's son having landed with about 200 men and 2000 spare arms at Arisaig, about thirty miles north and west from Fort William. The Lords-Justices have directed Sir John Cope (as was his own intention) to assemble as many troops as he could get together and march directly to the place where the enemy were to rendezvous. It is uncertain how soon the necessity of affairs here may oblige your Royal Highness to make a considerable detachment of your army for the defence of His Majesty's dominions. Have everything ready, upon the first notice from H.M. or hence, or if the motions of the enemy in Flanders should allow you to make a detachment, without waiting for any directions for the purpose. On Friday next H.M. gives directions for his yachts to proceed immediately to Helvoetsluys, H.M. having declared his intention to set out for England as soon as he shall hear of their arrival there.

Cumberland rejoined, August 27—

> I am surprised to see this romantick expedition revived again, and that it has taken place as far as the landing of any troops in Great Britain. But I don't doubt but that Sir John Cope will be able to put a stop immediately to this affair.... I am glad to hear of the king's return to his British dominions. I have sent to Sir John Ligioner to meet him at Utrecht.

On August 28 Lord Harrington wrote from Helvoetsluys—

> The king arrived here yesterday, I thank God in perfect health, but is detained by contrary winds, and I have therefore had

an opportunity of knowing His Majesty's pleasure relating to sending a detachment immediately home. The representations of your Royal Highness, together with all that has been urged by Sir John Ligonier in your name, have been maturely weighed by the king, before whom I have laid an account of what passed between the Pensionary and the principal members of the Republic at the Hague, whom I found extremely alarmed at the thought of such a weakening of the combined army in Flanders at this most critical juncture, and ready to give up the game in despair if it should take place.

Upon consideration, therefore, His Majesty has determined to suspend that step at present, and is now enabled to do so without inconvenience by the resolution which has been obtained of the States General to send over as soon as possible the 6000 men due by treaty to H.M.'s assistance, the first four battalions of which, amounting to 2700 men, will be at Willemstadt in order to their embarcation on Wednesday next—*viz.*, three for Gravesend and one for Leith. (This treaty, concluded between Great Britain and the States-General on April 14, 1719, provided for the dispatch of 6000 Dutch troops to England in case of an invasion).

Cumberland did not answer this despatch until September 13:—

I am extremely rejoyced at the resolution taken by His Majesty to get those troops employed which composed the garrison of Tournai, and were useless to the common cause. This has saved the whole country, by preventing any detachments being made from this army. And in my own particular I have reason to be much more so, that His Majesty has been pleased to express to Sir John Ligonier his aprobation of my conduct during this campaign. This has been my only view hitherto, and allways be that of my life. Should the service in England require a detachment, I will take care to send such battalions as may be depended on.

The States General have often been charged with evading treaty obligations by sending troops to England in 1745 who were, to their knowledge, disqualified by the capitulation of Tournai. It now appears that the idea was King George's. The English Government's weakness is revealed in the next despatch from Whitehall:—

You will have the Hessians now very soon, and be enabled by them, as we hope, to keep your ground. You may be assured that, if we had not the strongest reason to apprehend a foreign invasion, the rebels in Scotland would not, with their present strength, have induced the king to weaken H.RH.'s army. But you will easily see that battalions ordered from thence were absolutely necessary here, when you consider how small a force remained in the three kingdoms, and that the 6000 men granted by the Dutch are absolutely tyed up from bearing arms, either against French or Spaniards.—Harrington to Fawkener, September 20.

News came of the surrender of Ostend while George II. was waiting for a favourable wind at Helvoetsluys. On August 22, 1745, the besiegers occupied the covered way after a night attack, in which the Regiment d'Eu suffered severely. General Chanclos displayed the white flag on August 24, after obtaining a truce for two hours to allow of the dead being buried. He thus related the humiliating story of surrender:—

August 21. This town is a heap of ruins. . . . The great fatigue, and entire absence of quiet, day or night, owing to bombshells and cannon-balls, put the garrison into very bad humour. And it is really not saying too much to call it "bad." I might even add that one must be an Englishman to put up with what we are suffering here! The enemy is sapping up to the covered way, and is attacking on our weakest side. Nearly all our cannon have been dismounted, many artillerymen have been killed, and survivors decline to work the guns.

August 24. On the night of the 22nd a general assault was made on our covered way by fifteen companies of grenadiers, supported by two battalions. The point chosen was the sea front at low water. We repulsed the enemy more than once, killing and wounding 500 men, and making prisoners of 2 captains, a lieutenant, and 30 odd grenadiers. At daybreak I assembled my commanding officers to obtain their opinion as to our situation. Everyone agreed that we could not hope to hold out for more than a few days.

I therefore hung out the white flag, and sent a lieut.-colonel and captain to Count Löwendahl with the capitulation enclosed. Four hours later he returned it, with his marginal notes, by my emissaries. I must confess, *monseigneur*, that I did not hope to secure such conditions. It is a great point gained—to save the garrison from becoming prisoners of war.—General Comte de Chanclos, commanding at Ostend, to Cumberland, August 25, 1745.

Under the capitulation granted with such suspicious haste, the garrison was to evacuate Ostend with all the honours of war—even by the breach if Chanclos wished—and be escorted to Austrian territory. Cumberland was rather prematurely jubilant in reporting these conditions.

I suppose before now you are acquainted with the surrender of Ostend. It is some alleviation to that bad news that the garrison has met with such honourable and usefull conditions, since it will procure us an augmentation of five battalions. I don't doubt that General Chanclos and the whole army have done their utmost to defend a place they were sensible was of so much importance.—Cumberland to Newcastle, August 26.

After the capitulation Lord Crawford wrote to Chanclos from the transport which brought him from Antwerp, expressing deep regret that he had come too late to share the labour and perils of the siege. (Earl of Crawford to General Chanclos, August 24). The reply contained very disheartening news:—

I have just come from Count Löwendahl, who seems most eager to see you, and you are at liberty to land if you wish. The hope I cherished of embarking my garrison in the English transports for Antwerp has vanished. Orders have come from the King of France that they are to be escorted to Mons by way of Bruges, Ghent, Audenarde, and Tournai. I have protested vigorously against this decision, but all to no avail.—Chanclos to Lord Crawford, August 26.

Lord Crawford rejoined:—

I am very sorry that I cannot have the pleasure of paying my respects to my old friend Count Löwendahl, to whom I beg you will give my best compliments. It is my duty to return to the army with all despatch.—Reply, August 31.

So urgent was the need of troops at home that the Regency ordered Chanclos to send three line battalions to London and the fourth to Leith, whence Sir John Cope was appealing for reinforcements. (Newcastle to Cumberland, August 31). This arrangement was upset by Saxe's transparent evasion of the terms on which Ostend had surrendered, and a marked coolness arose between the rival leaders.

On September 2 Cumberland wrote to the Duke of Newcastle:—

> I am very sorry that, by Marshal Saxe's equivocation, the garrison is prevented from returning to England as soon as the Lords-Justices might have expected it. You will see by this copy of their march route that they will be out of the enemy's hands only on the 11th, and then they will be at Mons. As I have had a complaint from Brigadier Mordaunt that the garrison of Ostend had received at Ghent and elsewhere some insults by words from the officers of the Irish Brigade of Fitz-James, and that a detachment of that brigade was to escort them to Ghent, I have complained to Marshal Saxe of the indecency of that behaviour, and have likewise let him know that the interpretation they have taken on themselves to put upon the capitulation was a very unjustifiable one.

The marshal substituted a French battalion for Fitz-James's Irishmen as an escort of the British prisoners, while he warmly resented the imputation hurled at his adopted country by Cumberland:—

> If your Royal Highness would but consider our treatment of British troops throughout this campaign, you would do me greater justice. You would perceive that I do not deserve the reproaches insinuated in the letter which you did me the honour to address to me. Besides, we are not in the habit of insulting anyone: to do so is not a national characteristic—quite the contrary.—Marshal Saxe to Cumberland, September 2.

Cumberland returned to the charge on September 13. He reminded Saxe of his undertaking to restore the Frankfort Convention to its pristine force as soon as the Belle-Isles were set at liberty. Though England's part in the contract had been punctually fulfilled, the marshal had dispatched his English and Hanoverian prisoners on a tour through Flanders. They would be delivered at a fortress where no one was waiting to receive them, at a time much beyond the limits specified in the Cartel. As these unfortunate people were defenceless, and had a long march before them, the duke expressed a wish to send an escort of fifty horse to protect them from insults and keep them in discipline.

Saxe vouchsafed no reply to this letter. He had a bad case, and was probably nettled by the insinuation that the captives would be treated uncivilly. Cumberland next invoked the intervention of Marshal Belle-Isle. He pointed out that France was bound, under the Cartel of Frankfort, to restore prisoners of war exchanged within fifteen days. In other words, they ought to be sent back by the shortest route. He now learned that the Anglo-Hanoverian captives were to travel by unheard-of lines of march. For example, men confined in the Castle of Ham were to reach Mons by way of Noyon, Châlons, and Verdun. How, he asked, would Marshal Belle-Isle have liked to return to France vid Cadiz or Germany? (Cumberland to Marshal Belle-Isle, September 12). Expostulations were fruitless, and Sir John Cope was left to fight the Highlanders without reinforcements which might possibly have turned the scale in his favour.

The fall of Ostend served as a prelude to that of Nieuport, memorable in history for its obstinate resistance to the French in 1489, and the Battle of the Dunes, wherein Maurice of Orange defeated the Spaniards under its walls (1600). Very different was the spirit shown by its garrison when Löwendahl summoned them to surrender. Without waiting for the usual hail of shells and round-shot, the governor capitulated on September 5, 1745. Cumberland's despondency found vent in the despatch announcing this new reverse:—

> Sir John Ligonier will be better able to inform you by word of mouth than I can by letter the many difficulties I have met with in this campaign, and to assure you that it would have been far more to my satisfaction and for the king's honour if the worthy marshal (Königsegg) had commanded the whole army, and I had only had the command of the right wing under him. For the nominal command, without any real power either to the marshal or me, makes the service here go on so heavily that I have often wondered it did not come to a standstill.—Cumberland to Newcastle, September 2.

He was about to lose the mentor to whose tact and guidance he owed so much. The veteran Königsegg's career was drawing to a close. He thus addressed Lord Harrington on September 14:—

> Your Excellency may remember the alacrity with which I journeyed to the Netherlands when, at H.B.M.'s request, I was ordered thither by the queen, my august mistress. I am free to

admit that, in complying, I consulted my zeal for her service and that of her high Allies without thinking of personal advantage or remembering my gouty disposition.

This campaign has convinced me that I undertook a task wholly beyond my strength. I was prostrated by the fatigues of marching, and especially by those which I underwent at Fontenoy; and my strength was so exhausted by a fit of gout which I had soon afterwards that I am unable to walk four steps without leaning on another person's arm, and cannot keep my saddle for an hour while riding at foot's pace.

You will agree, my lord, that one who is reduced to such a state is incapable of the vigilance and activity which a general must display—above all in battle. One must be on horseback day and night to reconnoitre the country, visit outposts, and watch the enemy's movements. A leader who can issue orders only on reports made to him by others is liable to commit irreparable mistakes.

A man of my age,—I am now in my seventy-third year,—disabled by gout and worn out by the incessant toil of fifty-two years' service, can scarcely hope to regain his strength once it has been lost. When a certain period of life has been reached, Nature places no further resources at the individual's command. He becomes useless to the State and himself. Such is my unhappy plight, which compels me to seek repose. I have, with all humility, informed the queen, my mistress, that I find it impossible to serve any longer; that I must return to Vienna at the close of this campaign; and wish to restore my health as best I can by a regimen of hot baths and asses' milk, which I was obliged this year to interrupt.

I flatter myself that the queen, who is aware of my zeal for her service, will comply with this request. But knowing her manner of viewing all that concerns the interests of her high Allies, and especially her respect for H.B.M., I am equally sure that she will not permit me to leave this country without His Majesty's consent. I would, therefore, beg your Excellency to obtain this royal favour on my behalf, by explaining all the motives which compel me to quit a career which I have followed with passionate devotion.

At the same time, I may assure you that I shall in nowise be missed by the army. During this thorny campaign H.R.H. the

Duke of Cumberland has, by his vast labours and indefatigable activity, acquired a degree of experience and local knowledge which few generals have attained after many years' service. Not less has he won by illustrious birth the love and confidence of the troops, who admire his valour and prudence, as well as the excellent discipline which he maintains. Thus he has gained the heart of the entire country. H.R.H. is well able to add the reality of supreme command to the title which he already possesses. I may add that since the Battle of Fontenoy, wherein his bravery was so conspicuous, I have been incapable of independent action, and that we owe to his care, alertness, and prudence the excellent dispositions which have enabled us to hold Brussels and Antwerp against an enemy whose strength is vastly superior to our own.

I crave your forgiveness, my lord, for trespassing on your precious time with so lengthy a letter, but flatter myself that you will give some weight to our old acquaintance, which I shall always remember with the highest esteem and veneration, and with which I have the honour to be unalterably, my lord, your Excellency's very humble and obedient servant,

      Marshal Comte de Kinigsegg (*sic*).

This laudation of his favourite son went straight home to King George's heart. His principal Secretary of State replied on September 23:—"I have lost no time in laying your letter before his Majesty, and may assure you that he is grieved to learn that the state of your health will not permit you to endure the fatigues of another campaign. As no one is more convinced than His Majesty of the merit which you have acquired by long and honourable service, and of the loss the common cause will suffer by the retirement of so experienced a leader, it is with real sorrow that His Majesty is compelled to accede to your wish, but he hopes that your Excellency will be able to hold the field until both armies have taken up winter quarters.

The praises of His Royal Highness contained in your letter have given the greatest pleasure to the King, who is so well aware of your probity and solid judgment. To have deserved the applause of Marshal Königsegg will add lustre to the reputation of this worthy young prince. As far as I am personally concerned, and am permitted to do so in this letter, I may inform your Excellency that I am deeply grateful for your remembrance of our old friendship, which for my part I will always cherish. I wish you heartily all the happiness which you hope to realise on retiring from so laborious and distinguished a career, and am, your Excellency's most humble obedient servant,

Harrington.

While the Flanders campaign was ending in a complete fiasco, things wore a still blacker aspect in Scotland. Sir John Cope had orders to concentrate at Stirling and push on to Fort Augustus, in order to crush the rebellion in its birth. Leaving two dragoon regiments at Edinburgh, he plunged into the Highlands with 1400 men and a few light guns. On reaching Dalwhinnie (August 19) he learnt that Prince Charles Edward had occupied the Correyairack Pass in greatly superior strength, blocking his route to Fort Augustus. Commonsense should have inspired him to fall back on the Forth, in view of disputing the enemy's advance on Edinburgh. Cope held blindly to his instructions, and continued his march to Inverness, where the Argyll Campbells were mustering to support him. This fatal blunder opened a passage for the Highlanders to Scotland's capital. At this crisis Charles Edward showed something of a leader's instinct. Disregarding his friends' advice to pursue Cope, he sped onwards to Edinburgh by way of Blair Atholl and Perth.

Partisans flocked to his standard at every halting place, and among them was Lord George Murray (1695-1760), sixth son of the Duke of Atholl. Mature years and lofty birth gave this great captain prestige in the eyes of Charles Edward's followers, which was enhanced by the rarest personal gifts. Murray, indeed, combined the most opposite characteristics—daring carried to the verge of rashness when any substantial advantage might be gained; "sage counsel in cumber"; an intuition of approaching danger which amounted to instinct; a lifelong experience of war and affairs.

Like most men of action, he brooked no interference, and scorned the opinion of others. In his relations with the prince he was tactless and dictatorial, while infinite harm was wrought by his frequent bickerings with other leaders, especially the young Duke of Perth and Captain John Roy Stewart. Thus Murray was never cordially trusted by the prince, who requited his services with gross ingratitude. Lord George Murray was, indeed, the real hero of "the '45." Very different would have been its results had he been permitted to act unhampered by jealousy and the meddling of inferior men.

The young prince possessed the magnetic charm which comes of a kindly heart. Personal beauty, grace, and accomplishments conspired with the halo of a great cause and Right Divine to make him perfectly irresistible. Marching at the head of his clansmen, he shared all their hardships, and equalled the best in endurance. But he already showed symptoms of the besetting vice which clouded his old age. Brought up in Rome under priestly influences, he never understood the temper of the English people, or grasped any of the intricate problems which beset him.

The Highlanders' approach to Edinburgh spread wild alarm among supporters of the reigning dynasty. The Lowland population, however, had too keen a memory of Stuart persecution to welcome a claimant to the crown who represented abhorred principles of government in Church and State alike. As a body the Scottish nobility were hostile, or at the best indifferent; and Archibald, Duke of Argyll, kept the great clan of Campbell staunch to the Protestant succession.

The motley host encountered but feeble opposition at Edinburgh. Panic seized the Town Council, and all hope of resistance vanished with the precipitate flight of Cope's dragoons. On September 16, 1745, one of the city gates, which had been left unguarded, was rushed by Lochiel's men. Next morning the prince took up his abode at Holyrood Palace, and at 1 p.m. King James III. was proclaimed in his presence at Edinburgh Cross. The castle, however, held out, and was never captured by the Jacobites.

With Scotland in revolt, the Cabinet could no longer delay recalling troops from Flanders. Lord Harrington wrote on September 15:—

> The rebels in Scotland have found means to steal by at a distance from the king's troops, which were moving on through the Highlands to give them battle, and were, when the last letter came away, in full march for Edingburgh, having left Sir John Cope by that motion two or three days behind them. It is, therefore, His Majesty's pleasure that your Royal Highness should ... give orders for the marching of ten of the best English battalions directly for Willemstadt, to be commanded by Sir John Ligonier, who is to take them to Gravesend with the utmost expedition. You are requested to explain the reasons to the generals-in-chief of the allied army. His Majesty will continue to exert himself for the common cause, hoping, by the blessing of God, with these succours speedily to end the present alarms at home, so that the troops may return.

This despatch reached Cumberland at a banquet given at Brussels to celebrate the election of Maria Theresa's husband as King of the Romans (September 13, 1745). This dignity was a steppingstone to the purple, and he was chosen Emperor of Germany at Frankfort, October 4. The triumph of the Coalition's candidate put Cumberland into better spirits. He replied, September 20:—

> I must do both the Marshal and Prince Waldeck the justice to say that they were equally concerned for the occasion, and the diminution of our present small force. The ten battalions which I have named for this service are the three of Guards, Sowle's (11th Foot), Pulteney's (13th), Charles Howard's (19th), Bragg's (28th), Douglas's (32nd), Johnson's (33rd), and Cholmondeley's (34th). I can assure His Majesty that last Fryday I had the satisfaction to see the whole army under arms, and can with the greatest truth say that the battalions were equally fine and in good order; but if there were any prefference to be given, it was to these ten, which I have pick'd out for that very reason.

The review alluded to was held on September 17, on an extensive plain near Vilvorden. General Orders prove that it was an unqualified success:—

> *September 18.* It is H.R.H.'s pleasure to declare that he is so thoroughly pleased and satisfied with the clean appearance and good order of the troops he saw yesterday, that he orders it to be signified to all ye officers that he is extremely obliedged to them for their care.

During these festivities the French displayed increased activity in the interior of Flanders. On September 16 Saxe reinforced Clermont-Gallerande at Enghien, and sent him eastwards through Austrian Hainault *via* Braine le Comte and Nivelles. Another strong detachment was dispatched to operate on the line of the Sambre and isolate the Dutch garrison at Namur. Louis XV., after visiting Ostend, returned to Versailles, leaving Saxe in supreme command, with the option of taking up winter quarters when he pleased. But he had reasons of State for protracting the campaign in Flanders, the King of Prussia having insisted on the necessity of occupying the attention of Austria by further aggressions.

Cumberland informed the Secretary of State on September 30 that his hussars had intercepted letters from Paris enjoining Saxe to besiege Ath, the Allies' sole remaining stronghold in Western Flanders. This operation, he added:

> It was at last resolved to undertake, much against the advice of that marshal. It was invested yesterday by Count Clermont-Gallerande with 24 battalions and an uncertain number of squadrons. They propose tomorrow night to break ground, and reckon to take it in a fortnight. Count D'Estrées, with 28 squadrons, 500 *Grassins*, and 300 *Uhlans*, is advanced to this side of the Dender, towards Enghien, which helps to cut us off from our battalions at Mons. We are occupied in settling winter quarters, and would be much obliged if you would search in your office for all tariffs, as well of King William's as of the last war, attested copies of which would be very usefull now we are likely to be crowded in our quarters.

The exodus from Flanders was in full swing when this despatch was dictated. On September 24 Generals Pulteney and Cholmondeley started with five battalions for Willemstadt, where transports were in waiting, and Sir John Ligonier followed next day with the remainder. Returns show that the ten regiments were far stronger than at Fontenoy. The Guards' battalions numbered 799, 700, and 706, officers and men included, the strength of the line regiments averaging 760. Those who were fated to remain longed to quit an irksome position, and events in Scotland were watched with intense interest. As became the heir-presumptive of Maccallum Mhor, Major-General John Campbell of Mamore tendered his services on the Hanoverian side. He wrote:—

> The duty and regard I owe the king, my master, and the gratefull sense I shall ever retain of his repeated favours, calls upon me at this time of danger to offer what some may call indiscreet advice, without first consulting the Duke of Argyll, who is the head of my family; but I have to plead with him that in such cases no time is to be lost. Be that as it will, I am determined to beg your lordship will be so good as to acquaint His Majesty that I am ready in any shape of resenting the insult offered to him, his family, and the libertys of my country by the unnatural rebellion begun in Scotland, and that if His Majesty thinks I can, upon this unhappy occasion, be of the smalest use, that he will doe me the honour to imploy me in any shape.
> If the Duke of Argyll could but be led into making this thought or proposall of mine his own, and will only give me full powers

in his country, I realy think I can be of some service in drawing his people together, should there be any occasion for it. I am not so conceited as to think of, or desire, any particular command. I humbly offer my services as a volunteer, having served in that status in the year 1715, as *aide-de-camp* to the last Duke of Argyll, at the latter end of that campaign. If the affair is over, and General Cope has met with, burnt, and destroyed (*sic*), I beg you will commit this to the flames without saying anything.

I don't want to make a merit of what I take to be the duty of every honest man. The duke (of Cumberland) is most justly adored, beloved, and respected by the army, so that if the crown of England is to be fought for, His Majesty cannot have so good a general under him. Should any number of troops be ordered out, pray think of this. The trouble of this proceeds from a zeal I have for the welfare of my king and country. I wish for peace; I find myself unfitt for war; but in every circumstance of life you will find me what I profess....

P.S.—My lord, I find I have omitted a very material point, which is the want of arms among all the people in Scotland who are known to be well affected to H.M. and government. But more particularly in that part commonly called the Duke of Argyll's country. I know that the late duke was fond of the Disarming Act, and under it, absolute in his own country, gave positive orders to those intrusted with his affairs to comply strictly with the Act, and even threatened them if they did not. This, I am perswaded is the reason of the present duke's leaving the country—no arms, or any power of putting arms into the people's hands.—Major-General John Campbell to Lord Harrington, Vilvorden, September 23.

There was no resisting such an appeal. Lord Harrington replied, October 1:—

His Majesty was pleased to express a very particular satisfaction in your zeal for his service, and has ordered Mr Pelham to endeavour to manage the matter so with the Duke of Argyll that your proposition may come, as you suggest, from His Grace, the King approving entirely himself that you should be employed upon that command.

Campbell rendered yeoman service during the Scottish campaign.

Before Culloden he brought hundreds of his clansmen to the royal standard, and was sent by Cumberland to keep the Western Highlands in order during his own advance northwards. After the battle he was zealous in unearthing concealed weapons in Appin and Glencoe, and showed no less vigour in tracking the fugitive prince. (Chambers, *History of the Rebellion,* chap. xxv.) Of a different order was the Judas-like information sent home by Cumberland on September 27:—

> Since the disturbances in Scotland, one Walford, a quartermaster in the King's Own Regiment of Horse, has owned that he was anxious for some friends in England who he knew were disaffected, and he feared would throw themselves into dangerous courses; and that his father could raise 2000 men. I had him brought to me today, when he owned that his father, Thomas Walford of Wem, in Shropshire, can raise 2000 disaffected men, and that Lainford or Langford Hall, near Newport in Shropshire, is inhabited by Papists, and that it is suspected powder and arms are concealed there. This man said that a post or two ago he wrote to his father to dissuade him from taking any part against the royal family.

Orders were given for searching the house indicated, but the result has not been recorded. (Harrington to Cumberland, October 8).

The impending departure of our Flanders contingent was seized by Sir Everard Fawkener as a means of pushing his master's interests and his own. As far back as September 18 he showed more than usual hypocrisy in informing the Duke of Newcastle that:

> We are extremely mortified at the recall of troops, yet there is a thorough acquiescence in the reasons for it. H.R.H. executes the orders he receives on the subject, so that the troops will be ready before there will be transports to receive them.... I hope your Grace will do justice to the zeal and diligence of my master on this important occasion.—Fawkener to Newcastle, September 18 and 27.

We have seen that Cumberland anticipated an easy triumph for Sir John Cope's regulars over the undisciplined horde opposed to them. His foresight was once more at fault. That unlucky general brought his little force by sea from Inverness to Dunbar, where he was joined by his dragoons. On September 18, he started for Edinburgh with 1400 foot, 600 cavalry, and 6 guns. But a large proportion of the infantry were mere depot companies; the dragoons raw levies; while the artillerymen were sailors, who in those days were very far from being "handy men" ashore. Prince Charles Edward led 2400 clansmen from their camp at Duddingston on September 20, and in a few hours the two armies came in contact at Prestonpans. The rest of the day was spent in manoeuvring, to Cope's advantage, for he contrived to cover his front with marshy ground.

During the night-bivouac Charles Edward learnt that the morass was traversed by a path, and that he could form up on Cope's left flank. A flank march began three hours before sunrise on September 21, 1745; and when the reveille beat, poor Cope saw two lines of Highlanders advancing from a quarter which he deemed secure. There was still time to throw back his left and form with Gardiner's and Hamilton's dragoons on either flank, facing the enemy. Hardly was the line of infantry dressed ere the clansmen struck it obliquely on the right, sweeping all before them. Hamilton's dragoons went about before the human avalanche reached them, and Gardiner's followed suit, riding down the gunners in their headlong flight. Their colonel, a splendid type of the Christian soldier, (see note following), put himself at the head of a handful of infantry, and fought with desperation until he was mortally wounded by a Lochaber axe.

★★★★★★

> James Gardiner (1688-1745) had covered himself with glory in Marlborough's wars. Converted by a vision in 1719, he became a burning and shining light in the little band of Methodists who wrought a second Reformation during the eighteenth century.

★★★★★★

The Battle of Prestonpans was decided in a few minutes: 400 British infantry were killed; 700 captured, with their guns, treasure-chest, and baggage. Sir John Cope fled to Berwick-on-Tweed, carrying the news thither of his discomfiture. He was the butt of innumerable satires. It is only fair to his memory to quote the opinion of a recent expert:—

> Sir John Cope really did all he could under the circumstances. ... Stalk round him the Highlanders did, as a tiger would glide round a solitary bull, but like that animal, the unfortunate Cope was always ready, facing the foe.—Major-General Sir Alexander Tulloch, *Culloden and the '45*. Inverness: 1896.

In informing Cumberland of "the unfortunate success of His Majesty's arms against the rebels in Scotland," Harrington announced the first instalment's safe arrival, and pressed for further draughts:—

> Send the eight battalions of British troops remaining in camp to Willemstadt, where they will find transports waiting to convey them to Newcastle-upon-Tyne in order to join the corps marching northward under Marshal Wade; and also hold the nine squadrons of dragoons ready to march at the first notice of transports being ready. They must carry tents, camp equipage, and everything necessary for taking the field immediately on landing, as none of these things can be furnished here without great loss of time. As they will march direct to Scotland, the king thinks it will be better to put the Scotch battalion now in your Royal Highness' camp (the Black Watch) into Antwerp and Brussels instead of the English, and to send over nothing but English.—Harrington to Cumberland, October 6 and 8.

Early in October the Chevalier de St George sent his son a quantity of money and arms, including six small cannon. With this timely help, and the crowds who flocked to his standard when he returned in triumph to Edinburgh, Charles Edward found himself at the head of a serviceable little army of 6000 men. About half were Highlanders; and he had 500 cavalry, as well as tents, pack-horses, and everything necessary for a winter campaign. He had some reason to expect active co operation from France, for the Duc de Richelieu was designated to command an expedition fitting out at Dunkirk for an invasion of England by its eastern coast.

These preparations deceived Hanoverians and Jacobites alike; but they were probably a mere feint, intended to embarrass the English Government, or to give Louis XV. an excuse for conferring a marshal's baton on his favourite. The French had their hands full in Flanders and Germany; their Channel Fleet was far inferior to our own, and the fate of the last attempt at invasion was by no means encouraging. Some light is cast on the true inwardness of French designs by a report of October 12 from an anonymous agent at Dunkirk, whose style and handwriting show that he was a person of some distinction:—

> The Court of France has not yet taken Scottish affairs to heart, and the small amount of help which one foresees will be given to the Pretender will be at the expense of Spain. ... I know this to be a fact from a friend of mine, who is the Pretender's agent, and went to Versailles to solicit help on his behalf. He told me

this when he returned on October 8. I do not think he wished to deceive me, for he could not do so for long. It appears that, for the present at least, the Pretender will receive assistance only through the agency of privateers and smuggling vessels, which carry him arms and perhaps money, and will take away a few Irishmen at a time in the French service, as well as Highland deserters from the Duke of Cumberland's army.

This view is confirmed by a despatch from Lord Harrington of October 9, announcing the capture of a Spanish vessel, piloted by an Irishman, with 2500 muskets, several tons of ball, a vast amount of powder, and several chests of silver.

Although Charles Edward found comparatively few adherents south of the Forth, he was under the illusion that all England would receive him with open arms. On October 31, therefore, he set out on an adventurous march on London. Two days earlier Wade had arrived at Newcastle with an intercepting force, which included the bulk of the Flanders detachment. During his progress northwards he sent Harrington a letter received at Northallerton from a Scottish sympathiser:—

> By our last express from Edinburgh we are informed that the rebels are decamped and gone into quarters in the city and suburbs, and it is the prevailing opinion that they will not leave it till they are drove out; or, which is more probable, that so soon as our army enters Scotland they will endeavour, by takeing another rout and speedy marches, to get past them into England. By the very best accounts I can get, they do not exceed 8000, including volunteers. Though this is a small force, they are by no means to be despised, for they are to fight with a rope about their necks, determined to die with their swords in their hands rather than be hanged up like traitors.—J. A. Gilchrist of Dumfries to Marshal Wade, October 20.

This forecast was accurate enough, but the aged Marshal was unable to grasp its full significance. As early as October 20 Whitehall was perturbed by a false alarm that the Jacobites were already advancing on London:—

> The danger to H.M.'s dominions daily increases, and the force which we have to oppose the rebel army now marching into England from the north is by everybody thought insufficient...

I have the king's commands to signify to your Royal Highness that you do as soon as possible send away to Willemstadt all the British foot remaining in your army, including the battalions which you have anywhere in garrison, that of Ostend if it be returned from duress, and the whole corps of British prisoners if delivered. . . . Sir John Ligonier's Regiment of Horse (7th D. G-.), Lieut.-General Hawley's (1st Royal Dragoons), Bland's (3rd Hussars), and the remainder of Sir Robert Rich's (4th Hussars).—Harrington to Cumberland, October 20.

The released prisoners were not yet available. They had reached Mons after a tortuous journey, but D'Estrées and Clermont-Gallerande were hovering, hawk-like, in its vicinity. Cumberland sent Sir John Hawley to the rescue with 4000 cavalry, 600 Dutch grenadiers, and the Free Companies. This strong detachment formed a flying camp at Halle. During a reconnaissance in force they met a foraging party from D'Estrées' position at Enghien, and drove them back with heavy loss. D'Estrées retired precipitately, giving Hawley an opportunity of extricating the prisoners from Mons. (Cumberland to Harrington, October 7). Cumberland thus related their progress:—

I hope by the 18th October to have the greater part of the prisoners at Louvain; but they have been so disorderly and riotous on the march that I have sent Brigadier Douglas with 300 British dragoons, and with a power of holding courts martial, for the better quieting of these disorders. Last Friday Brigadier Mordaunt marched into camp with the five English battalions that were in Ostend. . . . The detached battalion of Guards is in no condition to serve, owing to the age of the officers.—*Ibid.*, October 11.

Ath was the only fortress in Western Flanders which still flew the Austrian banner. Löwendahl opened trenches before it on October 1, and the Dutch governor surrendered after enduring a hail of bombs and red-hot shot for eight days (October 9). The garrison, which included Lord Sempill's (25th Foot), marched out with full military honours and joined the allied army at Brussels. (*Ibid.*, Vilvorden, October 11).

Campaigning in Flanders was clearly at an end: the prisoners were restored, the garrisons evacuated by British troops. Cumberland's position as leader of an army deprived of its staunchest element became quite intolerable. His eagerness to strike a blow for the interests of his

> Vilvoorden Oct ye 12th 1745 N.S.
>
> I received yours of the 7th instant with pleasure at the safe arrivall of the ten battallions that vent from hence under your comand & your own personall safe arrivall which I take great share in. but the bad news from Scotland shock'd me doubly, because of the bad behaviour of the Kings troops there a the success of these infamous Rabells, I flatter myself that your battallions won't behave so & hope that the King will do me the favour to let me come to them as I am agoing to detach five battallions & nine Squadrons of Dragoons from hence for England The Hessians are all come up & in good order & the rohrus prisoners are within six days march halting days included. Pray let your correspondance be continued & let me know all that may be trusted pa paper & you will much oblige your most affectionate friend
>
> William

FACSIMILE OF A HOLOGRAPH LETTER OF WILLIAM AUGUSTUS, DUKE OF CUMBERLAND.

family at home found vent in an autograph epistle to Ligonier, which was evidently meant for the royal eye:—

> I received yours of the 7th instant with pleasure at the safe arivall of the ten battallions that went from hence under your comand, and your own personall safe arivall, which I take great share in; but the bad news from Scotland shocked me doubly, because of the bad behaviour of the king's troops there and the success of these infamous rabells. I flatter myself that your battallions won't behave so, and hope that the king will do me the favour to let me come to them, as I am agoing to detach five battallions and nine squadrons of dragoons from hence for England.... Pray let your correspondance be continued, and let me know all that may be trusted to paper, and you will much oblige your most affectionate friend, William.—Cumberland to Sir John Ligonier, October 12.

On the same day he entreated Lord Harrington's friendly offices:—

> I beg your lordship to use your utmost interest that His Majesty may permit me to return to England, where there is now the greatest prospect of my being able to render him service, all being over here. As on the success of your negotiations my ease of mind depends, I beg of you to send me the king's determination upon it as soon as possible.

On October 14 the duke became more insistent. After announcing the departure of eight additional battalions, including the Guards who had garrisoned Ostend and the Black Watch, he went on:—

> I flatter myself with the hope that I shall receive before this can arrive H.M.'s gracious permission for my return. Every argument that I presst in my last bears every day more in my favour; and should not my last instances have prevailed, I most earnestly recommend it to you to renew your application to the king that I may have His Majesty's leave to employ my duty and affection to H.M. and my country, where they now seem most to be called for; and indeed it would be the last mortification to me, when so much is at stake at home and brought to the decision of arms, to be out of the way of doing my duty there. The

campaign is near at an end here, the French being now moving into their winter quarters.—Cumberland to Harrington, October 14.

A reply was long in coming, and Fawkener must needs put in his oar:—

> Your lordship will have seen with what alacrity the orders for sending troops are obeyed, and I can assure you it is accompanied by the most perfect acquiescence in the reasons for demanding them.... If you send again, it must be for His Royal Highness, for little else now remains. He is impatient to oppose himself to the abominable rebellion, which to me appears the most monstrous one there is yet an instance of—that a nation rich, at ease, and happy (for Scotland was in a higher degree than there is any instance in history), should at once, unprovoked, revolt in favour of an absolute tyranny, and to destroy a religion they profess! false, stupid, and inconstant people! But I hope the better part of the nation will not be tainted by the mad spirit that is gone forth, and that, by the assistance of the army drawn from here, they may bring back those who have so giddily and traitorously fallen off.—Fawkener to Harrington, October 18.

This egregious missive crossed a despatch from Whitehall which must have gladdened Cumberland's heart:—

> I have not failed to recommend to His Majesty, in the manner your Royal Highness was pleased to order me, your request of now being allowed to return home; and I have the pleasure to acquaint you that the king consents to your doing it the moment the troops shall have entered into winter quarters. Your Royal Highness will easily conceive that, whilst there was an appearance of any further operations, the king, who has so great a confidence in your conduct, could not think of withdrawing you from so important a command as you had.... In consequence of this permission from the king, I hope and am persuaded that your Royal Highness will find yourself immediately at liberty to return hither.
>
> P.S.—The king has been pleased to order a yacht, with a sufficient convoy, to sail immediately to Willemstadt and attend your Royal Highness's orders; ... and upon your departure, it

is His Majesty's pleasure that you should leave the command of the British troops and those in the king's pay to the Earl of Dunmore, H.M. having great confidence in his Lordship's capacity to discharge that trust, and that you should likewise leave in Flanders General Hawley, and such other officers as you think proper.—Harrington to Cumberland, October 19.

Ere the receipt of this joyful news Cumberland had sent off the twelve remaining battalions of British infantry. (Cumberland to Harrington—his last despatch from Flanders—October 21). He followed on October 29. Three days later Marshal Königsegg set out for Vienna, leaving Prince Waldeck to conduct the debris of the allied army into winter quarters. Its strength was further reduced by orders recalling eighteen squadrons of British horse and dragoons, four companies of artillery, and the field-train, in quarters at Antwerp. (Harrington to the Earl of Dunmore, November 19 and 22). Lord Dunmore's command included little save the 6000 Hessians in British pay.

On November 11, he forwarded another report from the anonymous agent who had correctly gauged the extent to which France was prepared to go as fostering the Scottish rising. This man wrote from Liége, November 9:—

> Lord Clancarty's travelling companion, coming from France, where he had apparently left that nobleman, passed through this city on November 6. What a pity it is that no one has authority to follow these accomplices, to intercept them, or at least make capture of their despatches! I am convinced there are many mysteries to be unravelled. Such was the system adopted by Lord Stair during his ambassadorship in Paris, and the Court of St James often profited by his vigilance.
>
> ******
>
> Clancarty was one of a swarm of dissolute partisans who threw dust in their master's eyes and discredit on his cause with foreign courts.
>
> ******

Lord Dunmore added that the Hanoverian General, Ilten, described this emissary as "a fat little man of a fierce aspect, aged fifty." He contrived to reach England by way of Holland.

The new commander of a phantom British contingent was as impatient as his predecessor to quit a false position, and asked, rather querulously, for leave to return. (Dunmore to Harrington, December

10). At such a crisis, it was necessary to conciliate a Scottish peer. Lord Dunmore received the required permission, with a proviso that he must first superintend the embarkation of the 6000 Hessians for Leith. (Harrington to Dunmore, December 13, 1745).

Thus, ended a year as pregnant with disaster as the *Annus Mirabilis* sung by Dryden. Its annals record the most signal defeat ever inflicted upon a British army, a fruitless campaign, and the beginning of a civil war—of all calamities the most to be dreaded. Our consciousness of failure in the past, and of impotence in the face of coming trials, found expression in *A New Campaign*, published in September. (Campbell Maclachlan, W. A., Duke of Cumberland). After bewailing Fontenoy, the poetaster goes on:—

> *To veil the shame of this defeat*
> *Proceeding thence, she could but tell ye*
> *A tedious summer of retreat,*
> *Another action lost at Melle.*
> *But see, th' insulting Gallic bard,*
> *Of rough Dutch names exceeding fond,*
> *To Doornich (Tournai), adding Oudenarde,*
> *Ghent, Brugghen, (Bruges), Aelst, (Alost) and Dendermond.*
> *At last, most grating to our ears,*
> *Ere the campaign is at an end,*
> *The sudden sound outstrips our fears*
> *That tells the conquest of Ostend!*

CHAPTER 8

End of "The '45

Prince Charles Edward's attempt to oust the Hanoverian dynasty was a consequence of Fontenoy, and therefore an episode in the War of the Austrian Succession. The story of our country's part in that struggle is incomplete without a sketch of the Scottish rising, which sheds new light on the character of many actors in the greater drama, and has lessons of great value to the present generation.

In order to hoodwink Wade, who commanded 10,000 troops at Newcastle, the prince ostentatiously prepared to enter England by the east coast route. He led a division of his little army to Kelso, November 4. At the same time Lord George Murray made for Carlisle by the western road with artillery and baggage. Having thoroughly deceived the old marshal, Charles Edward quitted Kelso November 6, and three days later he joined forces with Murray near Carlisle. That city was invested on the morrow, and it surrendered after a five-days' siege, with great store of ammunition and supplies of all kinds.

Wade set out to relieve the garrison, but his army returned to Carlisle after floundering for some days in heavy snow. The Highlanders resumed their march on London, November 21, by way of Preston and Manchester. Here disillusion awaited them. They had been led to expect a warm welcome in England, but the populace everywhere looked askance at a movement which, in its eyes, was identified with absolutism and truckling to hereditary foes. At Manchester only 300 adherents joined the prince's banner, while the Tory squires of Yorkshire rose in arms against him. On reaching Macclesfield he learnt that the English army was dangerously close to his line of advance. Lord George Murray was, therefore, sent westwards with a portion of the invading army, as though Wales, not London, were the Jacobites' objective.

Meanwhile George II. and his ministers were straining every nerve to meet the crisis. As each regiment arrived from Flanders it was hurried into the Midlands, where an army was concentrating under Sir John Ligonier. On his breakdown, due to the strain of two campaigns in Flanders, he was replaced by the Duke of Cumberland, who reached headquarters at Lichfield, November 22. Three days later he detached Major-General Bland with a body of cavalry and Lord Sempill's regiment (25th Foot) to Newcastle-under-Lyme, in view of barring Lord George Murray's progress into Wales. On December 3 Cumberland pushed forward to Stone, in anticipation of the enemy's approach by the western route.

Murray's movement was but a feint, and its success surpassed his wildest hopes. Cumberland was as completely out manoeuvred as Wade had been. He concentrated at the very point desired by the invaders, and left the London road open to them. Having fulfilled his mission, Lord George rejoined the main body by a night march. Charles Edward's entire force slipped round the English right flank, and reached Derby, December 4, 1745.

When this master-stroke was reported to Cumberland at Stone, he recalled Bland's detachment and hurried southwards, in the hope of intercepting the Highlanders. On December 4 the rival forces were at Stafford and Derby; but Charles Edward was a day's march nearer London. His spirits rose with the news that Lord John Drummond's regiment and a few hundred Irishmen in the service of France had lauded at Montrose. Advices came, too, that 10,000 Frenchmen would soon be thrown on the east coast of England.

★★★★★★

News arrived that the rebels had given the duke the slip, and had got a day's march towards London; and soon afterwards a famous Jacobite squire, who, with great joy in his countenance, shook the landlord by the hand, saying, "All's our own, my boy; ten thousand honest Frenchmen are landed in Suffolk! Old England for ever! Ten thousand Frenchmen, my lad!"—Fielding, *Tom Jones*, bk. xi. chap. ii.

★★★★★★

The invaders' approach filled London with the direst panic. Every shop was closed, and a run on the Bank of England was stopped only by the stratagem of paying notes with sixpences. (The Chevalier de Johnstone, *Memoirs of the Rebellion*). But the cooler heads amongst Jacobite leaders saw that, as far as England was concerned, their game was up. Support promised from Wales and the southwest came not; and the Midlands were hostile, or at best indifferent. Their own forces did not reach 5000, while the enemy had three armies, each 10,000 strong, round London, at Stafford, and Newcastle. A council of war was convoked, and Lord George Murray's saner view of the situation prevailed over the young prince's optimism. A retreat was resolved upon with few dissentient voices, and on December 6 the little army turned its back on London with a heavy heart.

It was followed by Cumberland, who reached Coventry on the same day in a frantic effort to make up for lost time. On December 18, his cavalry came up with the Highlanders' rear-guard on Clifton Moor, beyond Shap. A night encounter took place, in which the pursuers lost 150 killed and wounded. They were handled so roughly that Cumberland halted perforce at Penrith for his infantry toiling in the rear. Thanks to Lord George Murray's vigilance, the retreat on Carlisle was accomplished at a cost of only 40 men. To linger in that stronghold was impossible with 20,000 foes within striking distance.

Charles Edward continued his retreat, leaving his tents and field-guns in the castle guarded by 400 Highlanders, who paid dearly for their leaders' folly in exposing them to certain destruction. He reached Glasgow after marching 580 miles in twenty-six days, and literally walking round two armies, each twice as strong as his own. From the unfriendly capital of Western Scotland, he moved northwards to Stirling, where he was joined by the Franco-Irish contingent, numbering 1200 men, and 3000 Highlanders. His army, now 9000 strong, laid siege to Stirling Castle, defended by stout-hearted old General Blakeney.

Cumberland had no difficulty in recapturing Carlisle. After wreaking vengeance on the hapless garrison, he posted to London and took command of a southern army mustering to repel the threatened French invasion. Sir John Hawley was appointed Commander-in-Chief in Scotland, and marched into Edinburgh at the head of 8000 men. This ruffian had a profound contempt for raw levies, which was common to generals of Marlborough's school, and a fixed idea that the Highlanders would not stand before a cavalry charge. Determining to raise the siege of Stirling, he marched, January 16, 1746, to Falkirk. Here he was joined by 1000 Argyll Campbells, bringing his force up to 8000 men. So confident was he that the rebels would not venture to attack him, that he rode off on the morrow to breakfast with Lady Kilmarnock at Callendar House.

After reviewing his army near Bannockburn, the Stuart prince announced his intention of attacking the English camp. His Highlanders mustered in silence, and took position on ground commanding it. Hawley returned to duty too late to retrieve the consequences of his neglect. He launched three dragoon regiments at a trot against the Scottish line. A volley, delivered at point-blank range, emptied many a saddle. Most of the horsemen promptly went about, and those who charged home were cut to pieces.

Then the victorious Highlanders turned their attention to the English infantry, already demoralised by their comrades' flight. In a few minutes the left and centre were driven pell-mell down the slope. On the right wing, however, Lieut.-General Howard's (The Buffs), Barrell's (4th Foot), Price's (14th), and Ligonier's (48th) were kept together by Major General Huske.

✶✶✶✶✶✶

John Huske (1692-1761) behaved gloriously at Dettingen as brigadier. In 1743 he became Major-General, and Colonel of the Royal Welsh Fusiliers. At Culloden he commanded the second line of foot. He was a brave, blunt veteran, whose sedulous care of his men won the affectionate nickname "Daddy Huske."

✶✶✶✶✶✶

Their fire took the Highlanders in flank and checked their pursuit. Darkness, with a storm of wind and rain, came at the nick of time, enabling Hawley's force to make their escape to Linlithgow. They left behind them baggage, tents, 7 out of 10 field guns, 400 killed, and about 100 prisoners. Among the dead was one who was mourned sincerely by both sides. Colonel Sir Robert Munro of Foulis, one of the heroes of Fontenoy, stood his ground when others gave way. Attacked by six clansmen, he wielded a half pike with such effect that two were killed ere he succumbed to numbers. Colonel Francis Ligonier was another victim of Hawley's incompetence. He died soon after Falkirk of exhaustion and pleurisy, leaving a reputation as unsullied as his brother's.

Not until the morrow did the Highlanders grasp the full extent of their victory. Then, instead of marching on Edinburgh, they wasted precious weeks in besieging Stirling Castle. Their engineer-in-chief was a Frenchman of Scottish extraction, whose patronymic, Mirabelle de Gordon, became "Mr Admirable" in the mouths of the deluded clansmen. He mounted siege guns at points where no cover was available, nor earth for filling fascines. General Blakeney saw that the besiegers were guileless of engineering craft, but knowing the importance of detaining them at Stirling, he made no sign until they opened fire. Then, with a few well-directed salvoes, he levelled their futile batteries to the ground.

★★★★★★

William Blakeney (1672-1761) was a Limerick man; served under William III. and Marlborough in Flanders, and became colonel of the Inniskilling regiment (37th Foot) in 1737; Governor of Minorca when it was besieged by Richelieu in 1756, but compelled to surrender after Admiral Byng's ineffectual attempt at succour. Public opinion always runs to extremes. Byng was greeted with a howl of indignation at home, and suffered an ignominious death. Blakeney was lauded to the skies, and George II. insisted on raising him to the Irish peerage. Walpole says that he came to court in a hackney carriage with a soldier behind it. "As he has not only lost his government, but was bedridden while it was losing, these honours are a little ridiculed." (See *Memoir of the Life of General W. Blakeney*. London and Dublin: 1757.)

★★★★★★

When news of Falkirk reached London, the Cabinet decided that Cumberland was the only man in England who was capable of dealing with such a crisis. He was no longer needed to cope with a French invasion. Sea-power was on our side, and the most pessimistic of King Georges advisers were convinced that Richelieu's transports would not venture from Dunkirk. The duke arrived at Edinburgh, January 30, 1746, and took over supreme command from crestfallen Hawley, whom he permitted to retain that of the cavalry. In thirty hours he was again in the saddle, eager to relieve the garrison of Stirling.

He arrived within sight of the fortress a day too late to fall on the besiegers. Charles Edward, finding the Castle impregnable, planned an advance on Edinburgh. But many of his followers had retreated to their homes, gorged with plunder, and the rest were discouraged by Mirabelle's failure. The chieftains unanimously insisted on retreating northwards, and their leader yielded after a dignified remonstrance. On February 1, his camp broke up with unnecessary haste, and the little army marched in two columns on Inverness.

Lord George Murray urged that a stand should be made in the Atholl country; and the English army might well have found a Thermopylae in its passes. He was overruled, and the clans, still 7000 strong, continued their retreat. Inverness was occupied, February 18, 1746, after slight resistance, and the succeeding weeks were given to capturing English posts as far as Blair-Atholl and the Spey. But the Hanoverian Government held their foes in the hollow of their hand. On the north and west Lord-President Forbes was mustering thousands on their side.

******

Duncan Forbes of Culloden (1685-1747) became President of the Court of Session in 1737. He was a patriot of the loftiest type. Devoted to the Hanoverian cause from a belief that its success made for his country's welfare, he invariably urged conciliation in dealings with the opposite faction. Hence he was regarded with unworthy suspicion by Cumberland's clique. His self-sacrifice met with such ingratitude that he died brokenhearted soon after the return of peace.

******

The 6000 Dutch auxiliaries were no longer available. They had belonged to the garrisons of Tournai and Termonde, and were thus precluded from serving against France or Spain. The arrival of French troops on the scene of action brought the capitulations into force, and the Dutchmen were repatriated. 6000 Hessians, however, had arrived at Leith from Flanders, under the Prince of Hesse-Philipsthal and Lord Crawford.

******

The State Papers (vol. xviii. F.O., Military Expeditions) contain a curious report from Colonel John Stewart, who was sent from London to superintend their embarkation at Willemstadt (December 26, 1745). They insisted on taking 8 chaises, 77 chariots, 11 waggons, 2384 horses, and baggage in a volume utterly beyond the transports' burden. How the problem was solved is not recorded.

******

They garrisoned Perth and Dunkeld, protecting Cumberland's rear. From the south-east that indefatigable leader was advancing to crush the handful of his father's enemies.

The duke wintered at Aberdeen, engaged in restoring discipline in his dejected forces. He had grasped the rationale of British defeat. His regulars, fettered by cumbrous equipment, were no match for the clansmen, who received bayonet-thrust on target and then wielded the terrible broadsword with crushing effect. Cumberland introduced a new drill of his own devising. Each soldier was taught to fix his attention not on the Highlander who had singled him out, but on that foeman's right-hand man, whose uplifted sword-arm left his right side defenceless. By this simple device he restored superiority to the bayonet. (Hill Burton, *History of Scotland*, vol. viii., chap. xcii.)

On April 8, 1746, the environs of Aberdeen were sufficiently clear of snow to warrant an advance. Cumberland reviewed his army in the order of battle which prevailed at Culloden. It mustered 15 weak line battalions, 7200 men all told; 3 dragoon regiments, including 900 sabres; and 600 Argyll Campbells. In the first line, under Lords Albemarle and Ancrum and Major-General Bland, stood the Royals (1st Foot), Cholmondeley's (34th), Price's (14th), Campbell's (21st), Monro's (37th), and Barrell's (4th).

The second line, commanded by Major-General Huske, included Howard's (The Buffs), Fleming's (36th Foot), Ligonier's (48th), Bligh's (20th), Lord Sempill's (25th), and Wolfe's (8th). A reserve, under Brigadier Mordaunt, of Pulteney's (13th Foot), Battereau's (disbanded in 1748), and Blakeney's (27th), formed in the rear. On the right flank were posted a squadron of Cobham's Dragoons (10th Hussars) and Kingston's Horse (disbanded); on the left, the remainder of Cobham's and Lord Mark Kerr's Dragoons (11th Hussars). The artillery mustered eighteen 3-pounders.

Cumberland halted at Nairn in his march on Inverness, April 15, and his birthday was celebrated by frugal libations.

> ½ Anchor of brandy to be given to each regiment of foot and to ye artillery as soon as possible. It is to be divided equally among ye men.—G. O., April 15, 1746. The "anker" was a Dutch liquid measure, now obsolete in this country, containing 7 to 9 gallons.

Charles Edward, meanwhile, assembled his 6000 clansmen and 1200 Franco Irish auxiliaries on Drumossie Moor, an upland five miles east of Inverness. Lord George Murray pleaded in vain for a position on the right bank of the Nairn, south of Drumossie, with mountainous country in the rear, and ground unsuitable to the formation of the order of battle so dear to the military heart. On April 15 scouts brought intelligence that the English Army was carousing at Nairn, twelve miles from the prince's position, and his evil genius prompted him to plan a night attack. It failed because it involved ten hours' work at a season when only seven of darkness could be reckoned on.

The Highlanders heard the reveille's ominous boom while they were still three miles from Nairn, and returned starving and spent with fatigue to their bivouac. There was still time for a retreat to the river Nairn, where they might have awaited reinforcements hastening from Badenoch. Murray's advice was once more rejected. The army clung to its position on Drumossie Moor until withdrawal was impossible.

At 11 a.m. on April 16, 1746, an alarm was given that the English Army was approaching. Frantic efforts were made to collect the scattered clansmen, many of whom had wandered as far as Inverness in search of food. The prince could muster no more than 5000 tired and hungry followers to encounter 9000 veteran troops, who were well fed and had enjoyed a good night's sleep.

Cumberland's address to his men ere they went into action was manly and inspiring. He invited all who were doubtful of their courage or the justice of his cause to quit the ranks, and assured them of his free pardon for so doing; for, he said:

> I had much rather be at the head of one thousand brave and resolute men than ten thousand among whom there are some who, by cowardice or misbehaviour, may dispirit or disorder the troops, and so bring dishonour and disgrace on any army under my command.—Ray, *History of the Rebellion.*

The simple tactics of Culloden have been too often described to need detailed notice in these pages. The battle commenced at 1 p.m., and was decided in less than an hour. On the Highland left three Macdonald regiments (Glengarry, Keppoch, and Clanranald) stood fast, because they had not been given the post of honour on the right, which had been theirs since Bannockburn. But the right and centre under Lord George Murray lost patience, and threw themselves on the English left. They penetrated the first line, but were stopped by a hail of bullets from the second.

The Highlanders' flank was protected by a wall, which was breached by the Argyll Campbells to admit a flank attack by Lord Mark Kerr's and Cobham's Dragoons. A simultaneous charge made by the English cavalry of the right wing completed the clansmen's rout. They retreated in two divisions. One body made for the mountains in good order with pipes playing. Another fled pell-mell towards Inverness, pursued by the dragoons, who burned to revenge their discomfiture at Prestonpans and Falkirk. According to Cumberland's official narrative—

Lord Ancrum was ordered to pursue with the horse as far as they could, and which he did with so good an effect that a considerable number were killed in the pursuit. As we were on our march to Inverness, and were near arrived there, Major-General Bland sent me the enclosed paper, (see note following), and I immediately received the French officers and soldiers as prisoners of war. Major-General Bland also made great slaughter, and gave quarter to none but about fifty French officers and soldiers he picked up in the pursuit. By the best calculations we can make, I think we may reckon the rebels lost 2000 men upon the field of battle and in the pursuit, as few of their wounded could get off. (Cumberland to the Duke of Newcastle, Inverness, April 18, 1746).

******

Note:—It was thus conceived:—

Inverness, April 16, 1746.
Sir,—The French officers and soldiers who were at Inverness surrender themselves prisoners to H.R.H. the Duke of Cumberland, and hope for everything that is to be expected from English generosity.
(Signed)   Cusack, Murphy, Le Marquis de Giles, Dehan, D'Obrian, Macdonald.

******

The Highland right wing suffered most severely. Of the 2000 clansmen who dashed against the English left, barely half survived. Cumberland lost only 310 in killed, wounded, and missing. He made 548 prisoners, including 222 French troops and Irish piquets, who had been most useful throughout the campaign.

Vae metis! was the cry at Inverness on the morrow of Culloden. General Orders directed—

A captain and fifty men to march immediately to the field of battle, and search all cottages in the neighbourhood for rebels. The officers and men will take notice that the publick orders given yesterday were to give us no quarter.

This bloodthirsty suggestion was founded on the following General Order, issued under the prince's instructions by Lord George Murray:—

Parole, Righ Shemuis.
It is his Royal Highness' positive orders that every person attach

himself to some corps of the army, and remain with that corps until the battle and pursuit be finally over, and to give no quarter to the Elector's troops on any account whatsoever.—Campbell Maclachlan, W.A., *Duke of Cumberland*; see also Wright, *Life of Wolfe*, chap. iv.

It must not be forgotten that the English Guards vowed, at starting from London, that they would neither give nor take quarter. (Horace Walpole to Mann, November 29, 1745). Such are the evil passions let loose by civil war.

No good purpose would be served by reviving the memory of reprisals which tarnished the victor's laurels, and branded him with the nickname "Butcher." Allowance must be made for his idiosyncrasies and the temper of his time.

★★★★★★

Ibid., August 1746: "It was lately proposed in the City to present him with the freedom of some Company. One of the aldermen said aloud, 'Then let it be of the Butchers'."

Byron, *Don Juan, canto* i., "The Butcher Cumberland."

★★★★★★

Cumberland was, as we have seen, a strict disciplinarian, and his choler was raised to white heat by insubordination in any form. Filial love, his own dynastic interests, forbade him to extend mercy to rebels. And there was a strain of hardness in the eighteenth-century heart which is unintelligible to a generation imbued with humanitarian dogmas. The criminal law of 1746 was written in letters of blood. Our ancestors implored Divine mercy on "all prisoners and captives," but they showed none whatever. Within half a mile of the seat of civic revelries stood Newgate, an earthly hell: the populace delighted in cruel sports, and still more barbarous punishments. Let us be thankful that we live in a gentler age, and fall not into the common error of judging characters that belong to history by canons of which they had not the remotest conception!

It is quite certain that the young duke was credited with many atrocities which were the work of his subordinates. A hideous story is retailed by Chambers, (*History of the Rebellion*), to the effect that Cumberland ordered James Wolfe to pistol a wounded Highlander who stared at him insolently. It is branded as a libel by the concluding sentence, which affirms that Wolfe lost his chiefs favour by refusing to stain his hands with so odious a crime. Now, we have unimpeachable evidence that the future hero of Quebec enjoyed Cumberland's friendship long after Culloden. In 1750 he wrote—

> If ever he (the duke) commands the army of this country in its defence, I shall wish to be with him, and glad to contribute something to his success. (Wright, *Life of Wolfe*, chap. viii.)

And again—

> If I don't keep a good watch on myself, I must be a little vain, for the duke has of late given me such peculiar marks of his esteem and confidence that I am ashamed not to deserve it better.—*Ibid.*, chap. xiv.

As a matter of fact, Wolfe was not Cumberland's *aide-de-camp* during the Scottish campaign, but Hawley's. That ruffian was perfectly capable of ordering a helpless prisoner to be slaughtered in cold blood; and he was at the bottom of those outrages which give Culloden so sinister a ring in modern ears. Equally groundless are the charges of rioting and wantonness preferred by Chambers.

> Duke William and his myrmidons . . . spent their time in a round of festivities, . . . and their camp exhibited all the coarse and obstreperous revelries of an English fair.—*History of the Rebellion.*

Thus writes the historian of the Scottish rising, and he adds more revolting details. Cumberland's General Orders prove that the high standard of discipline maintained in Flanders was in nowise relaxed:—

> *Inverness, April 19.* It is H.R.H. orders yet no man go above a quarter of a mile out of camp, several outrages and disorders having been committed which he will not permit on any account.
>
> *April 21.* The men of Pulteney's, and one of Campbell's Argyleshire men, confined for plundering, are to be sent to the Provost and tryed by general court-martial tomorrow morning.

On May 5 Roger Weigh, of Wolfe's regiment, was sentenced to receive "1200 lashes at the head of each brigade at five different times for morauding and stealing of meal," and terrible floggings were administered on the same day to seven other culprits convicted of similar offences. Superior officers were, indeed, excepted from the inhibition of plundering. Hawley swept the house he occupied at Aberdeen of all its contents, worth £600, and sent them by sea to London!

Cumberland's orders, however, display his invariable regard for good order and the comfort of his troops. Gaming and horse-stealing were rigorously repressed; nor were religious observances a dead-letter:—

> *Inverness, April 19.* Divine service tomorrow in camp, at 10 o'clock, and thanksgiving for the defeat of ye Rebells. All officers and soldiers to attend. Divine service at H.R.H. quarters tomorrow at 12.

Culloden rang out the death-knell of the Stuart cause. Lord George Murray, who was its mainstay, resigned his commission as Lieutenant-General, telling his young chief some unpalatable home-truths. In his opinion the expedition should not have been undertaken without more definite pledges of assistance from France, and the choice of a battlefield at Culloden was a "fatal" one. After five months of wanderings, which form one of the most thrilling pages in history, Charles Edward boarded a French vessel on Loch Nanagh, and landed September 20, 1746, at Roscoff, near Morlaix.

The genius of Sir Walter Scott has invested "the '45" with a glamour which obscures its practical lessons from the present generation. Sir Alexander Tulloch asks pertinently—

> Should not the last invasion of England be a warning to those who consider an army unnecessary except for the protection of naval bases and attacks on other countries? The Highlanders' march southwards was no mere raid by a handful of mounted men. The little army had an ample amount of field-artillery and a complete baggage train, carrying even tents to lessen the speed of its advance; and yet, in spite of such drawbacks to rapid movement, it arrived within six marches of the capital.
> If a hostile force ever does land on the English coast, the objective point will be the same—*viz.*, London; but the length of the march would not be one-quarter of what the Highlanders accomplished in the teeth of two opposing armies, each double their strength. With the Highlanders the capture of London would only have been the commencement of the great work in view—the restoration of the Stuarts. In the present day the seizure of the heart of the empire would be a catastrophe which is startling even to think of.—Tulloch, *Culloden and the '45.*

The reaction in London from Black Friday was extreme. All England burst into a blaze of loyalty, and Cumberland was hailed as his country's saviour.

✶✶✶✶✶✶

So in the chapel of old Ely House,
When wandering Charles, who meant to be the third,
Had fled from William, and the news was fresh,
The simple clerk, but loyal, did announce,
And eke did roar right merrily two staves,
Sung to the praise and glory of King George.
—Cowper, *The Task*, vi.

✶✶✶✶✶✶

British gratitude generally assumes a material shape. The faithful Commons voted him a perpetual pension of £25,000, bringing his appanage up to £40,000 a-year. Like greater generals, he was destined to experience the fickleness of public opinion:—

> His popularity ended with the Rebellion: his services were forgot, and he became the object of fear and jealousy. The severe treatment of Scotland after the defeat of the rebels was imputed to his cruel and sanguinary disposition; even the army had been taught to complain of the unnecessary strictness of his discipline—that they were treated rather like Germans than Englishmen. All his good qualities were overlooked, false facts were adduced against him, and false conclusions drawn from them.—Waldegrave, *Memoirs*, 1754-58.

British influence on the Continent was paralysed by the Scottish revolt, and Marshal Saxe was able to undertake a winter campaign which astonished Europe. He spent Christmas at Ghent in the wildest revelry. Nightly performances were given by Favart of the Opéra Comique, whose troupe always followed Saxe's headquarters; and the encounters of fighting-cocks, imported from England, were nearly as popular. Graver business began in 1746. On January 30 Brussels was invested, in the teeth of an unbroken army under Prince Waldeck at Malines. It capitulated after a three weeks' siege—the garrison, 15,000 strong, becoming prisoners of war. Then Vilvorden was captured, with the whole Dutch field artillery and immense magazines for supplying the allied army.

Saxe received another ovation on returning from this brilliant campaign (March 11). Louis XV. embraced and kissed him at an audience.

He was given the life enjoyment of Chambord. That grandest of royal demesnes was built by Francis I. at a time when medieval gloom was pierced by the blaze of the exuberant Renascence. Its massive central keep is encrusted with domes, pinnacles, and all that fancy and colour could suggest. Chambord realises Rabelais' Abbey of Thelema—

> In its exterior—unity, the solemn harmony of towers, their belfries and chimneys fashioned like oriental minarets, grouped round a central *donjon*.

Chambord was completely furnished from the royal stores; and Saxe had amassed sufficient wealth by the sale of passes in Flanders, (Barbier, *Journal*, vol. ii.), to resuscitate the pristine glories of his new domain. He took possession in April 1, and revelled in its many beauties for a fortnight ere rejoining his headquarters at Brussels.

Popular gratitude took a form which was peculiarly French, and proved embarrassing to its object. The French Pepys records that on March 18, 1746, Lulli's *Armide* was rendered at the Paris Opera to a crowded house. On Saxe's appearance in the balcony, a tempest of clapping and shouts, "*Vive M. de Saxe!*" broke out, which he acknowledged by bowing, right and left. The general enthusiasm infected the court faction opposed to Saxe. Madame de la Rocheguyon, a great lady allied to the Prince de Conti, sent him word that if usage permitted her sex to clap, she would be the first thus to express her sense of his great services. *Armide* was composed in honour of Louis XIV. In the prologue "Glory" appears, bearing a crown of laurels, and singing—

> *Everything on earth must yield*
> *To the august hero whom I love.*

After declaiming these words Mlle. Metz, who personified Glory, presented her laurel crown to Saxe. He seemed much surprised, and declined the tribute with many bows. But the Duc de Biron took the laurels from Glory's hands and placed them on Saxe's left arm. This graceful act was the signal for a fresh outburst of applause. (Barbier, *Journal*, vol. ii. Mlle. Metz received from Saxe a pair of earrings worth £500.

Soon the horizon darkened. George II. vowed vengeance on France for her support of the Jacobite rising, and opposition in Parliament was stifled by the prestige gained at Culloden. Peace was rendered still more remote by a Cabinet crisis. George II. hankered after his old favourite Granville, and brought him back to office at the cost of the Pelhams' resignation. The new Secretary of State found his position untenable in the Cabinet and Parliament alike.

After holding it for three days he resigned the Seals, forcing his master to humble himself and seek the Pelhams' aid. They returned to power, bringing with them William Pitt as Paymaster of the Land Forces. From that moment matters proceeded smoothly enough. Supplies were granted of nearly £9,500,000 to continue the war. Maria Theresa's subsidy was raised to £433,000, and smaller sums were doled out to a horde of German princes who sent contingents to an army assembling in Bohemia under Prince Charles of Lorraine.

Louis XV. was content with his gains in Flanders; and the election of Francis I. destroyed his real or fancied interests in Germany. He again made overtures for peace to Maria Theresa. The high-spirited empress refused to sheathe the sword, and Prince Charles of Lorraine led 50,000 Austrians across the Rhine. Saxe was once more the only hope of his adopted country. He was appointed *generalissimo*, and given a free hand in the ensuing campaign.

Its first-fruits were the citadel of Antwerp, which surrendered on May 31. No interference was attempted by Prince Waldeck. He retreated to Breda, formed an entrenched camp, and sought to join hands with Prince Charles, who had advanced to the right bank of the Meuse. Reinforcements poured in. The 6000 Hessian mercenaries who had assisted in pacifying Scotland and 13,000 Hanoverians reached Breda during May. Towards the end of June Sir John Ligonier brought a British contingent of six line regiments and four of cavalry.

******

The only existing corps which I have been able to trace are the Royal Scots Greys, Inniskilling Dragoons, and 7th (Queen's Own) Hussars, the Devonshire, Somersetshire Light Infantry, and Yorkshire regiments.

******

Waldeck now had 50,000 men available for field operations, and an equal force of Austrians were encamped within four days' march of Breda. With capable generalship the Allies' might have checked Saxe's victorious career. They remained quiescent, while Mons was captured (July 10). After the two armies, had effected a junction at Eindhoven, they allowed the French to take Namur (September 19) without striking a blow.

******

A miserable attempt to create a diversion on the French coast is unworthy of notice in the text. A squadron sailed from Portsmouth August 5, ostensibly for North America, but landed troops under General St Clair near the French East India Company's depot at Lorient. Those who wish to plumb the depths of our ignorance of warfare in 1746 are referred to Beatson's *Naval, &c, Memoirs*, vol. i., and Burton's *Life of Hume*, vol. i. chap. v. Versailles was greatly perturbed by this ridiculous raid, and Saxe received orders to make a detachment to the coast of Brittany, which did not reach him till after the Battle of Rocoux. This gross miscarriage was eclipsed by the fate of a French expedition under the Duc d'Anville, which sailed from Brest, June 22, to recapture Louisbourg. It returned to France after suffering fearful loss from preventable diseases.

******

Saxe was urged by "carpet generals" to end the war by a pitched battle. He laid bare the most secret springs of his action in a letter addressed to Louis XV. from his headquarters at Tongres:—

I have held Prince Charles, who is encamped within cannon-shot of this position; indeed, we are separated by a stream. However, I do not believe that he will attack me, and think I have effected a good deal in forcing him to abandon Namur to us without committing myself to a battle, whose issue is always doubtful when one cannot rely on the discipline of one's troops. The French are what they were in Caesar's day, and all that he depicts them—excessively brave, but inconstant.

They fight to the last man in a position after a first assault upon it has failed; and delight in outpost affairs, if only they can be kept together for the first few moments. They do not show well in manoeuvring on open ground. I must, therefore, be very circumspect in my dispositions. The private soldier is quick to recognise an advantageous post, and shows satisfaction by his gaiety and sallies. But your Majesty may consider this method of warfare wanting in dash. I am not the man to follow it in every conceivable case. Next campaign will, perhaps, give me an opportunity of changing it. Let us take one or two more strongholds, in order to safeguard our rear, subsistence, and convoys.—Marshal Saxe to Louis XV., undated: Pajol, *Les Guerres sous Louis XV*, vol. iii.

The time was at length propitious for one of those brilliant exploits in which the French soldier delighted. It was the Allies' purpose to winter in Liége and the Walloon country, Saxe's to dislodge and drive them across the frontier. Prince Charles and Waldeck crossed the River Meuse, in view of holding Liége without venturing too far from Maastricht. On October 10, their army encamped in two lines on a range of hills overlooking Liége, which were densely wooded and much broken by ravines. Ligonier's 24,000 British, Hanoverians, and Hessians formed the centre, covered by the villages of Rocoux, Voroux, and Liers. The right wing consisted of 49,000 Austrians under Prince Charles of Lorraine and Count Batthyani.

The left wing, of 24,000 Dutch troops, commanded by Prince Waldeck, extended from the village of Ans to Liége. Every hamlet covering their front was entrenched, while three batteries on the heights took Rocoux and Ans in flank. The Allies' position seemed at first blush very formidable, but Saxe was not slow to recognise its defects. With a front inordinately prolonged, it was not deep enough. Moreover, inequalities of ground prevented co-operation between the wings or succour from reserves. His plans were quickly formed. They were to attack the Allies' left and centre in great force, and to keep their right wing motionless, in a situation which forbade the Austrians to assist their comrades or pursue his own army in case of a reverse.

******

After completing his arrangements Saxe sent for Favart, who directed his opera company, and thus addressed him: "I am going to entrust you with a secret which you must keep faithfully tonight. It is my intention to offer battle tomorrow, but no one suspects it. After the performance, this evening you will give out that the theatre will be closed tomorrow on account of victory. . . . Go and put what I have told you into eight or ten verses—not more—which your charming wife will sing to some military tune."

The house was packed that night, and instead of the usual orders of the day, Mme. Favart announced a battle and victory in eight doggerel lines. Saxe was not present, but he said to D'Espagnac, "We shall win a victory, for the human heart is concerned! Powder and bullets tomorrow! Goodnight."—*Théâtre du Maréchal Saxe en Belgique*, 1748; quoted by Pajol, vol. iii.

******

On October 11, 1746, Saxe pushed reconnaissances in force towards the Allies' left, and thus learnt all he wished to know regarding their position. Its keys were Ans on the left, and Liers, Rocoux, and Voroux in the centre. At 3 p.m. D'Estrées and the Comte de Clermont led 4 brigades against Ans and the adjacent suburb of Liége, which they carried at the bayonet's point. The Allies' left was turned. Meanwhile Saxe was massing 12 brigades for an onslaught on Liers, Rocoux, and Voroux, held by 12 battalions of British, Hanoverians, and Hessians. This should have been delivered simultaneously with the left attack. It was delayed by Clermont-Gallerande's insubordination. He had orders to lead 3 brigades against Liers, but kept them halted in the rear.

> Saxe sent him five or six *aides-de-camp* in succession without result. At last Clermont-Gallerande went himself to the marshal to proffer some excuse. The latter refused to see or hear him until he was in possession of Liers. He returned at a foot's pace to his brigades, but finally attacked. (Barbier, *Journal*, vol. ii.)

At 3.30 the 12 brigades charged forward in three columns. They recoiled under a fearful fire from small-arms and artillery loaded with musket-ball. Saxe was cool, and even jocular, while bullets were flying thick as hail. Animated by so splendid an example, his troops sprang forward once more. At 4.30 Rocoux and Voroux were carried by sheer weight of numbers; and Liers, pulverised by artillery-fire, was perforce evacuated. Thus the Allies' centre was pierced. D'Estrées' brigades appeared on the heights of Vottem, commanding their left. A general retreat was begun by the Dutch and a few thousand renegade Bavarians who had joined them just before the engagement.

The British, Hanoverians, and Hessians were drawn into the vortex of flight. The whole mass streamed across the Meuse by three pontoon bridges at Visé, leaving Saxe master of the field. But for the approach of night, the centre and left would have been cut to pieces. While their comrades were struggling desperately against tremendous odds, the 50,000 Austrians were kept inactive by intervening valleys and an equal French force, which watched their every movement. They retired in good order on Maastricht. The Allies' losses were comparatively small. Accurate statistics are not available, for an unknown number of Bavarians were drowned in the Meuse. The whole casualties were between 4500 and 5000. Those of the French were 3518 in killed, wounded, and missing.

Rocoux was an infantry battle, for the ground was quite unsuited to cavalry manoeuvres. The glory of an heroic defence rests with the British, Hanoverian, and Hessian battalions. On the French side, Marshal Saxe bore off the palm for his well-planned scheme of attack and the brilliant personal courage which he displayed in executing it. While numbers and gallantry on either part were equal, his strategy and tactics turned the scale. On the following day Sir John Ligonier wrote—

> I think this affair, to give it the right name, cannot be called a battle, for I question whether a third of the army was engaged.—Ligonier to the Earl of Sandwich, October 12, 1746.

These words are an unconscious condemnation of his colleagues' generalship. After this disastrous termination of their third campaign in Flanders, the Allies' sought winter quarters, Breda being occupied by the British contingent. Saxe hastened to the court at Fontainebleau, in order to rebut charges brought against him by the Prince de Conti. This haughty scion of the royal family had shown some ability as a general, and captured Charleroi, August 2, 1746.

After this exploit he joined forces with Saxe. At a council of war he raised his voice in favour of an immediate pitched battle. Finding Saxe of a different opinion, he exclaimed that, as a lieutenant-general and prince of the blood, he would receive orders from no one! His antagonist invoked his own authority as *generalissimo*, and both parties referred their dispute to the king's decision. The result was a moral victory for the hero of Rocoux. While Conti's wounded pride was salved by the empty title of Commander-in-Chief, Saxe was permitted by royal edict to style himself "Most Serene Highness," and was presented with six captured guns to grace Chambord. Public opinion, too, was on his side. Barbier writes:

> We all know the marshal has almost the whole court against him from base jealousy. . . . Everyone blamed the Prince de Conti. A young man of twenty-eight should have deemed it an honour to sit at the feet of a past master in the art of war.—*Journal,* vol. ii.

France fondly hoped that peace would be secured by this glorious campaign; but George II. and Maria Theresa were bent on continuing a bootless struggle. Supplies amounting to £9,325,253 were granted by Parliament, and the system of lavishing British gold that German princes might fight their own battles was again adopted. In his speech from the throne, November 18, 1746, King George declared:

> It shall be my particular care to exert our strength at sea in the most effectual manner.

The nation's spirit, downcast by so many reverses, rejoiced to learn that Great Britain was at length to bestir herself on an element which was hers by birth-right. Nor was the royal pledge unfulfilled. A newborn energy was seen at the Admiralty, which was governed with wholesome despotism by George Anson, and William Pitt inspired a measure of his own ardent soul into every branch of the administration.

✶✶✶✶✶✶

The career of Vice-Admiral George Anson (1697-1762) proves the immense influence of those occult forces which we term "luck" upon human affairs. In 1740 he commanded a buccaneering expedition against the Spanish settlements, which does not come within the scope of this work. Suffice it to say that, after circumnavigating the globe, he returned in the *Centurion*—sole survivor of six vessels that started—on June 15, 1744. On reaching St Helens he learnt that he had traversed a French squadron during a dense fog! His booty, valued at a million and a quarter, was carried through London streets in thirty-two waggons decked with flags. See his *Voyage Round the World*, 1748, and *Life*, by Sir George Barrow, 1839.

✶✶✶✶✶✶

Too late in the day did Louis XV. give some attention to his neglected navy. In the spring of 1747 two squadrons were fitted out at Brest under the Marquis de la Jonquière. The one was destined to complete the conquest of British possessions in India, the other to recapture Louisbourg. They were to sail in company until the danger zone was passed.

Our Admiralty's intelligence had been reorganised by Anson, and no movement in French ports escaped its notice. When a cruiser brought news of the intended expeditions Anson, and Warren of Louisbourg fame, left Spithead to intercept them with seventeen sail-of-the-line and a cloud of smaller vessels.

They cruised off Finisterre until May 14, 1747, when thirty-eight French sail were signalled steering S.W. Only ten were line-of-battle ships, the rest frigates and armed Indiamen. Anson hoisted the signal for line of battle; but Warren's acuter instinct told him that the enemy would attempt to escape. He boarded the flagship and persuaded the vice-admiral to substitute a signal for a general chase. The Frenchmen were soon overhauled, and after a gallant struggle with overwhelming odds against them, six of their men of war were captured.

******

The revolution wrought in our navy since 1744 was evidenced by an anecdote to be found in Beatson's *Naval Memoirs*. When the *Bristol* began to engage the *Invincible*, Captain Fincher of the *Pembroke* hailed the *Bristol* and requested Captain Montagu to put his helm astarboard or the *Pembroke* would run foul of him. To this Montagu replied, "Run foul of me and be d——d; neither you nor any man in the world shall come between me and my enemy!"—(Vol. i.) *L'Invincible* and *La Gloire* were among our prizes. A better-known story records the neat epigram perpetrated by La Jonquière when he handed his sword to Anson—*Vous avez vaincu l'Invincible, et la Gloire suit.*

******

The same fate attended four Indiamen, but La Jonquiere's resistance enabled most of his convoy to regain port. Great capital was made out of this success by the Ministry. Anson received the king's personal thanks and a peerage; Warren was made a Knight of the Bath.

La Jonquière's defeat had more momentous consequences than any episode of the war. It was an important link in the chain of events which wrested India from French hands to place it in our own. In 1741 the Peninsula was still nominally subject to the *Padisha* of Delhi; but his feudatories had thrown off active allegiance and carved out kingdoms for themselves. The French and English East India Companies occupied factories by sufferance, where European cloth, cutlery, and gewgaws were exchanged for silks and muslins from Indian looms. Calcutta was our chief commercial centre in the Gangetic Delta.

It was overshadowed by Chandernagore, on an upper reach of the River Hughli. On the Coromandel coast we had established ourselves at Madras, Fort St David, and Cuddalore; but our rivals showed far greater activity at Pondicherry. Chandernagore was the creation of Jean François Dupleix (16971763). This extraordinary man was the son of a director of the East India Company; but paternal wealth alone would not have made him dictator of French India. He was versed in all the arts of administration and diplomacy. His intellect was subtle and far-seeing; his energy proof against any discouragement. And Dupleix had qualities of heart which placed him on a loftier pedestal. He was noble, sympathetic, and generous; incapable of jealousy or envy.

On assuming charge of Chandernagore in 1731, he found the settlement at its lowest ebb. Some small craft pursued a languid trade with Europe, often sailing half-loaded. Dupleix grasped the advantages of extending commerce to other Indian ports and the China seas. He dedicated a considerable private fortune to developing the "country trade," as it was afterwards styled. So successful was the new departure that in less than a decade Chandernagore owned seventy large ships, which plied between India, China, and Arabia.

In 1741 he became Governor General of French India, and removed to Pondicherry. Dupleix had sounded the depths of the oriental heart. Knowing that it was to be won by a stiff upper lip and external magnificence, he declared himself to be the Great Mughal's *Nawab*, entitled to a retinue of 4500 horse. Never was there a time when a strong hand was more sorely needed at the helm.

Native princes tolerated the foreign adventurers by reason of the wealth which they brought into the country, but despised them as representatives of an unwarlike calling. Southern India was seething with anarchy. Anwaruddin, *Nawab* of the Carnatic, occupied the hinterland, and defied the moribund dynasty of Delhi. At this crisis Dupleix learnt that hostilities between Great Britain and France were imminent. With the news, however, came a fatuous despatch (September 18, 1743) enjoining him to halve expenditure, and, above all, to reduce his outlay on fortifications.

These orders were boldly disregarded by the governor-general, who lavished his personal fortune on strengthening Pondicherry. He appealed for help to the *Nawab* of the Carnatic, who informed the British authorities at Madras that he would not allow an attack on their rivals. Dupleix was not satisfied with this negative advantage. He sent the only ship at his disposal to implore succour from the Isle of France. In this dependency, now styled Mauritius, and Bourbon (Réunion) France possessed stations for commerce and privateering midway between Europe and India, while Great Britain had no ports of call. They were ruled by a man as remarkable as Dupleix.

Bertrand François Mahé de Labourdonnais (1699-1753) began life as a common sailor, and worked his way upwards by sheer merit. In 1735 he was appointed Governor of the Isle of France and Bourbon. After seven years of highly successful administration he returned to Paris on leave, and gained Cardinal Fleury's ear. So convincing was his eloquence that the French Government was induced to fit out five sail-of-the-line in view of trying issues with their British rivals in the Far East. But the purblind East India Company took alarm. They were only merchants, forsooth; why should they not preserve neutrality in India?

These half-hearted counsels chimed in with Fleury's natural timidity. The expedition was countermanded, and a unique opportunity was lost of asserting French supremacy. Labourdonnais returned to his charge in mute despair. He none the less responded to the appeal from Pondicherry, threatened by an English fleet. There was but one king's ship at Port Louis. Labourdonnais impressed every trading vessel that came into harbour; stripped his batteries to arm them; trained Indians, and *Caffres* from Madagascar, in musketry and handling great guns. In a few months eight vessels partially armed sailed from Port Louis under Labourdonnais' command. On gaining the Coromandel coast he beat off an English squadron more heavily armed than his own, and on July 1746 he relieved Pondicherry.

France now possessed two men of genius at the capital of her nascent empire. Their energy, patriotism, and capacity were equal. Dupleix was an accomplished administrator. Labourdonnais thrilled with a sense of power; he was an accomplished seaman, and accustomed to command. Friction is often produced by the contact of men of action. Colonel Malleson wrote in 1868:

> We have seen in our day, how blind to all perceptions of right, how oblivious even of the ordinary obligations of politeness, how open to the malignant suggestions of whisperers and sycophants, wounded vanity will make even those who in other respects soar far above their fellow-men."

******

History of the French in India. Malleson alluded to an ignoble dispute which convulsed the Indian Olympus in 1866. Sir William Mansfield, Commander in Chief, accused a subordinate of stealing his stores of jam and pickles. Sides were taken by his colleagues, and the "Simla Scandal" assumed portentous dimensions. My readers may recall a more recent instance.

******

At first relations between the two strong men were cordial enough. Both agreed that Madras must be attacked. Labourdonnais was appointed to command an expedition against the English settlement, and Dupleix supplied all his requirements with alacrity. Then a rift in the lute appeared. Labourdonnais seemed to be hypnotised by his colleague's presence. He delayed sailing until the Pondicherry council lost patience. Peremptory orders were given him either to start for Madras or yield command to a junior officer.

The English settlement could offer no effective defence. Governor Morse was immersed in his ledgers, and incapable of breaking the bonds of routine. The fortifications had been neglected, and barely two-thirds of a garrison of 300 were fit for duty. Despite his weakness, Morse rejected overtures for neutrality from Dupleix on the score that he was without instructions on the subject from home. This refusal sealed the fate of Madras. On August 15, 1746, a French squadron appeared in the roads; Labourdonnais landed troops, September 3, mounted batteries, and cannonaded Fort St George from his ships. On September 21 Morse hung out the white flag.

The *Nawab* of the Carnatic now called to mind his pledges. He threatened armed intervention unless the French relinquished their prize. Dupleix evaded it by informing the indignant prince that he had conquered Madras on his behalf, and would transfer the settlement to him when its surrender was completed. Meanwhile the future of Madras was eagerly discussed between Labourdonnais and the English council. There were three possible methods of dealing with it. Madras might be proclaimed a French colony. This idea did not commend itself to Labourdonnais.

Another port within half-a-day's sail of Pondicherry was unnecessary; and then Madras would probably be restored at a general peace. It might be razed to the ground—but a hundred sites as suitable for commerce were available on the Coromandel coast. Nothing could prevent the English from establishing themselves elsewhere at a smaller cost than the amount of ransom which they were perfectly willing to give for Madras. The third expedient was preferred. Labourdonnais and Morse agreed in principle that the settlement should be restored for a payment of £440,000.

Dupleix and his council had acknowledged Labourdonnais' exploit by a vote of thanks, and the conqueror had attributed his success to Dupleix's care in meeting all his requisitions for men and material. Now arose a conflict of interests and ideals which destroyed all semblance of amity. Dupleix hated the English with a fervour bred of half a century's competition for the Indian trade, and was loath to relinquish a chance of dealing them a mortal blow. The fall of Madras would bring about that of Fort St David. The destruction of Calcutta was a necessary sequence, and his own creation, Chandernagore, would be sole mistress of trade in the Gangetic Delta.

The Pondicherry council, therefore, scouted the suggestion that Madras should be ransomed. This rebuff prompted Labourdonnais to throw down the gauntlet. He concluded a treaty with the English council, which provided for the restoration of Madras in return for bills of exchange on London amounting to £440,000. At the same time, he stipulated for a personal "gratification" of £40,000.

This transaction places Labourdonnais on a lower moral plane than his colleague; but it does not lie with Englishmen to judge him too severely. The founders of our empire in the East were by no means insensible to the attractions of lucre. Clive's extortions after Plassey exceeded Labourdonnais' wildest dreams. The vitals of India were preyed upon by Barwell, Verelst, and their fellows. Warren Hastings himself stooped to fish in troubled waters through the agency of a native agent. The fearful famine which ravaged Bengal in 1770 was due in part to a "corner" in grain contrived by Europeans in high places.

On October 11, 1746, Labourdonnais sent an unsigned treaty in the terms arranged to the Pondicherry council for ratification; while he, somewhat inconsistently, asserted his independence of that body. Dupleix asserted his claim to supreme command by despatching a commission to Madras, with instructions to form a council for administering the new acquisition. Labourdonnais placed them under arrest and continued his negotiation with Morse. But while he carried matters with a high hand, he had serious qualms for the immediate future. The stormy season was approaching. It was unsafe to keep his squadron in open roads, while self-interest forbade him to quit Madras until the treaty was ratified. He condescended to flatter the man whose authority he had set at nought, and implored his approval of the treaty provided that its execution was deferred until the following spring.

Dupleix was inclined to temporise; but at this critical moment his hands were strengthened by the arrival of three French warships. Labourdonnais was informed that he had a deliberative voice in the Pondicherry council, but must obey its behests. His reply was the execution of a treaty (October 12, 1746) by which he bound himself to retrocede Madras in three days on payment of the stipulated ransom.

On the morrow his worst anticipations were realised. A terrific cyclone swept the coast, and three of his vessels foundered with 1200 souls on board. Labourdonnais sent his treaty to Pondicherry, with an intimation that he would hold the council jointly and severally liable for its execution. Then he busied himself with characteristic energy in repairing his damaged squadron. When all was ready he boarded the flagship in a storm and set sail for the Isle of France without touching at Pondicherry.

Among the reasons urged by Dupleix for refusing to sanction the restoration of Madras was the pledge which he had given to the *Nawab* of the Carnatic. Anwar-ud-din pressed for its fulfilment, emphasising his claim with an army of 10,000 horsemen. The governor-general was placed in a sore dilemma. If he delivered Madras intact to the *Nawab*, how could he prevent its sale to the English? To destroy its defences under the very eyes of the *Nawab's* forces was to excite his indignation.

Hitherto the native princes had arrogated a superiority over the foreign merchants who traded with their subjects which no one dreamt of contesting. It was a fundamental maxim with both East India Companies to avoid hostility with rulers of the land at any cost. After anxious deliberation, Dupleix instructed his council at Madras to keep the French flag flying, without risking a collision. Thereon the *Nawab's* army advanced to the suburb of St Thomé and attempted to establish a blockade. This step was too much for the patience of Paradis, an able Swiss officer who commanded the French garrison.

On November 4, 1746, he attacked the native horde with 1000 troops, of whom 230 only were Europeans. The result was a foretaste of Plassey. Anwar-ud-din's horsemen were unable to face a disciplined force barely a tenth of their strength. The proud edifice of Mughal might proved to be a house of cards. The foreign adventurers who had sued humbly for a share of India's commerce became predominant factors in the struggle for hegemony. The foundations of our empire in the East were laid at St Thomé. Dupleix gauged the new situation at a glance. Labourdonnais' treaty had been publicly disavowed. He now asserted that Madras was a French possession by right of conquest, and named Paradis as governor. Treasure and public stores of all descriptions were confiscated, and English residents who refused allegiance to the King of France were deported to Pondicherry as prisoners of war. These arbitrary measures elicited a remonstrance from the sufferers, and among the signatories was Ensign Robert Clive.

French prestige in India was exalted by this master-stroke. Anwar-ud-din executed a treaty which confirmed the French in the possession of their new territory, and ratified it during a State visit to Pondicherry. Dupleix might now have laid foundations firm and strong for a French empire in the south. Had Paradis been charged with expeditions to reduce Fort St David and Cuddalore, nothing could have saved the last strongholds of British power. Our naval force in Indian waters was at its lowest ebb, and Calcutta itself could not have held out for long. The claims of seniority, however, outweighed those of common-sense. The attacks on Fort St David and Cuddalore were intrusted to incompetent men, and invaluable months were lost by their failure. Great Britain's sea power was established by Anson's victory off Finisterre. Warships flocked to the Coromandel coast, and our remaining settlements defied attack.

At this crisis in India's fortunes the British Cabinet were striving to roll back the tide of victory in Flanders. Cumberland was despatched to The Hague with full power to treat for Dutch support. So well did he succeed that a convention was signed in January 1747, by which Holland undertook to furnish 40,000 men for a new campaign, and to pay two-thirds of its cost. Great Britain promised 13,800, Hanover 16,400, Austria 60,000. The allied army—on paper—reached a total of 130,000, but only 112,000 concentrated in February at Breda. Cumberland again enjoyed the empty title of Commander-in-Chief, while the Dutch and Austrian contingents were controlled by Prince Waldeck and Marshal Batthyani. Two months were occupied in fitting this motley host to take the field.

On April 20, the British contingent was formed into six brigades. We had five dragoon regiments—the Royal North British (Scots Greys), Rothes' (Inniskillings), the Queen's (7th Hussars), and the Duke's, disbanded in 1748. The Guards again formed a separate brigade, Colonel Laforey and Lord Panmure commanding two weak battalions of the 1st and 3rd Regiments, which left depot companies in London. The line regiments were Lieut.-General Howard's (The Buffs), the King's Own (8th Foot), Pulteney's (13th), Major-General Howard's (19th), the North British (21st) and Royal Welsh Fusiliers, Crawford's (25th), Douglas's (32nd), Johnson's (33rd), Flemming's (36th), Dejean s (37th), and Conway's (48th).

Equal determination was shown on the French side. On March 14, 1747, a council of war held at Versailles resolved to carry the war into Holland. Saxe was intrusted with every detail, created governor of the conquered provinces, and vested with the rank of Marshal-General. His plan of campaign embraced the formation of two army corps. The first, under Löwendahl, was to operate in Dutch Flanders and besiege

Sluys and Fort Philippine, which defended the seaport of Ghent. The second, commanded by the marshal-general, would concentrate at a centre which threatened Southern Holland, as a preliminary to the siege of Maastricht.

The allied generals held frequent councils of war without arriving at any decision. According to his wont, Cumberland pressed for immediate action, and could not conceal the disgust excited by his colleagues' vacillation. Batthyani was jealous of Waldeck, and the pair agreed only in thwarting the young Commander-in-Chief. On May 1, however, the army marched towards Antwerp with a vague idea of recapturing it.

While the enemy were engaged in bickerings, Löwendahl captured Sluys, Philippine, and other Dutch strongholds in rapid succession. The conquest of Western Flanders secured Saxe's left from attack. It placed the whole canal system under his control, and gave him the means of massing his whole force for a crushing blow.

Its political results were still more decisive. Hitherto the Dutch had regarded themselves as mere auxiliaries. Louis XV. forced their hand by declaring war against the Republic (April 17, 1747). The prospect of invasion produced a ferment in the Netherlands which culminated in revolution. On May 4, Prince William of Orange Nassau, a son-in-law of George II., was elected Hereditary Stadtholder. The Dutch Republic with all its glorious memories was a thing of the past. The British and Austrian generals were sorely hampered by their allies' preoccupation in internal politics.

When at length the advance on Antwerp began, its object was thwarted by Löwendahl, who threw himself into the citadel with a formidable force. After much fruitless manoeuvring, the Allies abandoned their enterprise as they had retired from Lille in 1744. They were content to cover Maastricht, while dysentery and desertions robbed them of a fifth of their strength.

Cumberland still insisted on a forward policy, urging that an army of 81,000 men and 250 cannon could carry all before it in the field. He was opposed, tooth and nail, by Batthyani and Waldeck, who had bitter memories of Fontenoy. With discord raging at headquarters, the Allies could do little but watch the movements of Marshal Saxe.

That great leader repeated the Fabian tactics which had been so effectual in 1744. His army was kept in comfortable cantonments on the frontier of Hainault, awaiting the king's arrival. On May 31 Louis XV. reached Brussels and reviewed his army of invasion, numbering

140,000 men. All preparations completed, Saxe marched his forces towards Maastricht on June 22. At the same time Cumberland put his dispirited army in motion with a view of establishing headquarters at Tongres. He was forestalled by Saxe in that point of vantage, and compelled to fall back on Maastricht.

After manoeuvring for a week, the opposing armies at last came in contact. The Allies, 90,000 strong, made for Herdeeren Heights. Again they were anticipated by Saxe. Leaving ten battalions at Tongres, he advanced with 120,000 men and seized the Heights, placing himself between the enemy and Maastricht. On July 2, 1747, order of battle was formed on both sides. The Allies extended in three lines: Austrians on the right, Dutch in the centre, British, Hanoverians, and Hessians left wise, resting on Maastricht. The key to their position was Laffeldt, in front of their first line. Saxe disposed his infantry in two lines facing the enemy, on rising ground, while his cavalry were similarly ranged in the plain below. Louis XV. watched the battle from Herdeeren Heights.

It began at 10 a.m. with a furious onslaught on Laffeldt, held by British and German infantry. Thrice was it carried, and as often were the French hurled back by fresh regiments drawn from the first line in the rear. At length Saxe gathered all his forces for a supreme effort. Heading the regiment Le Roi in person, he led six infantry brigades against Laffeldt, supporting these by a concentrated fire of guns of position, the Royal Vaisseaux, and the Irish Brigade. After a prolonged struggle numbers told, and the French gained a footing in Laffeldt. Now Cumberland brought up his whole left wing to sustain the battalions which were struggling to oust the foe from Laffeldt. They were taken in flank by four infantry brigades, and driven back in some disorder. The key of our position was carried at noon.

Still Cumberland did not despair of the day. He ordered the Dutch cavalry to create a diversion by charging from the centre. This was the crisis of the battle. Saxe launched his *Carabiniers* against the Dutchmen, who went about, riding over five infantry battalions on their way to recapture Laffeldt.

Pursuing their advantage, the French cavalry pierced our centre, completely rending the army in twain. Nothing now remained but a retirement on Maastricht. A retrograde movement was begun by the left and centre under severe pressure from the enemy's cavalry. Few indeed of our harassed infantry could have reached the Meuse had not Sir John Ligonier, who had been gazetted "General of Horse,"

Performed an action of most desperate gallantry, which prevented the total destruction of our troops, and almost made Marshal Saxe doubt of his victory.—Horace Walpole, *Memoirs of George II*, vol. i.

Heading the Royal North British, Rich's, Rothes', and the Queen's Dragoons, he charged the pursuing cavalry with such fury that they were rolled back in confusion, losing five standards. Ligonier was unhorsed in the *mêlée*, and made prisoner by a *carabinier*, to whom he offered his purse and diamond ring. The chivalrous Frenchman declined these *spolia opima*, asking only for his captive's sword. Relieved from overwhelming pressure, the Allies' left and centre succeeded in passing the Meuse by pontoon bridges, and found shelter under the guns of Maastricht.

While their comrades were being handled so roughly, Batthyani's 27,000 Austrians on the right wing were held in their position by the French left. They scarcely fired a shot, and retreated northwards in good order after the rout of the Dutch cavalry. Saxe was blamed by his enemies, the "carpet generals" of Versailles, for not sending his cavalry in pursuit of the retiring Austrians. In this instance the charge so often levelled at him of reluctance to end hostilities appears to rest on a solid basis.

Both armies lost heavily by the needless slaughter of Laffeldt. The Allies had 6000 casualties. They abandoned 16 cannon, and 2000 prisoners were made during the brief pursuit. On the French side 20 superior officers were killed or wounded, amongst them Colonel Dillon, who had shown such gallantry at Fontenoy. They admitted having 8700 men placed *hors de combat*. The greatest carnage took place in and around Laffeldt, which was defended with their wonted staunchness by 10,000 British infantry. The French historian of Louis XV.'s wars pays a splendid tribute to these forgotten heroes:—

> Above all, the English worked wonders in attempting to hold Laffeldt, which was attacked five times before it was carried. Their resistance would have daunted troops less accustomed to victory than ours. They resembled that famous column—that stubborn rock which we had to mine at Fontenoy. This characteristic of the English infantry is a tower of strength. They seem to be untouched by human emotions in the hour of battle; their calmness is unshakeable; their cohesion resists attack. "What splendid infantry!" cried Marshal Bugeaud; "happily for

their foes, there are not many of them!" He instanced their prowess during the Peninsular War. I found them just the same at Inkermann—impossible, and inspiring terror by their coolness and courage.—General Comte Pajol, *Les Guerres sous Louis XV*, vol. iii.

The Duke of Cumberland again displayed a full measure of this bulldog bravery. While striving to rally the Dutch cavalry he was within an ace of being taken prisoner, as indeed was Marshal Saxe. This curious episode is described by Colonel the Hon. Joseph Yorke, who served Cumberland as *aide-de-camp* at Fontenoy and Laffeldt:—

> His Royal Highness did wonders: I believe in my conscience the strength of his own arm saved him from being a prisoner. He was in the middle of a French squadron, and, one of the troopers going to lay hold of him, he gave him such a cut with his sword that if he did not cut his arm off 'twill not be of much use to him the rest of his life. His family and servants ran to his succour, and brought him off. . . . M. Saxe was as near being taken by the Scotch Greys; as he says, one of them had his pat upon his shoulder, and he was forced to run for it.—Colonel Yorke to Colonel Barrington, Camp of Richelt, July 11, 1747 (Chequers Court Papers).

In the view taken by public opinion at home, Cumberland had already given ample proof of physical courage. It was high time that he should show the higher qualities demanded of a leader. Fontenoy and Laffeldt have, indeed, many features in common. On each occasion the day was lost mainly because Cumberland omitted to use all the forces at his command. In both battles one of the wings were impassive spectators of a conflict which needed every man within reach. In both lukewarm co-operation on the part of our Dutch allies contributed to our defeat, while British valour shone out with undying lustre. French heroism was equally splendid. The Irish Brigade once more proved that a potential bulwark of our empire had been turned against us by insane religious persecution. The far-famed *Carabiniers*, and the infantry regiments Le Roi, Vaisseaux, and Bettens, repeated their exploits at Fontenoy.

Sir John Ligonier was brought into the presence of Louis XV., who had watched the battle from Herdeeren Heights.

"Sire," said Marshal Saxe, "I present to your Majesty a man who has defeated all my plans by a single glorious action."

The captive was most graciously received. Louis assured him that he greatly admired the English people, who, he said, not only paid but fought for all. It is pleasant to add that the carabinier who had behaved so generously received a life-pension. In the course of conversation with this great cavalry leader, Louis XV. expressed a strong desire to end a war which had seriously impaired his naval strength and brought ruin on the kingdom's maritime commerce. (Beatson's *Naval Memoirs*, vol. i.) Ligonier was much *fêted* in the French camp, and soon released on parole with a message for Cumberland, which paved the way for the Treaty of Aix-la-Chapelle.

CHAPTER 9

Siege of Pondicherry

The issue of Laffeldt was not decisive enough to warrant an immediate attempt to capture Maastricht. Saxe turned his eyes to Bergen-op-Zoom, as a more vulnerable point in Holland's defensive armour. It was a virgin fortress, and had sustained two regular sieges. In 1688 Coehorn had brought all the resources of his art to bear on the task of rendering the stronghold impregnable. With a garrison of 10,600 men, amply supplied, and sea communications with England open, the great engineer's dream might well have been realised. Unhappily for the Coalition, these resources were controlled by a governor of eighty-six, who had been a thorn in our generals' side since 1744. General Cronstrom's obstinacy and incompetence produced the most disastrous episode of an inglorious war.

Löwendahl was intrusted with the siege of Bergen-op-Zoom, while D'Estrées held the Allies in check above Maastricht and hindered them from crossing the Meuse. Trenches were opened July 14, 1747. Vainly did the garrison strive to pierce the iron wall by sorties and vigorous cannonading. The besiegers were hampered more seriously by an unbroken army close at hand, which sought to relieve Bergen op Zoom. On August 8 Prince Waldeck made a night attack on the French left wing, which was repelled with difficulty. Convoys on their way to the trenches were intercepted by the Allies, whose left was pushed as far as Oudenbosch, north east of the beleaguered fortress.

Cumberland was urged by the panic-stricken Dutch to save the main bulwark of their country. He marched from a position between Maastricht and Liége with the intention of joining hands with Waldeck. On the other side, Saxe received positive orders from Versailles to capture Bergen-op-Zoom at any cost. A check at that cri-

WOLDERMAR DE LOWENDAL

sis would have destroyed the fruit of two successful campaigns. On September 13, 1747, Löwendahl took one of those desperate resolves which spell either victory or overwhelming disaster. Although the main defences were intact, he ordered a general assault.

After a tremendous bombardment, his grenadiers rushed forward in three dense columns. It was 4 a.m.: the garrison were wrapped in sleep when the salvoes began. Hurriedly summoned to their posts, they offered a feeble resistance, and the besiegers gained a footing in the *enceinte*. Old Cronstrom was enabled to escape by the self-sacrifice of two Scottish regiments in Dutch service, which were almost annihilated. At 9 a.m. all was over, and the survivors streamed out of the city by a bridge of boats.

Then began a scene of horror which finds few parallels in modern warfare. Löwendahl permitted the slaughter and pillage of defenceless citizens, and his connivance remains an indelible blot on his memory.

******

According to Barbier, many grenadiers obtained booty worth 14,000 or 15,000 *livres*. "We hear that jewellery, plate, and equipages sold at slaughter prices. The Jews who follow our army alone profit on such occasions, money being very scarce with officers."—*Journal*, vol. iii.

******

This siege cost the defence nearly 5000 in killed and wounded, of whom 3000 fell in the general assault. The French had 5259 casualties; but it is a remarkable fact that only 479 occurred on September 13. This brilliant exploit won for Löwendahl the coveted grade of Marshal. It was conferred with some reluctance. Stories of his cruelty reached the king's ears, and the detested foreigner was dubbed "Verres" by the carpet generals of Versailles.

Louis' hesitation was overcome by Saxe's bluntness, he remarked:

Sire, there is no middle course; you must either hang him or make him Marshal of France.

There is some reason for suspecting that both soldiers of fortune were implicated in these misdoings. In judging them, we must not forget that the opposite faction was both virulent and unscrupulous. Harassed beyond bearing by the intrigues of d'Argenson and Conti, Saxe exclaimed, "If war be a matter of inspiration, do not vex the oracle!" Breathing-time was given him by the approach of winter, which suspended operations on both sides. The British contingent, reduced to 8 battalions and 7 squadrons, went into quarters at Amsterdam and Rotterdam.

While Bergen-op-Zoom was approaching the crisis of its fate, the British Ministry sought to appease public wrath by increased activity at sea. In August 1747 news came to the Admiralty that nine line-of-battle ships, under Chef d'Escadre de l'Etenduère, had left Brest for Rochelle, where a fleet of merchantmen awaited convoy to the West Indies.

Rear-Admiral Hawke was ordered to intercept them with fourteen ships of the line. At 10 a.m. on October 25, 1747, he fell in with the French squadron escorting 250 merchant vessels westwards. Hawke formed line of battle ahead and made for the enemy under full sail. Though de l'Etenduère had only 556 guns against 784, he was undismayed by the tremendous odds. His first thought was for the defenceless traders under his protection. After providing for their safety as far as was possible, he too formed line of battle ahead, and calmly awaited the foe. Hawke penetrated the French admiral's scheme for facilitating his convoy's escape.

******

Edward Hawke (1705-81) came of middle-class stock, and, wanting "interest," he rose but slowly in his profession. He was one of the few post-captains who behaved creditably in Mathews' action near Toulon (1744). His victory off Finisterre was eclipsed by a subsequent feat worthy of Nelson himself. On November 20, 1759, he intercepted a fleet under de Conflans intended for the invasion of England. Regardless of foul weather, a rocky shore on his lee, and gathering darkness, he pursued de Conflans into Quiberon Bay and utterly defeated him. Hawke's outspoken criticism of the Admiralty's methods delayed the reward for this great victory. He was not raised to the peerage until 1771.

******

Signals were hoisted for a general chase, and in half an hour the opponents were exchanging broadsides. After a smart engagement six French line-of-battle ships were overpowered and taken. De Vaudreuil, commanding *l'Intrépide*, 74, proved worthy of his vessel's name. Seeing his chief hard beset in the 80-gun ship *Tonnant*, he went to the rescue through the whole British fleet. Their only chance of escape was to set all sail and steer for Brest. Night came to favour this bold design. *L'Intrépide* took her disabled consort in tow, and, after beating off the

Marlborough, the pair reached Brest in safety. The gallantry displayed in this engagement constitutes a crushing indictment of the French Government. What might not Louis XV.'s navy have effected had it received a tithe of the attention lavished on his army? While the British people rendered justice to the self-devotion of de l'Etenduère and his captains, their enthusiasm was excited by Hawke's signal victory.

******

His despatch smacked strongly of the British tar. "As the enemy's ships were large," he wrote, "they took a good deal of drubbing." English was not George II.'s strong point. When the report was read to him, he asked what a "drubbing" meant. At that moment the Duke of Bedford entered the closet. Now he had quite lately been severely handled during a political fracas at Lichfield Races. Lord Chesterfield slyly suggested that the duke might possibly explain the ambiguous expression. George II. had heard the story. He laughed heartily, and said that he understood its signification well.—Beatson, *Naval Memoirs*, vol. i.

******

Spurred to new exertions, the Ministry determined to oust the French from India. Rear-Admiral Boscawen was selected to command an expedition destined to capture Pondicherry. Though still comparatively young, he had gained a great reputation for energy and professional skill.

******

Hon. Edward Boscawen (1711-61) was third son of Viscount Falmouth. He won his spurs at the capture of Portobello and Carthagena in 1741, and was wounded in Anson's engagement. In after life he destroyed the Toulon fleet in Lagos Bay (August 18, 1759). Boscawen was much admired by his sailors, who styled him "Old Dreadnought."

******

In November 1747 he sailed from England with six men-of-war and eleven armed Indiamen, carrying 1500 regulars. At the Cape he was reinforced by six Dutch warships and 400 soldiers. Then he steered for the Isle of France, with a view of extirpating that hornet's nest. Discouraged by the enemy's activity in planting batteries at every possible landing-place, Boscawen had recourse to a council of war. That weak-kneed body decided that the Isle of France was impregnable, although it afterwards leaked out that the French garrison could not have long withstood so large a force.

The admiral pursued his voyage to India, arriving at Fort St David, August 10, 1748. Here he was joined by our Indian squadron under Rear-Admiral Griffin, and found himself in command of the most imposing fleet ever seen in Eastern waters. It was manned by 5220 men available for land service, of whom 4000 were Europeans. Boscawen cast anchor, August 18, two miles south of Pondicherry. His troops were reinforced on landing by 2000 cavalry, sent by *Nawab* Anwar-ud-din to support the side which he deemed the stronger.

The fortifications of Pondicherry were still incomplete, and only 1800 men of its garrison, numbering 3000, were Europeans. A prompt attack would probably have succeeded. Boscawen's engineers wasted eighteen days in laying regular siege to a detached fort, and they encountered several repulses ere it was evacuated. This respite was employed by Dupleix and his henchman, Paradis, in perfecting the main defences.

On September 10, 1748, the siege began in earnest. It was conducted with an amazing lack of common-sense. Approaches should have been made from the northern side, where Pondicherry was most vulnerable. Our camp would then have been pitched close to shore, whence ground suitable for spade-work extended up to the covered way. The engineers selected a base on the northwest of the fortress. It involved an attack on the strongest side, which was further protected by an intervening swamp.

The siege-train, and supplies of all kinds for an extensive camp, were dragged for three miles through a sea of mud in the hottest weather, and exposed to constant attacks from the enemy. Ground was broken no less than 1500 yards from the covered way, and work was interrupted by daily sorties. In one of them Paradis was slain. This was a grievous loss to the garrison, for that brave and resourceful Switzer was the heart and soul of the defence. Dupleix stood boldly in the breach. He knew nothing of warfare from its practical side, but what cannot genius effect? Taking command of the garrison, he inspired each and all with his own fiery enthusiasm. Their spirits revived, and the besiegers were harassed by night attacks. On one occasion our entrenchments would have been rushed but for the presence of mind exhibited by Ensign Clive.

After infinite labour four batteries were completed by the engineers, and on October 7 firing began at the extreme range of 800 yards. The garrison's fire proved superior, and Boscawen was fain to admit that the land attack was ineffectual. He resolved to try the effect of broadsides from his ships. The two-deckers were warped within 1000 yards of the sea front, and much ammunition was wasted ere the admiral discovered that his wall-sided craft rolled too heavily in the land swell for accurate gunnery. Further progress on shore was barred by the inundated area; and nine of our heaviest breaching cannon had been dismounted by the besiegers.

Boscawen saw that he had undertaken a task utterly beyond his resources. Moreover, the rainy season was in full swing. Trenches were flooded, hospitals gorged with sick men. At any moment, a cyclone might sweep down the coast and sink or scatter his war-vessels. On October 11, 1748, a council of war unanimously resolved to raise the siege of Pondicherry. With a heavy heart Boscawen destroyed his batteries, shipped heavy guns and stores, and left the scene of so much futile labour. The siege had cost us 1065 European lives. The *Sepoys* suffered little, for they had been employed to guard approaches, and fled at the first appearance of danger.

Though Boscawen did not show his wonted self-reliance during this expedition, blame for its non-success must rest on the engineering staff. Löwendahl had made the French *Corps du Génie* the first military school in Europe. Until its reorganisation in 1757, the engineer branch of our Board of Ordnance was destitute of technical skill and strangled by routine.

The year 1748 opened with brighter auspices for exhausted Europe. Peace had been in the air since September 1746, when a Congress assembled at Breda; but negotiations were broken off in the following June. They were renewed by George II. when Ligonier reported the overtures made him by Louis XV.

Lord Sandwich met the French Minister of Foreign Affairs at Liége, and it was arranged between them that another Peace Congress should be held at Aix-la-Chapelle. (John, fourth Earl of Sandwich, 1718-92, is best remembered as the inventor of a convenient form of food). The sessions began in January 1748. Great Britain was represented by Sandwich and Sir Thomas Robinson, afterwards Lord Grantham; France by the Comte de St Severin. (Alphonse-Marie, Comte de St Severin d'Arragon, 1705-57, was chief of an illustrious Neapolitan family, and naturalised only in 1735, he was emphatically an honest man and a lover of peace, but wanted penetration). Count Kaunitz was the Austrian plenipotentiary, and laid the foundations of his fame as a statesman at Aix-la-Chapelle.

Louis XV.'s instructions to his agent were in themselves the strongest condemnation of this unjust and needless war. He wished to deal, forsooth, not as a tradesman but as a king, and was content to revert to the *status quo ante bellum*. This concession went far beyond the Allies' wildest hopes, and mutual goodwill was alone needed to secure a common basis of action. This element was not conspicuous at Aix-la-Chapelle. Defeat had soured the spirits of the Coalition and bred mutual distrust.

This war was the grave of the Anglo-Dutch alliance, which had endured for sixty years. Maria Theresa was profoundly dissatisfied with Great Britain, which exacted full value for her subsidies, and was more eager to humble France than safeguard Austria's domestic interests. Holland, too, aroused the high-spirited empress's wrath by insisting on her treaty rights to garrison the Barrier fortresses of Flanders, which she had been unable to preserve. The old grouping was clearly obsolete. Its *rationale* was intelligible enough while the traditional hostility between Habsburg and Bourbon prevailed.

Flanders was the arena marked out by nature for that struggle; the torrent of invasion was diverted from German soil, and the resources of France were sapped by naval defeats. The war which was drawing to a close had brought a new and far more formidable enemy into the field. Maria Theresa foresaw that Prussia would one day contest the hegemony of German lands with their hereditary chief. She turned from the Maritime Powers to France, which had reached the acme of her military strength.

The foundations of the Franco Austrian alliance, which startled Europe eight years later, were laid at Aix la Chapelle. Kaunitz drew nearer to his French colleague, in the hope of overcoming prejudices which had lasted for three centuries. Some progress had been made towards a secret understanding between them, when he learnt from Lord Sandwich that he had been forestalled by Great Britain and Holland. In point of fact, peace preliminaries were settled by France and the Maritime Powers on April 30, 1748. On this discovery, the vials of Maria Theresa's wrath were poured on her quondam allies; and France became the *tertium gaudens,* so envied by diplomacy. St Severin told his master that:

> The great advantage of the whole course of negotiations lay in the fact that, for years to come, Austria and Sardinia would not forget the trick which the Maritime Powers had played them.—J. Franck Bright, *Maria Theresa.*

While diplomatists were wrangling at Aix-la-Chapelle, Saxe completed his preparations for another campaign. His voice was raised in effectual protest against any relaxation in efforts to bring Holland to her knees. Peace, he said, lay at Maastricht; which was invested, April 15, on both banks of the Meuse. After a fortnight's incessant labour in the trenches Löwendahl, who commanded the right approaches, drove the garrison into their interior works. Sapping began, accompanied by the usual hail of shot and shell. Frequent sorties took place, one of which had some success owing to the insubordination of a French officer. The Vicomte de Lautrec was ordered by Löwendahl to post his grenadiers in ambush near a spot which the garrison would pass.

As a senior lieutenant-general he arrogated the right to disregard these orders, and the grenadiers were placed elsewhere. A night attack was delivered, in which both working and covering parties suffered severely. The new-made marshal's temper was proof against any trial. He told de Lautrec in courteous terms that he could not help reporting the mishap to Versailles. (Barbier, *Journal*, vol. iii. De Lautrec was disgraced, but we find him raised to the Marshalate in 1757).

The Allies had mustered such forces as they could still command at Roermonde, north of Maastricht. The depletion of their reserves of men compelled them to look far afield. Russia was then governed by Elizabeth Patronal, a personal foe of Frederick II., and surrounded by anti-Prussian advisers. By playing on her headstrong temper, Great Britain and Holland were able to take 37,000 Russians into their pay. These new auxiliaries were carried to Lubeck on their own galleys; but instead of proceeding by sea to Willemstadt, they started for Roermonde by land.

At the earnest entreaty of Marshal Batthyani, Cumberland was once more appointed Commander-in-Chief. He left London at the end of February 1748. Troops and artillery followed slowly, and the Guards did not land at Willemstadt until August was well advanced. At the outset of their last campaign the Allies could muster no more than 35,000 men. They were hampered, as of yore, by divided counsels. The young *stadtholder* was phlegmatic; Cumberland unconventional and eager for action,

The brothers-in-law forgot their differences when news was brought to Roermonde that preliminaries of peace had been signed at Aix-la-Chapelle (April 30). In fact, diplomatic delays had been abridged by the enemy's activity in attacking Maastricht, and the nightmare was conjured away which had oppressed Europe for seven weary years. Cumberland promptly sent an *aide-de-camp* to Saxe's camp with proposals for an armistice, the formation of a neutral zone, and the surrender of Maastricht. They were accepted by Louis XV., and on May 10, 1748, Holland's last mainstay opened its gates to Löwendahl.

Although Marshal Saxe welcomed Cumberland's peace overtures, he was by no means satisfied with the turn taken by negotiations at Aix-la-Chapelle. His forebodings found utterance in a letter of May 15, 1748, to the Comte de Maurepas, Minister of Marine:

> In matters political I am only a chatterbox; and if the military situation compels me to discuss them betimes, I don't quote my own opinion as being particularly sound. What I know, and what you ought to know, is that the enemy, however numerous they may be, cannot again penetrate these territories, which I should be very sorry to give up. They are, indeed, a dainty morsel, and when our present woes are forgotten we shall regret having abandoned them. I am ignorant of finance and of our national resources, but I am aware that the rate of interest in England at the close of the last war was only four *per cent*. It has lately reached the unprecedented pitch of twelve *per cent!* As commercial credit is the backbone of England and Holland, I conclude that both are on their last legs. This is not the case with ourselves.
>
> We have intrinsic resources, and can get along very well without money. I think we ought to make some sacrifices to keep such a province as Flanders, which gives us magnificent ports, millions of subjects, and an easily defended frontier. Such are my thoughts, though I don't pretend to know anything of your confounded politics. I see that the King of Prussia has got all he wants, and is to retain Silesia, and I only wish we could imitate him. After all, he is not so strong as we are: his geographical position is infinitely worse. He can be gripped by the head or heels, and has furious neighbours who love him no more than ourselves. We have none of those disadvantages, and it appears difficult, if not impossible, for any power to make us disgorge what we have won.—St René Taillandier, *Maurice de Saxe*.

These remonstrances had no effect with Louis XV., who would not hear of any departure from the peace preliminaries exchanged on April 30. The parleyings at Aix-la-Chapelle proceeded smoothly enough. At one moment a rupture was threatened, owing to the steady advance of our Russian auxiliaries. Louis XV. declared that, should it continue, he would demolish the fortifications of Bergen-op-Zoom and Maastricht. A compromise was effected on August 11, 1748, by which the Muscovites were sent back to their *steppes*, while France undertook to disband 37,000 of her own troops.

The Treaty of Aix-la-Chapelle was signed by Great Britain, France, and Holland on October 18, 1748, and afterwards by the other belligerents. Its terms were based on a mutual restoration of conquests. France surrendered the rich territory in Flanders and Holland which Saxe's strong right arm had won for her. She further consented to the demolition of Dunkirk's sea defences. Great Britain disgorged Louisbourg and Cape Breton, the only solid return for her immense sacrifices, and—more humiliating still—she was compelled to give hostages for their evacuation. She regained Madras, but was by no means satisfied with this part of the bargain.

In 1748 the nucleus of our Eastern empire was considered "a petty factory in the East Indies, belonging to a private company, whose existence had been deemed prejudicial to the Commonwealth," (Smollett, *Continuation of Hume*, vol. iii.). King George II. obtained a general guarantee of the Hanoverian Succession. The Pragmatic Sanction was also guaranteed, except as regards Silesia and Glatz: Prussia was allowed to retain those spoils of war, which were destined to be a bone of contention seven years later. Such were the terms of Aix-la-Chapelle which concerned British interests. The treaty made no reference to our frontier disputes with France in North America, nor did it attempt to regulate the right of search claimed by Spain in Western waters. None of the issues for which Europe had drawn the sword were solved, and a leaven of discord was left to germinate in the Seven Years' War.

Maria Theresa sullenly accepted accomplished facts, with a secret resolve to regain her ravished provinces by force of arms. The British funds rose on intelligence that peace had returned; for our ancestors were convinced against their will that, on the Continent at least, France was invincible. We have ever been impatient of reverses, and prone to intoxication on victory. The nation's heart was wrung by the long agony of disappointed hopes, and tears of humiliation mingled with the rejoicings for Aix-la-Chapelle.

It remains only to trace the subsequent careers of the chief actors in this stirring drama.

The vessel which carried Labourdonnais homewards in 1747 was captured by a British cruiser, and he was brought to London. The author of an agreement to restore Madras was hailed as a champion of our commerce in the East. His proud spirit revolted at the equivocal attentions paid him by the court and city alike. Learning that he was accused of fraud and insubordination at home, he obtained the Ministry's permission to exculpate himself. On reaching Paris he was thrown into the Bastille, where he lingered for three years in close confinement.

Denied all means of communication with the outer world, he described his stormy career on handkerchiefs glazed with rice water, using a pen fashioned from his copper drinking-vessel and ink made of coffee-grounds. The publication of these memoirs created a revulsion of feeling in his favour. Labourdonnais was acquitted and released in 1752, only to die of a broken heart on September 9 of the following year. Still more miserable was the fate of his illustrious foe. Dupleix gained immense prestige throughout India by his successful defence of Madras. He was concerting measures to extirpate British influence when despatches arrived directing him to suspend hostilities and restore his conquest.

Aix-la-Chapelle was a thunderbolt for the governor-general; but his protests were disregarded. Madras was given up to Boscawen with fortifications restored, and fitted to become a centre of anti-French intrigues. Dupleix sought to counteract them by forming a coalition of native princes, for his exploits had wrought a revolution in the status of European merchants. They were compelled to maintain standing armies, and to meet the cost by hiring out troops to native candidates for power. Intervention in Indian politics was essential to their new born prestige. Dupleix was steadily building up a French empire in Southern India when he fell a sacrifice to English jealousy. Recalled to France at the instance of our East India Company in 1754, he spent nine years in vainly suing for a repayment of 1,300,000 *livres* devoted from his private fortune to fortifying Pondicherry. On November 7, 1763, we find him writing—

> I have sacrificed youth, fortune, life, to enrich my masters in India. . . . My services are treated as fables; my demands denounced as ridiculous. I am considered the vilest of mankind. I live in the most deplorable indigence; the little property that remained to me has been seized. I must seek a respite from the court, to avoid being dragged to prison.—Quoted by Malleson, *The French in India*.

Three days later this much-injured man died, a victim to the ingratitude and cowardice of his government. But Dupleix "had against him that crime of genius which so many men have expiated by misery, by exile, by death." (Baron B. de Penliven, *Histoire de la Conquête de l'Inde par l'Angleterre*). Our condemnation of the statesmen who requited his great services with persecution and neglect must be tempered by the reflection that all bureaucracies are swayed by the baser attributes of our nature.

William Augustus, Duke of Cumberland, never again commanded a British army in the field. His ever-active mind found employment in beautifying Windsor Great Park, of which he was appointed Ranger. To him Londoners owe Virginia Water and the spurious ruins which adorn its purlieus. His racing stable was the finest in all England, and his name is written large in the annals of the Turf. During the Seven Years' War (1756-63) he was named Commander-in-Chief of 40,000 Hanoverians, Hessians, and Brunswickers, which mustered at Bielefeld to defend Hanover from Marshal D'Estrées. After several months of fruitless manoeuvring, the two armies came in contact at Hastenbeck, July 26, 1757.

Cumberland's mind was vigorous as ever, but his frame had grown unwieldy, and his sight was so bad that he was compelled to trust to other men's reports. Relying on the assurance of a Hanoverian quartermaster general that a certain wood which covered his left was impracticable, he neglected to defend it with an abatis. At this very point his position was turned by D'Estrées, who captured his principal battery and forced him to retreat with a loss of 1200 men. No other course remained but to negotiate with a greatly superior foe for the preservation of Hanover.

On September 8, 1757, Cumberland, armed with the fullest powers, concluded the Convention of Kloster Seven, by which he undertook to disband his army, the Hanoverian contingent alone excepted. In French opinion, which was subsequently voiced by Napoleon, this agreement was too favourable to the vanquished side. It excited a storm of indignation at home, and was disavowed by George II. Cumberland was made a scapegoat by the Ministry, and was so discourteously received by his father on returning to London, that he resigned every public office.

Saint-Simon remarks that "there is nothing so difficult as to maintain a wise and disdainful silence under unmerited disgrace." Cumberland proved that he possessed one at least of the elements of greatness by the philosophy with which he suffered opprobrium. In the late Lord Sherbrooke's words—

> The Duke of Cumberland always said that he had been most unjustly praised for Culloden, and most unjustly depreciated for his capitulation at Kloster Seven; so that, upon the whole, he considered justice had been done to him.—Mr Robert Lowe's Budget Speech, April 20, 1871.

In 1761 paralysis deprived him for a time of the faculty of speech; but he recovered to render one more public service. In 1765 his nephew, George III., persuaded him to treat with William Pitt for the formation of a Ministry. The negotiations failed in their immediate object, though they led to the advent of Lord Rockingham's Administration. Ere the new advisers of the Crown were settled in office, Cumberland passed beyond the reach of his innumerable foes. He died suddenly, October 31, 1765, from the consequences of a clot of blood on the brain.

The time has come for a frank recognition of the fact that he did not deserve the fierce obloquy which has pursued him beyond the grave. His General Orders resemble Wellington's; for they breathe the same intolerance of disloyalty and lack of discipline, the same appreciation of the steady and faithful soldier. With all his faults, William Augustus, Duke of Cumberland, merits the gratitude of Englishmen for the share he took in forming that incomparable infantry which is the backbone of their military strength.

Sir John Ligonier succeeded Marshal Wade as Lieutenant-General of the Ordnance in 1748, but was unjustly deprived of office by a court intrigue, which transferred it to a worthless Duke of Marlborough. In 1757 the veteran's *amour propre* was salved by the appointment of Commander-in-Chief, in succession to Cumberland. In the same year he was created Field-Marshal, and Viscount Ligonier of Inniskilling, and in 1766 he received an English earldom. He passed away, April 28, 1770, at the patriarchal age of ninety-one, having served his adopted country for sixty-seven years, and taken part in nineteen sieges and twenty-three general actions without receiving a single wound! Horace Walpole, who was by no means prone to enthusiasm, wrote of this splendid soldier—

> He had all the gallant gaiety of his nation. Polished from foppery by age, and living in a more thinking country, he was universally loved and respected.

******

Horace Walpole, *Memoirs of the Reign of George II,* vol. ii. Field Marshal Earl Ligonier's tomb may be seen in Westminster Abbey, with his portrait in profile, and medallions of the four British Sovereigns whom he served so faithfully. In April 1874, *The Times* reported that his correspondence with many, perhaps most, of the celebrated men and women of the eighteenth century had been sold in one lot for £26, 10s.!

******

Unlike Lord Ligonier, Sir Peter Warren did not long enjoy the fruits of a brilliant career. His well-earned booty made him the wealthiest commoner in England. He entered Parliament, was consulted by court and city alike, and beloved by his countrymen of all degrees. This useful and honoured life was closed by a fever, which carried him off in 1752 at the age of forty-nine.

******

Warren purchased 300 acres of land on Manhattan Island at his marriage, and the city fathers of New York presented him with the fee-simple of another tract, which is now built over. If his heirs had not disposed of this property, their descendants would now realise the Johnsonian "wealth beyond the dreams of avarice."

******

In marked contrast with these noble lives was that of Sir John Hawley. In his case proved incompetence was no bar to royal favour. He became colonel of the 20th Regiment, Commander-in-Chief in Ireland, and Governor of Portsmouth. Hawley's declining years were spent at West Green, a handsome "Queen Anne" mansion near Hook in Hampshire, which was paid for by the spoils of war. There still remain traces of a raised path which he made to the house of a comrade in arms. He died at eighty, in March 1759; and his will, which reveals the man's innate truculence, made a deep impression at the time:—

> I direct and order that, as there is now a peace and I may die the common way, my carcass may be put any where—'tis equal to me; but I will have no more expense or ridiculous show than if a poor soldier, who is as good a man, was to be buried from the hospital. The priest, I conclude, will have his fee—let the puppy have it. Pay the carpenter for the carcass-box, &c.

The great captains with whom Cumberland presumed to measure

swords preceded him to the grave. Löwendahl's war services ended with the capitulation of Maastricht. The remainder of his life was given to study and the enjoyment of a large fortune amassed in Flanders. We obtain some interesting glimpses of him in the pages of contemporary chroniclers. On November 1748 Saxe's *Uhlan* regiment was reviewed by Louis XV. in the Plain of Sablon, near Neuilly.

Among the host of spectators was a Mme. de la Poupelinière, whose husband had detected her in an intrigue with that incorrigible Lovelace, the Duc de Richelieu. After the manoeuvres, she implored Saxe's and Löwendahl's intercession with M. de la Poupelinière. They good-naturedly accompanied her to his house, and used every argument at their command to procure his forgiveness. Finding him inexorable, they took the fair and frail one to her mother. (Barbier, *Journal*, vol. iii.) Another reference reveals the soul-debasing atmosphere of the old court. Casanova visited France for the first time in 1750, and wormed himself into the royal circle at Fontainebleau. He thus describes the public dinner of ill-used Marie Leczinska:—

> I enter a splendid hall, where I see a dozen courtiers promenading, and a table large enough for at least as many guests, which, however, was laid for a single person. "For whom," I ask, "are all these preparations made?" "For the queen; here she comes."
> I see the Queen of France, unrouged, simply dressed, her head covered with a huge bonnet, her demeanour elderly and pious. Approaching the table, she courteously thanked two nuns, who placed a plate and fresh butter thereon. She then took her seat, whereupon the dozen courtiers formed a half-circle at ten paces from the table. I joined them, and imitated their respectful silence.
> Her Majesty began to eat without looking at anyone, but keeping her eyes fixed on her plate. Liking one of the dishes served, she took a second helping, and then glanced round the circle in front of her, doubtless in order to discover whether any of the spectators was entitled to be the depository of her impressions. She hit upon her man, and said, "Monsieur de Löwendahl!" As this name was uttered I saw a magnificent creature step forward, bow profoundly, and reply "*Madame.*"
> The Queen: "I believe this ragout to be a *fricassee* of chicken."
> Löwendahl: "I am of the same opinion, *Madame.*"
> After this conversation, carried on in a most serious tone, the

queen continued her repast, and the marshal backed to his place on tiptoe.... I was delighted with this glimpse of the renowned warrior to whom Bergen-op-Zoom had opened its gates; but I felt humiliated to see so great a man obliged to give his decision on a chicken stew in the same tone as a judge assumes when he pronounces sentence of death.—Casanova, *Memoirs*, vol. ii.

Löwendahl died in 1755, at the same age as the century. Had he survived to serve the country of his adoption in the ensuing war, its fortunes might have been very different. Of him it may be said, with all his failings:

> There were giants on the earth in those days.

This judgment applies to Maurice de Saxe. Deprived by an ignoble peace of his offices of Governor-General of Flanders and Marshal-General, he retired, heart-sick, to Chambord. Under the deteriorating influence of civil life the man of action relapsed into the dreamer and voluptuary. Once settled in the royal *demesne*, he began to refashion it as his ruling passions dictated. Barracks for 1200 men were added, and a theatre, which cost 600,000 *livres*. Valfons, who had served him as *aide-de-camp*, has left a fascinating picture of his manifold activity:—

"In 1749 I spent some days at Chambord with Marshal Saxe, who lodged me in Marie de Medici's bedchamber. On four successive mornings the great man condescended to take his seat by my bedside and discuss every detail of his campaigns with the simplicity which stamps the hero. The *château* was worthy of its illustrious tenant. He lived like a prince there, on an income of 100,000 crowns derived from various offices; had set up cavalry barracks, a stud, and a menagerie.

> While he was always weaving some chimerical dream or other, he plunged into amusements requiring an expenditure of physical energy. One moment he was hunting; *anon* he watched the progress of improvements, in which he sometimes took a hand. Above all things he loved to drill his regiment, which was kept in garrison by the king's special favour. Chambord was ruled by all the observances maintained in a fortress during war-time. The illusion was completed by the captured cannon and flags which adorned its gates. Besides, the marshal frequently gave concerts, indoors or on the lake.—St René Taillandier, *Maurice de Saxe*.

The regiment to which Valfons alludes was the *Volontaires de Saxe*, raised in 1743. It was recruited from the founder's countrymen in Saxony and Bohemia, and formed six brigades of 160 troopers—960 in all. They were organised as *uhlans* and dragoons. The first were armed with curved sabre and pistols, as well as a lance, which rested on the tip of the right jack-boot, and was driven home by a vigorous kick. The uniform was green; the helmet of gilt brass was encircled with a Russian-leather turban, and surmounted by a horsehair tuft, whose colour denoted the wearer's brigade.

These tufts were the origin of the coloured *pompons*, afterwards employed to distinguish regiments of the line. The dragoons' weapons were sabre and rifled carbine. They hovered in the rear while the *uhlans* charged, ready to support them or attack a pursuing enemy in flank. One troop was composed of negroes mounted on milk-white chargers. (Pajol, *Les Guerres sous Louis XV*, vol. vii.) Hospitality at Chambord was on a regal scale. Two tables were daily spread for eighty and sixty guests. The masters magnetic personality attracted all that was best in France to Chambord. Only eleven weeks before his death we find him describing a grand reception given to a princess of the blood, "with a dozen court ladies, comedy, ball. . . . All these people will stay a fortnight." (*Lettres de Maurice de Saxe a la Princesse d'Holstein, sa soeur*. Firmin Didot. 1831).

Despite these leanings to Asiatic magnificence, Saxe retained his charming simplicity to the last. He knew no respect of persons. At the theatre he laughed and chatted with anyone who addressed him, and Louis XV. often took umbrage at his soldierly frankness.

But mimic sovereignty in the heart of France was not enough for the adventurer of royal descent. His imagination outstripped the narrow limits of Chambord, and pined for shadowy realms across the sea. Ere the ink on the treaty of Aix-la-Chapelle was dry, Maurice de Saxe asked for the sovereignty of Madagascar, with the intention of colonising the island with poor Germans. Deterred by the immense cost of such an expedition, he obtained a grant of Tobago, a tiny island in the Antilles claimed by France. His dream of making it the nucleus of an American empire was thwarted by English and Dutch jealousy. Then his eye roved to Corsica, where a Westphalian adventurer had reigned for a few months in 1736. *Anon* we find him elaborating a scheme for transferring the Hebrew race bodily to virgin America!

Visions of kingship in some faery realm did not exclude the frenzied pursuit of pleasure. In 1748 he formed a *liaison* with Mlle. Verrières, who had lately achieved success in Parisian opera. The result was a daughter, christened Maria-Aurore after her maternal grandparents, who lived to be the mother of Armandine Aurore Dupin, known to fame as "George Sand." A more discreditable adventure marked the close of this stormy life. In 1746 Maurice fell madly in love with Madame Favart, the beautiful wife of his theatrical *impressario*.

******

Charles-Simon Favart (1710-92) was a manager and dramatist of considerable note. His wife, born Du Ronceray (1727-82), was much more than a first-rate actress. She united the most fascinating qualities of head and heart, and her benevolence was as inexhaustible as her gaiety.

******

Despite the temptations of their calling, the young couple represented the very best elements in the *bourgeoisie*, whose sound heart and homely virtues made them the salt of eighteenth century France. When his overtures were indignantly rejected, Saxe's wrath overstepped all bounds. Poor Favart was driven into hiding, and harassed with lawsuits; his wife was confined in a convent under a *lettre de cachet*.

******

The *lettre de cachet* was an essential feature of the old regime. It was a document under the privy seal, so folded that its contents were concealed, in contradistinction to the *lettres patentes*, which were open and sealed by the chancellor. *Lettres de cachet* were of two kinds: (1) Summons to public bodies for deliberation; (2) orders for the exile or imprisonment of individuals. In this reign the second variety was sold for 25 *louis* in blank. Thus, *lettres de cachet* were made a vehicle for private vengeance. These engines of oppression were swept away at the Revolution in 1790.

******

For years, this persecution lasted, covering the hero of Fontenoy with ridicule. Whether his ends were accomplished or not will never be known, but this episode remains a blot on his memory. Such is the fruit of unbridled passions, which intensify with advancing age, and have dimmed the lustre of many a strenuous career.

In the summer of 1749 Maurice de Saxe paid a flying visit to his half-brother, the King of Poland. His reception at Dresden was so flattering that half Europe suspected him of a desire to settle in his native land. Thence he journeyed to Sans Souci, where Frederick of Prussia welcomed him with open arms. Contrary to the methodical king's routine, he sat up till dawn, discussing things military with his illustrious guest. Frederick told Voltaire:

> I have learned much from his discourse, not of the French language, but of the warlike art. This marshal might be the professor of all the generals in Europe.

A life so feverish and many-sided, so wasteful of its mental and physical resources, was foredoomed to be cut short at the threshold of old age.

On November 30, 1750, France learnt with grief that her greatest general was no more. A tradition was long current at Chambord that Maurice de Saxe was mortally wounded in a duel with his old enemy, the Prince de Conti. In point of fact, his organism, worn out with manifold excesses, could not resist a violent attack of fever and congestion of the lungs. Löwendahl hastened to the deathbed, and strove in vain to convert his old comrade to Catholicism. He was as profound a materialist as the patient, but, like our own Faraday, he "kept a water-tight compartment in his brain." (This was Faraday's reply to a friend who asked him how he, a light of science, could hold forth at meetings of a strait-laced sect known as Glassites or Sandemanians).

Maurice de Saxe died as he had lived—with a soul full of reveries. Turning to his physician at the very last, he said, "Doctor, life is only a dream. Mine has been a beautiful dream—but it is too short!"

He was buried in the Protestant cemetery at Strasburg, the capital of the province which he had saved from Austrian invasion. His tomb, one of the wonders of the world-famous cathedral, was miraculously spared by a Prussian shell in 1870. The witty Mme. Du Boccage said:

> It is passing strange, that we are forbidden to sing *De Profundis* for a man who has made us sing so many *Te Deums*—Casanova, *Memoirs*, vol. ii.

Maurice de Saxe was tall and strong—so strong that his fingers could twist a nail into a corkscrew, and bend crown pieces double. During a visit to London he picked up and deposited in a passing scavenger's cart a street ruffian who insulted him. His swarthy features were lit with large blue eyes, and his smile was irresistible in its grace and sweetness.

Sympathy with others was the master-key which unlocked every heart. On the morning of Rocoux, while the whole camp was still wrapped in slumber, Maurice de Saxe watched the sun's rays breaking on that peaceful plain, and thought of the thousands of brave men whose last day had dawned. He poured out his very soul to a comrade, and burst into tears.

On another occasion he was advised by one of the "carpet generals" whom he despised so heartily to attack an outpost, which would not cost him more than a dozen soldiers. "I might try," he answered, "if it were a case of a dozen lieutenant-generals," and turned on his heel.

> Why was not that good and heroic heart always guided by lofty aspirations? When we analyse these robust natures on whom God has bestowed such powerful faculties, we long to find in them our ideal of a Man, and suffer because we find them so incomplete. We are consoled when for a moment we forget their weaknesses, and fix our attention on the nobler side of their character. Panegyrists of old time had an inkling of this method, but they pursued it without art or philosophy, and often disfigured their hero's personality by idealising it.
>
> The New Criticism forbids us to fall into such errors. I would depict reality in an honest spirit, without sacrificing my ideals. I would disclose a great soul with all its load of human misery, and raise it in the world's esteem by throwing a ray of light on its heroic side. Thus, will our common heritage be made the richer.
>
> I would isolate his peculiar virtues, and bring them into high relief in order to inspire purer lives, completer destinies than ever he enjoyed. Then, applying this method to the individual whose career I had endeavoured to relate, I would say—Let us ask our country's future to produce geniuses as active, as eager in the pursuit of glory; but active in other fields than war, eager for good in all its forms, and lovers of that glory which lifts man to God Himself. And as I am writing of an illustrious weaver of reveries, I would add an earnest prayer—May each of us, in his own degree and order, and having regard to the task intrusted to him by Providence, display that ardour which was the distinguishing mark of Maurice de Saxe!—St René Taillandier, *Maurice de Saxe.*

Appendix 1: Existing Regiments Which Fought in Flanders, 1743-47

Capitals refer to the battles in which each was engaged: Dettingen, D ;
Fontenoy, F ; *Rocoux,* R ; *Laffeldt,* L.

When raised.	Name of Corps.	Battles in which engaged.
1660	1st and 2nd Regiments of Life Guards	D, F.
1661	Royal Regiment of Horse Guards	D, F.
1685	1st (King's) Dragoon Guards	D, F.
1688	7th (Princess Royal's) Dragoon Guards	D, F.
1662	1st (Royal) Dragoons	D, F.
1678	Royal Scots Greys	D, F, R, L.
1685	3rd (King's Own) Hussars	D, F.
1685	4th (Queen's Own) Hussars	D, L.
1689	6th (Inniskilling) Dragoons	D, F, R, L.
1689	7th (Queen's Own) Hussars	D, F, R, L.
1660	Grenadier Guards	D, F, L.
1650	Coldstream Guards	D, F.
1660	Scots Guards	D, F, L.
1633	Royal Scots, Lothian Regiment	D, F.
1665	"The Buffs" (East Kent Regiment)	D, F, L.
1685	King's Liverpool Regiment	D, F, L.
1685	Devonshire Regiment	D, R.
1685	Suffolk Regiment	D, F.
1685	Somersetshire Light Infantry	D, F, R, L.
1688	Yorkshire Regiment	F, R, L.
1688	Lancashire Fusiliers	D, F.
1678	Royal Scots Fusiliers	D, F, L.
1689	Royal Welsh Fusiliers	D, F, L.
1689	King's Own Scottish Borderers	F, L.
1694	1st Battalion, Gloucestershire Regiment	F.
1702	1st Battalion, East Surrey Regiment	D, F.
1702	Duke of Cornwall's Light Infantry	D, F, L.
1702	Duke of Wellington's West Riding Regiment	D, F, L.
1702	Border Regiment	F.
1701	2nd Battalion, Worcestershire Regiment	L.
1702	1st Battalion, Hampshire Regiment	D, L.
1739	"The Black Watch," Royal Highlanders	F.
1740	Northamptonshire Regiment	L.

Appendix 2: British Officers Killed and Wounded at Fontenoy

From the Duke of Cumberland's Returns.

Corps.	Killed.	Wounded.
General Staff	Lt.-Gen. Hon. Sir James Campbell, K.B.; Major-Gen. Hon. H. Ponsonby.	Major-Gen. the Earl of Albemarle; „ Hon. Charles Howard; Brigadier George Churchill; „ Thomas Ingoldsby.
First Guards (Grenadier Guards)	Captains Harvey, Berckeley (*sic*), and Brereton; Ensign Sir Alex. Cockburn.	Lt.-Col. Lord Charles Hay; Captains Hildesley, Parkes, Pearson, and Bockland; Ensigns Nash and Vane.
Second Guards (Coldstream Guards)	Ensigns Cathcart and Molesworth.	Lt.-Cols. Needham, Corbet, Kellet, Moysten, and Lord Robert Bertie; Captains Townsend and Cæsar; Ensigns Burton and Vanburg.
Third Guards (Scots Guards)	Colonel Carpenter; Lt.-Col. Douglas; Captain Ross; Ensign Murray.	Lt.-Cols. Waldegrave and Fraser; Captains Laurie, Knevit, Maitland, Haldane, and Neil.
Royal North British Regiment (The Royal Scots, or Lothian Regiment)	...	Captains Thomson and Edmonston; Lieuts. Cockburn, Nairn, Elliot, Abernethy, and Grant; Ensign Jones.
Lt.-Gen. Howard's (The Buffs)	Quartermaster Cummins	Lieut. Tanner; Ensign Punceford.
Onslow's (The King's Liverpool Regiment)	...	Lt.-Col. Keightly; Major Gray; Captains Dalton, Loftus, and Ekins; Ensigns Cook and Thomson.
Sowle's (The Devonshire Regiment)	Captain Browne; Lieuts. Capel and Mowbray; Ensign Farrington.	Lt.-Col. Tullikens; Major Montague; Lieut. Hackstraw.
Duroure's (The Suffolk Regiment)	Colonel Duroure; Lt.-Col. Whitmore; Captain Campbell; Lieuts. Borkland and Laine; Ensigns Cannon and Clifton.	Major Coseley; Captains Rainsford and De Cosne; Capt.-Lieut. Goulstone; Lieuts. Salt, Robinson, Murray, Townsend, Millington, and Dalgarné; Ensigns Dagers and Pearce.

Corps.	Killed.	Wounded.
Pulteney's (The Somerset Light Infantry)	Captain Queenchant	Capt.-Lieut. Dan. Nicolas; Lieuts. W. Jones and Sam. Edhouse.
Major-Gen. Howard's (The Yorkshire Regiment)	Lieut. Legrand; Ensign Gibson.	Major Petitot; Captains Corkran and Douglas; Lieut. Coote; Ensigns Cheape, Martin, and Porterfeld.
Bligh's (The Lancashire Fusiliers)	Lt.-Col. Gee	Captains Meyrac and Maxwell; Lieuts. Bouchitière and Vickers; Ensign Hartley.
Scots Fusiliers (The Royal Scots Fusiliers)	Lieuts. Campbell, Houston, and Sergeant.	Major Colvil; Captains Latan, Olivant, Knatchbull, and Sandilands; Lieuts. Maxwell, Colvil, Bollenden, M'Gacken, Townsend, and Stuart; Quartermaster Stuart.
Welsh Fusiliers (The Royal Welsh Fusiliers)	Lieuts. Weaver, Pryce, Foster, and Isaac.	Major Lort; Captains Hickman, Carey, Bernard, Drysdale, Tayler, Sabine, and Johnston; Lieuts. Izard, Aubry, Clarke, Eyre, Roberts, Role, Berners, Gregge, Hawes, and Lort.
Rothes' (The King's Own Scottish Borderers)	Ensign Bonvillette	Lt.-Col. Kennedy; Major Dalrymple; Captains Worge and Lucas; Lieuts. Livingston and Hay; Ensigns Cockburn and Jones.
Bragg's (1st Batt. Gloucestershire Regiment)	Lieut. Cliffe	Lord George Sackville; Captains Sailly, Fitzgerald, Jocelyn, and Holt; Lieuts. Wright, Edgeworth, and Graydon; Ensigns Harman and Michelson.
Handisyde's (1st Batt. East Surrey Regiment)	Lt.-Col. Montague; Captains Baird and Pollock; Lieut. Dalway.	Lieuts. Stafford and Porter; Ensigns Worseley, Bramley, and Freeman.
Skelton's (The Duke of Cornwall's Light Infantry)	...	Captain Farquhar; First Lieuts. Lindsay, Martin, and Banks; Second Lieuts. How and Prescot.
Johnson's (1st Batt. Duke of Wellington's West Riding Regiment)	Lt.-Col. Clements; Lieuts. Graame, Colley, and Houghton.	Major Mure; Captains Godfrey, Lacey, Elles, Tighe, Gardner, Burrough, Otway, and Gore; Ensigns Rayner, Collis, Samson, and Descury.
Cholmondeley's (1st Batt. Border Regiment)	...	Lieuts. Cramer, Forrest, Mure, Cortney, and Hargroves; Ensigns Donallon and Stacey.
Sempill's (The Black Watch)	Captain John Campbell; Ensign Lachlan Campbell.	Captains Robert Campbell, Ronald Campbell, and James Campbell.
3rd Troop, Horse Guards (The Life Guards)	...	Lt.-Col. Lamelonière.

Corps.	Killed.	Wounded.
4th Troop, Horse Guards (The Life Guards)	...	Captain Hilgrove; Cornet Bardel.
2nd Troop, Horse Grenadier Guards (The Life Guards)	...	Major Brereton; Captains Elliott and Burton; Adjutant Thacker.
Regiment of Horse Guards (The Royal Horse Guards, Blue)	...	Colonel Black; Captain Lloyd; Captain-Lieut. Miget; Quartermasters Hudgson and Butt.
King's Regiment of Horse (1st Dragoon Guards)	...	Lieut. Brace.
Ligonier's Horse (7th Dragoon Guards)	...	Quartermaster Heath.
Royal Dragoons (1st, Royal, Dragoons)	...	Lt.-Col. Naizon; Cornets Hartwell, Desnieret, and Creighton.
North British Dragoons (The Royal Scots Greys)	...	Cornet Glasgo.
King's Own Regiment of Dragoons (3rd (King's Own) Hussars)	...	Captain Wade; Cornet Bland; Quartermaster Corbidge.
Queen's Regiment of Dragoons (7th (Queen's Own) Hussars)	Cornet Potts	Lt.-Col. Erskine; Capt.-Lieut. Ogilvey; Lieut. Forbes; Cornet Maitland; and Quartermaster Smith.
Stair's Dragoons (6th (Inniskilling) Dragoons)	Quartermaster Baird	...
Artillery . . .	Lieutenant Bennet	...

Appendix 3: References to the Plan of Battle of Fontenoy

INFANTERIE.

BRIGADES ET RENVOIS.	BATAILLONS.
1. LES deux Redoutes du Bois de Barri, défendues par le Régiment d'EU	2
2. Le Village, Église & Cimetière de Fontenoy, défendu par la Brigade de DAUPHIN & d'un Bataillon de BEAUVOISIS : à la Brigade de DAUPHIN s'est joint pendant l'Action un Bataillon du Régiment du ROY ; fait en tout	5
3. Redoutes entre Fontenoy & Antoing, soutenues par des Détachemens de DIESBACH & de BETTENS	0
4. Retranchemens d'ANTOING.	
5. La Brigade de PIEMONT, composée de quatre Bataillons de PIEMONT & un de ROYAL LA MARINE, gardoient les Retranchemens d'Antoing	4
6. Bataillon de BIRON, qui avoit été placé derrière la Brigade de PIEMONT, a été porté dès le commencement de l'Action en ligne entre Fontenoy & Antoing à la droite de CRILLON	1
7. NORMANDIE ; il n'arriva que pour les dernières charges que les Troupes du ROY ont faites : cette Brigade eut encore assez de temps pour s'y distinguer avec honneur	4
8. ROYAL CORSE	1
Deux autres Bataillons étoient dans le Château d'Elmont.	
9. BULKELEY } Brigades Irlandoises	
10. DILLON	
11. BERWICK	
12. LALLY	6
13. RUTH de chacune un Bataillon.	
14. CLARE	
15. ROYAL VAISSEAUX	3

BRIGADES ET RENVOIS.	BATAILLONS.
16. HAINAUT	1
17. ROYAL	3
18. SOISSONNOIS ayant LA COURONNE pour Chef de Brigade.	1
19. LA COURONNE	3
20. GARDES-SUISSES	2
Trois autres Bataillons étoient aux Retranchemens du Pont de Vaux.	
21. GARDES-FRANÇOISES	4
Deux autres Bataillons étoient aux Retranchemens du Pont de Vaux, & dès le commencement de l'Action deux Bataillons passèrent encore aux mêmes Retranchemens.	
22. COURTEN	3
23. AUBETERRE, Chef de Brigade de COURTEN	3
24. DU ROY	3
Deux autres Bataillons indiqués sous le même N°. étoient dans les Retranchemens du Village de Fontenoy.	
25. DIESBACH	1
Deux autres Bataillons étoient, l'un au service de l'Artillerie, & l'autre dans les trois Redoutes entre Fontenoy & Antoing.	
26. BETHENS	2
Les Bataillons de BETTENS & de DIESBACH faisoient la gauche de la Ligne formée entre Anthoin & Fontenoy.	
27. CRILLON avança jusqu'à la deuxième Redoute	3
28. TROUPES qui se portèrent sur la droite pendant l'Action aux chiffres 16, 17, 18, & 19 : ainsi l'on y verra HAINAUT, ROYAL, SOISSONNOIS & la COURONNE.	
a ROYAL LA MARINE.	
Aux Retranchemens d'Antoing	1

CAVALERIE.

Brigades et Renvois.	Escadrons.
29. ROYAL ROUSSILLON	4
30. LE PRINCE CAMILLE	4
31. CRAVATES	4
32. DE FIENNES	3
33. DE FITZ-JAMES	4
34. DE CLERMONT-PRINCE	4
35. DE BRANCAS	4
36. DU COLONEL GENERAL	4
37. CARABINIERS	10
38. GENDARMES de la Garde	4
39. CHEVAU-LEGERS	1
40. MOUSQUETAIRES	2
41. GARDES DU ROY	8
42. GRENADIERS à Cheval	1
43. BERRY	4
44. NOAILLES	4
45. PENTHIEVRE	4
46. PONS	4
47. BRIONNE	4
48. CHABRILLANT	4
49. ROYAL ETRANGER	4
50. DRAGONS DE ROYAL	4
Dans la Ligne entre Anthoin & Fontenoy.	
51. BEAUFREMONT	5
Dans la même Ligne.	
52. MESTRE DE CAMP DRAGONS	4
53. GENDARMERIE arrivée au moment du Combat	4
Les quatre autres n'ont rejoint que le lendemain.	
54. Maison du ROY, qui avoit été portée en reserve à Notre-Dame-aux-Bois.	
55. Maisons avancées du Village de Fontenoy hors les Retranchemens que nos Troupes brûlèrent sur le signal qui avoit été donné de l'approche des Ennemis.	

Troupes arrivés à la fin du Combat, & placées en seconde Ligne de Cavalerie.

56. LES CUIRASSIERS	4
57. EGMONT Cavalerie	4
58. TAILLERAND	4
59. ORLEANS Cavalerie	4
60. CLERMONT-TONNERRE	4
61. Le Régiment DU ROY Cavalerie	4
62. DRAGONS D'EGMONT	4

INFANTERIE.

	Bataillons.
63. TOURAINE	3
64. NIVERNOIS	1
65. AUVERGNE, Chef de Brigade de NIVERNOIS: Les GRASSINS répandus dans le Bois de Barri en observations par différens Détachemens tant à pied qu'à cheval.	

Troupes Ennemies.

A. Cavalerie . . . .

B. Infanterie qui se disposoit pour nous attaquer, & qui forma ensuite un Bataillon quarré.

C. Bataillon quarré qui enfonça jusque dans les deux premières Lignes de notre Infanterie, parce qu'elle avoit été dégarnie de monde, qu'on avoit envoyé pour garder les Retranchemens du Pont de Vaux, ainsi que je l'ai dit ci-devant aux No. 20 & 21.

} Troupes Angloises, Autrichiennes, & Hanoveriennes.

D. Deux Colonnes d'Infanterie qui par deux différentes fois vinrent attaquer de front le Village de Fontenoy par un feu épouvantable de 50 pièces de canon; mais ils y furent toujours repoussés avec une perte considérable.

E. Première disposition de la Cavalerie Hollandoise.

F. Cavalerie Hollandoise, qui s'est jointe à la gauche de l'Infanterie Angloise pour attaquer Fontenoy en flanc, mais elle essuya le même sort des Anglois.

G. Cavalerie Hollandoise, qui s'est retirée en deux Colonnes derrière leur Infanterie.

H. Première disposition de l'Infanterie Hollandoise.

I. Infanterie Hollandoise en deux Colonnes, qui s'étoient approchées pour attaquer le Bourg d'Antoing, y furent repoussées, de même que la Cavalerie, & restèrent l'une & l'autre dans leur dernière position pendant l'Action qui se passoit entre Fontenoy & le Bois de Barri.

REMARQUES.

Aux Postes d'Antoing, Fontenoy & les Redoutes, le nombre des pièces de canon est marqué au vrai par des lignes droites, à la reserve de l'une des deux Redoutes du Bois de Barri, où quatre pièces qui y étoient n'ont point servies, lesquelles sont marquées par des lignes de points.

Les Canons qui ont servis à la bataille sont placés en même nombre de petits Canons vis-à-vis des Brigades de la première Ligne.

Appendix 4: Services of the Irish Brigade During the War of the Austrian Succession

This compact little force exercised an influence which was out of all proportion to its numbers in the campaigns of 1745 and 1747. When war broke out, the Irish troops in French service included one cavalry regiment (Fitz-James's) of 240 sabres, and five infantry battalions (Bulkeley's, Clare's, Dillon's, Ruth's, and Berwick's), each numbering 685 men. At the close of Marshal Wade's campaign the non-commissioned officers' and privates' pay was augmented by 2 *sols per diem*. Thenceforward privates drew 8 *sols* 6 *deniers*, or 6 *livres* 1 *sol* 3 *deniers per mensem*, after deductions for rations.

The extra charge was met by retrenching 40 men from each battalion, and their average strength was thus reduced to 645. The 200 men discharged formed the nucleus of a sixth battalion, raised in the winter of 1744 by the Comte de Lally-Tollendal, and it was soon brought up to full strength by enrolling deserters from the British Army in Flanders. Thus, the brigade at Fontenoy consisted of six battalions and 3870 bayonets.

The Earl of Clare was inspector, and so great was his tact that the whole force formed, so to speak, a single regiment. Friction there was with the Royal Scottish on the delicate question of recruiting, but the Irish regiments worked together in complete harmony.

Their splendid gallantry at Fontenoy was acknowledged by rewards on an unprecedented scale. Lieutenant-Colonel Stapleton (Berwick's) was promoted brigadier; Lieutenant-Colonels Lee (Bulkeley's) and Cusack (Ruth's) were given pensions of 1000 and 600 *livres*. Crosses of St Louis were lavishly distributed, and wounded officers received gratuities of 200 to 600 *livres*. Fitz-James's Cavalry suffered as severely as the Foot, and was granted 74 horses from the Royal Remount Department to replace a portion of those which were slain during successive charges.

On the capture of Ghent (July 15, 1745) a vast quantity of British stores fell into the enemy's hands. The cloth and uniforms found in magazine were distributed to the Irish regiments gratis, enabling them to make a brave show in brand-new scarlet garb.

After the Fontenoy campaign the pickets of the Brigade were ordered to Scotland, but only those of Dillon's, Ruth's, and Lally's, with one squadron of Fitz-James's, succeeded in reaching Montrose. They were of great value to Prince Charles Edward, but were all slain or taken prisoners at Culloden. The rest of Fitz-James's troopers, and Bulkeley's, Clare's, and Berwick's pickets, were captured during the voyage by British cruisers.

The brigade saw no active service in 1746. It was dispatched to guard the Norman and Breton coasts against anticipated raids, such as the expedition to Lorient. In the ensuing campaign, however, it won additional glory at Laffeldt (July 2, 1745). Its losses were as heavy as at Fontenoy, and the rewards were on a yet more lavish scale. Brigadier Lord Dunkeld (commanding) obtained a pension of 3000 *livres*; Brigadier Cusack an augmentation of 1000 *livres*; Colonel Lee (Bulkeley's) was promoted brigadier; and pensions were given to Lieutenant-Colonels Grant (Clare's), Mannecy (?Manisty?) of Dillon's, Barnard (Berwick's), and Hogarty (Lally's). Major Carrol (Berwick's) and Captains Hennessy (Bulkeley's) and Arthur (Ruth's) were promoted lieutenant-colonel. A shower fell of crosses of St Louis, and wounded officers received life-pensions ranging from 200 to 600 *livres*.

Comte d'Argenson, Minister of War, acknowledged the Brigade's services at Laffeldt in the following reply to congratulations offered by M. de Bulkeley:—

> I have received with all possible esteem the compliments you were pleased to pay me on the occasion of the victory which the king has gained at Laffeldt. Justice compels me to own that I am your debtor, on account of the valour with which the Irish Brigade, and your regiment in particular, charged the enemy. Although your duties at Ostend did not permit you to be present at the battle, you are none the less a partaker in the glory which your regiment has won by these new proofs of its brav-

ery. I am aware that the harmony which prevails in it is chiefly owing to the attention of M. de Lee. (July 22, 1747.)

Unfortunately for British interests, the Brigade's courage and discipline were exerted on the enemy's side, and more than once did they turn the scale against us. Mr Mathew O'Conor's eloquent words find an echo in every heart which is not dominated by prejudice:—

> Let no one asperse the character of the Irish because they fought so often under foreign colours. Exiled, persecuted, and loyal, they lent their valour to the States which supported their dethroned kings, their outlawed religion, their denationalised country, their vow of vengeance, or their hopes of freedom. Viewed carelessly at a distance, their varied services seem evidence of an unprincipled praetorian race; examined in detail, with references to the creed, politics, and foreign relations of Ireland at each period, they only prove an amount of patriotism, piety, and valour which, concentrated at home to national service, would have made Ireland all we could wish her. (*The Irish Brigades,* Dublin, 1855.)

The Battle of Fontenoy, 1745
By James Grant

On the 7th of March, 1745, William Duke of Cumberland was commissioned as Captain-General of the British Army, being the third and last in succession after the Dukes of Marlborough and Ormond who has held that high rank. He was, moreover, appointed commander-in-chief of the Confederate forces, and at a Council of War held at Brussels it was agreed that these should be ready to take the field on a chosen day, if he approved; and on the 7th of April he reached the Belgian capital, and commenced his inspection of the troops.

To garrison the towns sufficiently it was computed that 18,000 men would be required; hence, from this cause and other detachments, the army did not muster more than 43,450 men.

Maurice Count Saxe, who commanded the French, had obtained great celebrity by the skilful manner in which he had managed his retreats in Germany. Not only had he shown great military talents, and coolness and intrepidity, but he also evinced the knowledge of a skilful commander. According to Voltaire, he brought into the field 35,000 more men than the Confederates; his strength being 106 battalions and 172 squadrons, while they had but 46 battalions and 90 squadrons.

The campaign opened with the investment of Tournay. The Duke of Cumberland and the Austrian general, Marshal Count Konigseck, marched for Halle, and on the 22nd of April were at Soignies.

Louis XV., accompanied by the *dauphin*, reached the camp before Tournay, when Marshal Saxe told the former that:

> He expected the Confederates were bold enough to give battle; therefore, as he was conscious that the French troops were unable to stand before the British forces fairly in the field, he was determined to depend upon stratagem rather than open strength, and accordingly made the best preparations for a brave

defence against a noble attack.—*Cumberland's Memoirs*.

The disposition of his troops was most advantageous.

To block up Tournay he left 18,000 men; the defence of the bridges of the Scheldt, and to keep the communications open, he assigned to 6,000 more. The siege of Tournay had been pressed vigorously when the Duke of Cumberland advanced to its relief unwisely, as he had only 53,000 men with which to make the attempt. The Dutch, who proved worse than useless in the campaign, were led by the Prince of Waldeck, a leader possessed of as little skill and experience as the former, who though Captain-General of the British Army, and so obese and unwieldy in figure as to be scarcely able to ride his horse, was only in his twenty-fourth year. Konigseck, who commanded our Austrian allies, was aged, and long past the time for campaigning; and thus led, the Allies advanced to engage one of the finest armies in Europe, led by the first general and strategist of the age, Count Saxe, Marshal-General of France and Duke Elect of Courland and Semigallia, an officer so esteemed in Europe that the Marshal Duke de Noailles was content to serve under him as his first *aide-de-camp*.

His army was led by five princes of the blood, and sixty-seven general officers, all of noble families; but at this time Saxe was so ill as to be unable to sit on horseback or wear uniform; thus he accompanied the troops in a litter.

He took up a position at Fontenoy, a small village which is situated on rising ground four miles east of Tournay, and on the left bank of the Scheldt. Along the summit of the eminence which there slopes upward from the plain, he formed his line of infantry. The village of St. Antoine, near the river, covered his right flank, and the defence of it was entrusted to the Regiments of Piedmont and Biron respectively, under the Counts De la Marche and De Lorges.

The wood of Barri covered his left; it was full of troops and guns. They had a battery at St. Antoine; another in their centre, at Fontenoy, entrenched and fortified; another at the wood; and, according to *Cumberland's Memoirs*, they had also batteries in rear of their wings:

> .... which were to open at a proper time, and make way for the horrible destruction expected from them by cartridge shot. They had cannon planted, almost invisible, on their intrenchments, pointed breast-high, and loaded so as to do dreadful execution; while their own forces were almost secure from danger, by being entrenched up to their necks.

There were also abattis of felled trees, fascines of baskets, and walls of turf.

The lines at Fontenoy were defended altogether by 260 heavy cannon and field-pieces. The village he committed to the Count de la Vauguyon, with the *Regiment du Dauphine*. On his left were the brave corps of the Irish Brigade, under the gallant Lord Clare. On their left were the French Marines, under the Count de Guerchi; and in their rear, was the Regiment of Angoumois, in the castle of Bourquembrai, on which a white banner with three *fleurs-de-lis* was flying.

It was impossible to turn the flanks pf the French, and to assail in front their superior force thus posted evinced either the extremity of rashness or of ignorance. Moreover, the reconnaissance made by Cumberland was most imperfect; yet he ordered his army, consisting, as we have said, of only 46 battalions and 90 squadrons, to advance at once to the attack. He had ninety pieces of ordnance; eight of these were mortars, but many were only three-pounder falconets. The whole position of Saxe rose with a gentle ascent from a flat and fertile plain, where the young grass was sprouting in the fields; and this he could sweep by the concentrated fire of 260 pieces of ordnance.

The night of the 30th of April was chilly, dark, and moonless, and mist was enveloping the banks of the Scheldt, the wood of Barri, and the slope of Fontenoy, when, at two o'clock on the morning of the first of May, the Allies began to advance over the open plain. The atmosphere was so still that they could hear the village clocks striking, as in the dark the columns of attack were formed.

The right wing was composed of British and Hanoverians, who, under General Zastrow, formed a portion of the centre, and were formed in four lines before a village named Veson. The left wing, composed of Dutch and Austrians, reached to the wood of Peronne. In front of Veson was a redoubt mounted with cannon, and manned by 600 Frenchmen; and this point Brigadier Ingoldsby had special orders to storm at the head of four battalions, while the Prince of Waldeck was to assail Fontenoy at the head of the Dutch. And with these orders to fulfil, the troops, encumbered by their knapsacks, blankets, kettles, and great-coats, stumbled forward in the dark, over hedges, through water-cuts and the growing grain, till they formed open column of regiments at quarter-distance columns of companies, and there deployed into line three ranks deep.

With the British Army in the field there now appeared a regiment of Highlanders for the first time—the famous Black Watch, now numbered as the 42nd. They were in the division of Ingoldsby. Their dress, being so well known, requires no description, save their bonnets, which were flat and blue and bordered then, as now, by the fess-cheque of the House of Stuart, with a tuft of black feathers. Their arms were a musket, bayonet, and large basket-hilted broadsword; these were furnished by government and such men as chose were permitted to carry a dirk, a pair of pistols, and around shield, after the fashion of their country. Their sword-belts were black.

Lieutenant-Colonel Sir Robert Munro was their leader on this day.

The Brigade of Guards was led by Sir John Ligonier, son of Colonel Francis Ligonier, a French Protestant refugee.

At a quarter to four a.m. the cannonade commenced, as the mist cleared away, and the earliest beams of day began to lighten the flat horizon, and it continued without intermission.

Sir John Ligonier was ordered to advance with the Brigade of Guards and seven guns, to check a destructive fire from the enemy's field artillery, and the moment they were silenced the whole line was to advance upon the French position.

The seven guns were grape-shotted, and the brigade advanced with bayonets fixed at a rapid pace. Several officers fell; two lieutenant-colonels, Douglas (son of Lord Morton) and Carpenter, of the Scots Guards, were unhorsed and killed at the same moment: but speedily the Guardsmen were among the French field-pieces, bayonetting and cutting down the gunners before they could limber up and retire. The *History of the War* says:

> The Guards and Highlanders began the battle, and attacked a body of French near Veson, where the Dauphin was posted. Though the enemy were entrenched breast-high, the Guards with their bayonets, and the Highlanders with sword, pistol, and dirk, forced them out, killing a considerable number.

The Guards and Black Watch then fell back and rejoined the first line, the formation of which was complete by nine o'clock; when Sir John Ligonier sent his *aide-de-camp* to acquaint the Duke of Cumberland that as the guns were silenced, "he was ready, and only waiting for the signal of Prince Waldeck to attack Fontenoy." The troops then moved forward with astonishing intrepidity to their respective points of attack.

The "advance" was then sounded by many a trumpet and bugle,

while, amid a stunning roar of musketry, the troops rushed on; the Dutch under Waldeck against Fontenoy, Ingoldsby to assail the redoubt in front of Veson, and the first line of British and Hanoverians, led by Cumberland in person, to attack the centre.

So quick was the rush, that the duke and other officers rode their horses at a canter; but their men fell fast on every hand while passing between Barri and Fontenoy, "the fire of the cannon making whole lanes through the ranks of the Confederates particularly the English."

Under this the Dutch, who covered their left, fell into disorder, and could be rallied no more during the day. The cavalry also became disorganised. The Earl of Crawford, colonel of the Royal Scots Dragoons, remarks that the conduct of the Dutch:

> .... had an extremely bad effect on the mind of the troops in general, though not so much on ours, who were the first ranged, and still marched towards the enemy, the noblest sight I ever saw, and never stopped till they got through a shower of bullets and musketry.

Brigadier Ingoldsby, who had special orders to carry the redoubts at the Bois de Barri, imagined the difficulty to be greater than it was; and instead of storming the works at once, and scouring the wood with the bayonet, he returned to the duke for artillery, thus affording the enemy time to strengthen the works. For this he was afterwards tried by a court-martial, but vindicated himself by denying that he had ever received orders on this occasion, and added that those he did receive were so contradictory that he did not know which to obey.

Led by the Duke of Cumberland, attended by Lord Cathcart, K.T., the first line succeeded in passing Fontenoy and the redoubt, and got within thirty yards of the enemy's muzzles. Receiving fire therefore, at this distance, "the British doubled up in a column, and advanced between the batteries," all of which were playing upon a spot not quite half a mile in breadth. The slaughter was indescribable. Whole ranks perished, but the intervals were closed up, and after two terrible rushes with the bayonet, they broke the brigade of French Guards, and hurled them back in disorder upon their supports, the Irish regiments of Lord Clare. The French cavalry now advanced, but went about, unable to face the fire that mowed down horse and man.

At this portion of the battle there occurred two episodes worth repeating. We find one in Voltaire, and the other in the *Records of the 42nd Highlanders,* which had been withdrawn from Ingoldby's division and attached to the Guards.

Voltaire tells us that the officers of the British Guards, when in the presence of the enemy, saluted the French by taking off their hats. The Count de Chambanne and Duke de Biron, who were in advance, returned the salute, as did all the other officers of the French Guards. Lord Charles Hay (son of the Marquis of Tweedale), a captain in the English Guards, called aloud—

"Gentlemen of the French Guards, fire!"

"Gentlemen," replied the Count d'Anterroche, lieutenant of grenadiers, "we never fire first; fire yourselves."

He continues:

> The British then commenced a running fire in divisions (platoons?), so that one battalion made a discharge, and afterwards another, while the first reloaded. Nineteen officers of the French Guards fell by the first discharge. Messieurs de Clisson, de Ligney, de la Peyre, and 95 soldiers were killed, and 285 were wounded; also 11 Swiss officers, and 209 of their soldiers, of whom 64 died on the spot. Colonel Courten, his lieutenant-colonel, 4 officers and 75 soldiers were killed, and 200 soldiers were dangerously wounded. The first rank being swept away, the three others, finding themselves unsupported, except by a regiment of cavalry at a distance, dispersed. The Duke de Grammont, their colonel and first lieutenant-general, who might have rallied them, was killed. Monsieur Luttaux, next in rank to De Grammont, did not reach the ground until they had abandoned it. The English advanced as if performing part of their exercise; the majors levelling the soldiers' muskets with their canes, to make their aim more sure.

In the *Records of the 42nd*, we find that this second attack was made about midday:

> When the Dutch again failed, and Lieutenant-Colonel Sir Robert Munro, with the Highlanders, was ordered to sustain the British troops, who were severely engaged with superior numbers.
>
> Sir Robert having obtained the duke's permission to let his men fight in their own fashion, they flung themselves flat on the ground when the French fired a volley, which thus swept harmlessly over them. Then, springing up, they poured in their fire, slung their mus-

kets, and in the smoke, rushed on with target and claymore. Doddridge in his *Life of Colonel Gardiner*, says:

> Sir Robert was everywhere with his regiment, notwithstanding his great corpulency, and when in the trenches, he was hauled out by the legs and arms by his own men; and it was observed that when he commanded the whole regiment to clap to the ground, he alone stood upright with the colours behind, receiving the fire of the enemy.

A little work entitled, *Conduct of Officers at Fontenoy Considered*, states that the Duke of Cumberland remarked the gallant conduct of the regiment, and observed a Highlander, who had killed nine men, making a stroke at a tenth with his broadsword, when his arm was torn off by a cannonball.

His Royal Highness applauded the Highlander's conduct, and promised him a reward of value equal to the arm.

The line of the French trenches was choked with dead and dying; while three-cornered hats, powdered wigs, weapons, and half-buried shot lay everywhere.

At this crisis, the British had decidedly the advantage over the left wing. The Duke de Grammont was killed by some English artillerymen, who, perceiving that he was splendidly mounted, conceived him to be an officer of rank, and made bets among themselves as to who would bring him down. His thigh was broken by a ball, and he expired on the field. For firing this shot, a *matross* named Baker received a pension of £18 *per annum*.

On the other side. Sir James Campbell, K.B., son of Lord Loudon, and colonel of the Scots Greys, fell at their head. A cannon-shot smashed one of his legs, and he expired just as he was being borne from the field, in his eightieth year.

The standard of this regiment was borne by Sir William Erskine, then a comet. His father, the lieutenant-colonel of the Greys, tied the standard to his son's right leg, and said, "Go, and take care of this; let me not see you separate, for if you return alive you must produce this standard."

After the battle, the cornet rode up to his father, and displayed the standard tight and fast, as in the morning.

Unsupported by cavalry, the British infantry bore down all before them, driving the French left 300 paces beyond Fontenoy, and making them, selves masters of the field, from the ground on which they stood to their own camp. But as the left retired, the columns wheeled back, or opened and uncovered two batteries of heavy guns, which poured on the British such a storm of cartridge shot in front and flank, that it was impossible to face it. Rallying, however, they completed the disorder of the French, who were fairly beaten; and had some fresh battalions from the reserve replaced those that had suffered from the masked batteries, or had the second line advanced to enable the cavalry to get past the redoubts, the enemy could not have recovered the day.

Colonel Mackinnon, in his *History of the Coldstream Guards*, says:

> According to the first plan drawn out, the French would have been taken in flank by Lord Crawford, who was to advance along the edge of the wood leading to the road of Leuse, where Prince Waldeck's regiments, with some hussars, had endeavoured to penetrate in the morning; and if the troops under Lord Crawford had been reinforced, instead of being withdrawn on the failure of the Dutch, the results of the battle would probably have been different. Lord Crawford himself gives it as his real opinion that orders were at one time issued for the retreat of the French. The left, although supported by the fire from the English artillery, did not succeed; and Fort Veson not being carried, the British were placed between a cross-fire of cannon and musketry, which obliged them to retire on the height of Fontenoy.

When the French infantry were fairly driven out of the village of St. Antoine, the Count de Saxe believed the battle was lost, and sent an officer with such tidings to the king and dauphin, who were seated on horseback at an eminence named "The Justice of our Lady in the Wood," where the royal standard of France was flying. The latter was immediately struck, by the order of Louis, as the officer begged that they would provide for their own safety by flight.

Guns were brought to bear on the British artillery, which in some degree slackened its fire, and gave time for the Irish Brigade to form. It was the last resource left to King Louis and Count Saxe. It was at the most critical period of that bloody day, when, after being harassed by the manoeuvres of the past night, when, after enduring a cannonade from more than 200 pieces of ordnance, after driving in the field-guns, after forcing a passage between Fontenoy and the wood of Barri, and after hurling the foe from the heights and village of St. Antoine, that the Irish Brigade, of immortal memory, came fully into action against the Confederates—the representatives of 30,000 Irishmen who had followed King James into exile—these were the veteran regiments of Clare, the Honourable Arthur Dillon, Count O'Lally, the Duke of Berwick, Rothe, and the Counts Buckley and Fitzjames; and the gallant Charles O'Brien, Lord Clare, was at their head. Fitzjames's regiment was a dragoon corps; and the regiments of Normandy and Vaisseaux were ordered to support them.

It must have been with emotions of a very mingled nature that some of the troops in that field, particularly the Highlanders, beheld the advance of the Irish exiles, who were all clad in scarlet uniform, with white breeches.

A yell rang along their ranks as the seven regiments came on, and their cry had a terrible significance. It was—

Cuimhnigidh ar Luimneac agus ar fheile na Sacsanach!
(Remember Limerick and Saxon faith!)

Pouring in a volley, they rushed on our toil worn infantry with the bayonet, after having successively routed the finest troops in the French service, who were now fated to be routed, and by the Irish! Mackinnon says:

No additional corps were sent to the relief of the British, whose compact formation had hitherto enabled them to repair the repeated losses occasioned by these incessant attacks. No fresh orders were issued; no cavalry was within reach to follow up the panic which had seized upon the enemy. The Dutch did not appear in any quarter, nor was there any probability of a sortie from Tournay to aid this isolated body. . . . . . . The encounter between the British and the Irish Brigade was fierce, the fire constant, the slaughter great; and the loss on the side of the British was such that they were compelled at length to retire.

The Duke of Cumberland lost all presence of mind, and his army fell back in undeniable confusion, cavalry and infantry all mingled together; and but for the steady stand made by the Earl of Crawford, with the 3rd Buffs and the Highlanders, to cover the rear, the defeated Allies had not crossed the Bruffoel so speedily, though some corps faced about to fire again at every hundred paces.

The army moved to Lessines, and encamped there near Aeth.

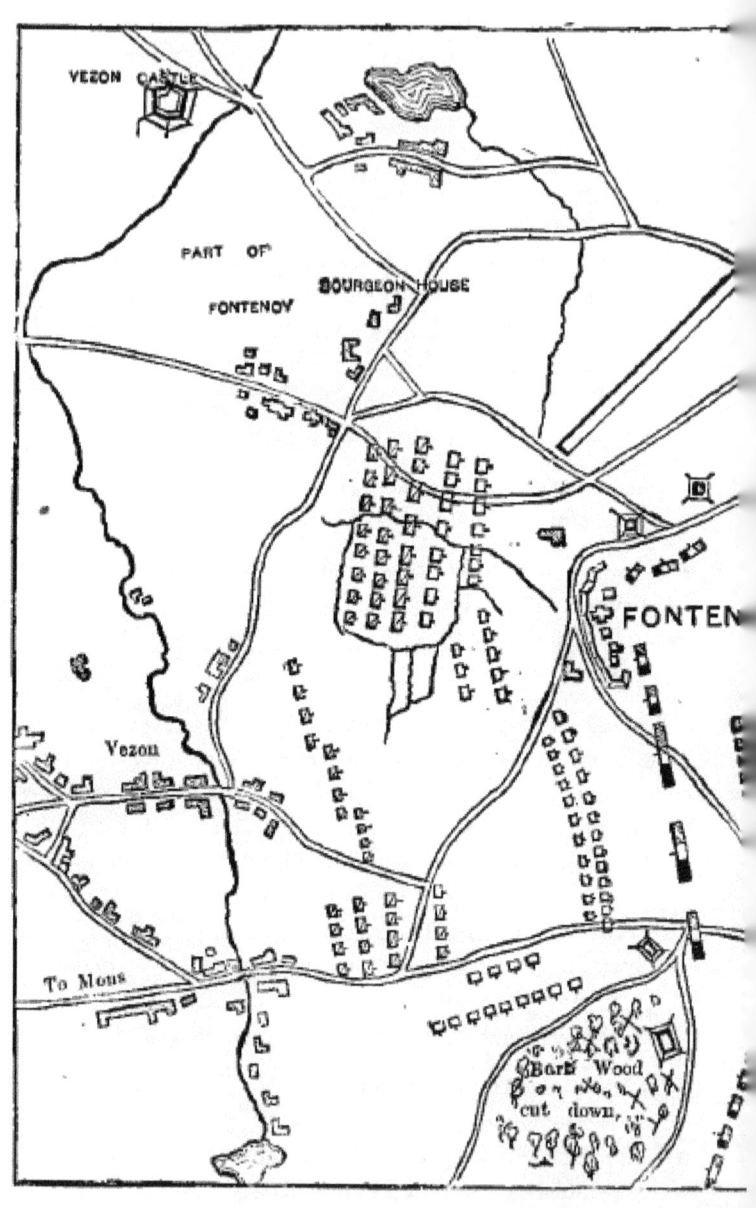

PLAN OF THE BATT

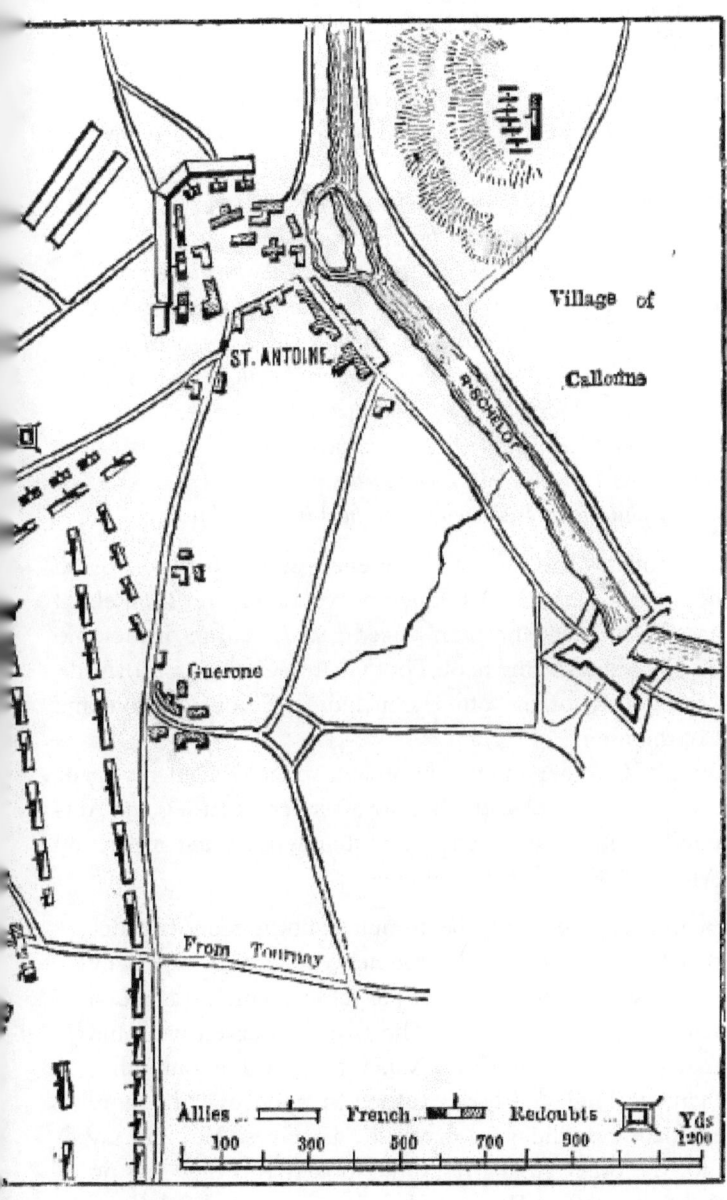

Louis is said to have ridden down to the bivouac of the Irish, and thanked them personally.

An Irish ballad, perhaps unknown in England, refers with exultation to Fontenoy:—

> *O'Brien's voice is hoarse with joy, as halting, he commands,*
> *'Fix bayonets—Charge!' Like mountain storm rush on these fiery bands;*
> *Like lions leaping at a fold, when mad with hunger's pang.*
> *Right onward to the English line the Irish exiles sprang.*
> *Bright was their steel—'tis bloody!—the muskets filled with gore;*
> *Through shattered ranks, and severed files, and trampled flags they tore.*
> *The English strove with desperate strength; they rallied, staggered, fled:*
> *The green hill-side is matted close with dying and with dead.*
> *Across the plain, and far away, passed on that hideous wreck,*
> *While cavalier and fantassin dash in upon their track.*
> *On Fontenoy, on Fontenoy, like eagles in the sun.*
> *With bloody plumes the Irish stand—the field is lost and won.*

Voltaire estimates the loss of the French in this battle at 8,000 men, while the Allies had 21,000 killed or wounded. Our Household Brigade had 724 officers and men placed *hors de combat;* of these no less than 437 belonged to the Scots Foot Guards. Of the Irish Brigade, there fell one-fourth of the officers, including Colonel Dillon, and one-third of the men.

The Duke of Cumberland was never able to face the enemy again, but lay timidly entrenched with his troops between Brussels and Antwerp. The following is the bulletin of Fontenoy, published at Paris on the 26th May, five days after the battle;—

> Our victory may be said to be complete; but it cannot be denied that the Allies behaved extremely well, more especially the English, who made a soldier-like retreat, which was much favoured by an adjacent wood. The British behaved well, and none could exceed them in advancing, none but our officers, when the Highland furies rushed in upon us with more violence than ever did a sea driven by a tempest. I cannot say much for the other auxiliaries; some looked as if they had no concern in the matter. We gained the victory, but may I never see such another!

From the Diary of the Rev. John Bisset, we learn that some of the cannon taken from the British at Fontenoy were afterwards sent over by France to the Highland army of Prince Charles, and were landed at Stonehaven.

When George II. heard of the conduct of the Irish at Fontenoy, he uttered that memorable imprecation on the penal code—

Cursed be the laws which deprive me of such subjects!

Such were the leading features of this memorable field; and hence the stirring words of Prince Charles Edward Stuart, when, soon after, he drew his sword before the disastrous Battle of Culloden—

Come, gentlemen, let us give Cumberland another Fontenoy!

The last survivor of this field was the well-known amazon, Phoebe Hessel, who served there as a soldier in the 5th Regiment, and received a bayonet-wound in the arm. She died in 1821, and her monument, which is still to be seen standing in the churchyard of Chelsea, states that she was born in 1713; so that, if the record be correct, she had attained the age of 108 years.

The Salute at Fontenoy

ALSO FROM LEONAUR
AVAILABLE IN SOFTCOVER OR HARDCOVER WITH DUST JACKET

THE FALL OF THE MOGHUL EMPIRE OF HINDUSTAN by H. G. Keene—By the beginning of the nineteenth century, as British and Indian armies under Lake and Wellesley dominated the scene, a little over half a century of conflict brought the Moghul Empire to its knees.

LADY SALE'S AFGHANISTAN by Florentia Sale—An Indomitable Victorian Lady's Account of the Retreat from Kabul During the First Afghan War.

THE CAMPAIGN OF MAGENTA AND SOLFERINO 1859 by Harold Carmichael Wylly—The Decisive Conflict for the Unification of Italy.

FRENCH'S CAVALRY CAMPAIGN by J. G. Maydon—A Special Correspondent's View of British Army Mounted Troops During the Boer War.

CAVALRY AT WATERLOO by Sir Evelyn Wood—British Mounted Troops During the Campaign of 1815.

THE SUBALTERN by George Robert Gleig—The Experiences of an Officer of the 85th Light Infantry During the Peninsular War.

NAPOLEON AT BAY, 1814 by F. Loraine Petre—The Campaigns to the Fall of the First Empire.

NAPOLEON AND THE CAMPAIGN OF 1806 by Colonel Vachée—The Napoleonic Method of Organisation and Command to the Battles of Jena & Auerstädt.

THE COMPLETE ADVENTURES IN THE CONNAUGHT RANGERS by William Grattan—The 88th Regiment during the Napoleonic Wars by a Serving Officer.

BUGLER AND OFFICER OF THE RIFLES by William Green & Harry Smith—With the 95th (Rifles) during the Peninsular & Waterloo Campaigns of the Napoleonic Wars.

NAPOLEONIC WAR STORIES by Sir Arthur Quiller-Couch—Tales of soldiers, spies, battles & sieges from the Peninsular & Waterloo campaingns.

CAPTAIN OF THE 95TH (RIFLES) by Jonathan Leach—An officer of Wellington's sharpshooters during the Peninsular, South of France and Waterloo campaigns of the Napoleonic wars.

RIFLEMAN COSTELLO by Edward Costello—The adventures of a soldier of the 95th (Rifles) in the Peninsular & Waterloo Campaigns of the Napoleonic wars.

AVAILABLE ONLINE AT www.leonaur.com
AND FROM ALL GOOD BOOK STORES

ALSO FROM LEONAUR
AVAILABLE IN SOFTCOVER OR HARDCOVER WITH DUST JACKET

THE 9TH—THE KING'S (LIVERPOOL REGIMENT) IN THE GREAT WAR 1914 - 1918 *by Enos H. G. Roberts*—Mersey to mud—war and Liverpool men.

THE GAMBARDIER *by Mark Severn*—The experiences of a battery of Heavy artillery on the Western Front during the First World War.

FROM MESSINES TO THIRD YPRES *by Thomas Floyd*—A personal account of the First World War on the Western front by a 2/5th Lancashire Fusilier.

THE IRISH GUARDS IN THE GREAT WAR - VOLUME 1 *by Rudyard Kipling*—Edited and Compiled from Their Diaries and Papers—The First Battalion.

THE IRISH GUARDS IN THE GREAT WAR - VOLUME 1 *by Rudyard Kipling*—Edited and Compiled from Their Diaries and Papers—The Second Battalion.

ARMOURED CARS IN EDEN *by K. Roosevelt*—An American President's son serving in Rolls Royce armoured cars with the British in Mesopotamia & with the American Artillery in France during the First World War.

CHASSEUR OF 1914 *by Marcel Dupont*—Experiences of the twilight of the French Light Cavalry by a young officer during the early battles of the great war in Europe.

TROOP HORSE & TRENCH *by R.A. Lloyd*—The experiences of a British Lifeguardsman of the household cavalry fighting on the western front during the First World War 1914-18.

THE EAST AFRICAN MOUNTED RIFLES *by C.J. Wilson*—Experiences of the campaign in the East African bush during the First World War.

THE LONG PATROL *by George Berrie*—A Novel of Light Horsemen from Gallipoli to the Palestine campaign of the First World War.

THE FIGHTING CAMELIERS *by Frank Reid*—The exploits of the Imperial Camel Corps in the desert and Palestine campaigns of the First World War.

STEEL CHARIOTS IN THE DESERT *by S. C. Rolls*—The first world war experiences of a Rolls Royce armoured car driver with the Duke of Westminster in Libya and in Arabia with T.E. Lawrence.

WITH THE IMPERIAL CAMEL CORPS IN THE GREAT WAR *by Geoffrey Inchbald*—The story of a serving officer with the British 2nd battalion against the Senussi and during the Palestine campaign.

AVAILABLE ONLINE AT **www.leonaur.com**
AND FROM ALL GOOD BOOK STORES

www.ingramcontent.com/pod-product-compliance
Lightning Source LLC
Chambersburg PA
CBHW031617160426
43196CB00006B/168